BROTHERS DOWN

BROTHERS DOWN

*Pearl Harbor and the Fate of the Many Brothers
Aboard the USS* Arizona

WALTER R. BORNEMAN

Little, Brown and Company
New York Boston London

Little, Brown and Company
Hachette Book Group
1290 Avenue of the Americas, New York, NY 10104
littlebrown.com

First Edition: May 2019

Little, Brown and Company is a division of Hachette Book Group, Inc. The Little, Brown name and logo are trademarks of Hachette Book Group, Inc.

The publisher is not responsible for websites (or their content) that are not owned by the publisher.

The Hachette Speakers Bureau provides a wide range of authors for speaking events. To find out more, go to hachettespeakersbureau.com or call (866) 376-6591.

Maps by David Lambert

ISBN 978-0-316-43888-9
Library of Congress Control Number: 2019932184

10 9 8 7 6 5 4 3 2 1

LSC-C

Printed in the United States of America

For Those Who Served—Brothers All

Contents

Contents

List of Maps

The Pacific, 1941

U.S.S.R.

Sea of Okhotsk

MONGOLIA

MANCHURIA
(MANCHUKUO)
Japan, 1937

Kuril Islands

Sea of Japan

Hokkaido

Japan, 1931

KOREA

Peiping
Tientsin

JAPAN

Yellow Sea

Tokyo

CHINA

Nanking
Shanghai

Japan, 1937

Kyushu

INDIA

East China Sea

Okinawa

Iwo Jima
(Japan)

BURMA

Hong
Kong

Formosa

Hanoi

Japan, 1940

INDOCHINA

Hainan
Japan, 1939

Mariana
Islands

Saipan (Japan)

*Bay
of
Bengal*

THAILAND

Japan, 1941

PHILIPPINES
(U.S.)

Guam (U.S.)

Bangkok

Manila

*Philippine
Sea*

Caroline Islands
(Japan)

Saigon

*South
China
Sea*

Truk

Palau
Islands
(Japan)

Singapore

Borneo

Admiralty
Islands
(Aust.)

Equator

Sumatra

Balikpapan

Hollandia

Rabaul

Solon
Isla

Java

NETHERLANDS INDIES
(Neth.)

Timor

NEW
GUINEA

Darwin

Port
Moresby

*Coral
Sea*

Townsville

*INDIAN

OCEAN*

Perth

AUSTRALIA

Brisbane

Canberra

Caled

Melbourne

80°E   100°E   120°E   140°E   160°E

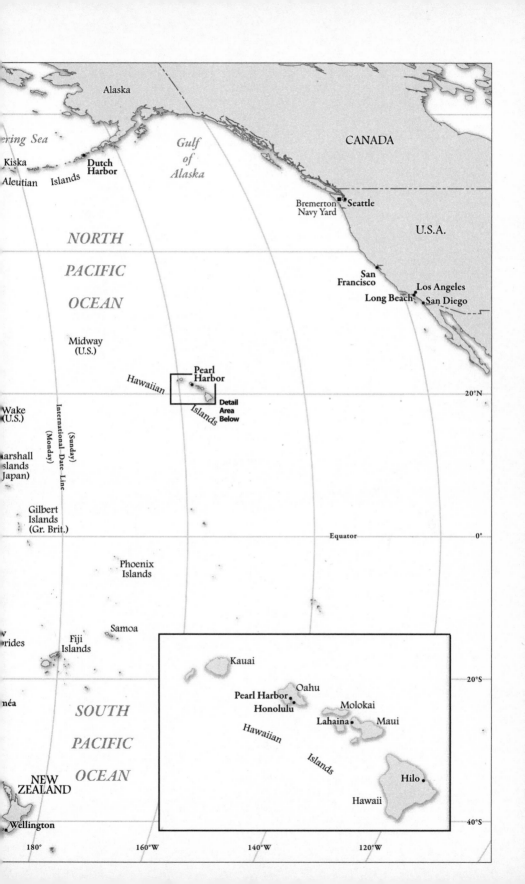

Cast of Characters

ON THE USS *ARIZONA*

Anderson twins John Delmar "Andy" and Delbert
    Jake from Minnesota
    Andy survived and searched in vain for Jake
Ball brothers Masten and William "Bill" from Iowa
    Masten survived; Bill died
Becker trio of brothers from Kansas
    Harvey survived; Marvin and Wesley died;
    younger brother Bob later enlisted in Navy and
    survived
Chandler brothers Edwin "Ray," US Navy, and
    Donald, USMC, from Alabama
    Ray survived; Donald died
Christiansen brothers Edward "Sonny" and Carl
    "Buddy" from Kansas
    Sonny died; Buddy survived

Czarnecki brothers Anthony and Stanley from
    Michigan
    Anthony survived; Stanley died;
    younger brother Henry later enlisted in Army and
    died
Free father and son, Thomas Augusta "Gussie" and
    William Thomas from Texas
    Both died
Giovenazzo brothers Joseph on *Vestal* and Mike on
    Arizona from Illinois
    Joe survived; Mike died
Heidt brothers Edward Joseph "Bud" and Wesley
    John from California
    Both died
Miller brothers George Stanley and Jesse Zimmer
    from Ohio
    Both died
Morse brothers Francis Jerome and Norman Roi
    from Colorado
    Both died
Murdock trio of brothers from Alabama
    Thomas survived, Charles Luther and Melvin
    died;
    younger brothers Verlon, then in Navy in Los
    Angeles, and Kenneth, who later enlisted,
    survived
Shive brothers Gordon, USMC, and Malcolm, US
    Navy, from California
    Both died
Warriner brothers Kenneth Thomas and Russell
    Walter from Wisconsin
    Both survived

Rear Admiral Isaac Kidd from Ohio
  Died on the flag bridge
  Commander, Battleship Division One; awarded
  Medal of Honor
Captain Franklin Van Valkenburgh from Wisconsin
  Died on the bridge
  Captain of the ship; awarded Medal of Honor
Lieutenant Commander Samuel G. Fuqua from Missouri
  Survived
  Damage Control Officer; awarded Medal of Honor
Major Alan Shapley, USMC, from New York
  Survived
  Outgoing commander, ship's Marine Detachment
Private, First Class, Russell Durio, USMC, from
  Louisiana
  Died
Musicians of the ship's band
  All died at their battle stations as ammunition
  handlers
Officers and enlisted men of the *Arizona*

AT PEARL HARBOR

Admiral Husband E. Kimmel, commander in chief,
  US Pacific Fleet
Lieutenant General Walter C. Short, commander, US
  Army forces in Hawaii
Lieutenant Commander William W. Outerbridge,
  captain of destroyer *Ward*
Joseph C. Harsch, *Christian Science Monitor* foreign
  correspondent
Wives and sweethearts of men on the *Arizona*

Cast of Characters

IN WASHINGTON, DC

Franklin D. Roosevelt, President of the United States
Cordell Hull, Secretary of State
Henry L. Stimson, Secretary of War
Frank Knox, Secretary of the Navy
Harry Hopkins, presidential advisor
Admiral Harold R. Stark, Chief of Naval Operations
General George C. Marshall, Chief of Staff, US
    Army

AROUND THE COUNTRY

Parents, wives, and sweethearts of men on the
    Arizona

Author's Note

Many of my books have focused on big-picture topics: major wars, an expansionist president, a controversial general, and the four men to hold the five-star rank of fleet admiral in the United States Navy. Behind those men and events, however, there were always the rank and file upon whose shoulders fell the implementation of broader strategies and goals. Frequently, their personal goals were to live to see another sunrise.

This was perhaps never truer than in the early months of World War II, when the horrors of war abruptly cascaded upon eighteen-, nineteen-, and twenty-something-year-old boys who had recently joined the United States Navy and Marines. Many suddenly found themselves on the front lines not out of any great surge of patriotic pride—although there was some of that—or out of a personal quest to see the world—a few were indeed rovers—but rather out of economic necessity.

Most came from the poverty of the Great Depression. Many were rural farm boys from large families whose absence around the family table meant one less mouth to feed. The five or ten dollars that many sent home monthly out of their pay of thirty-six dollars helped to feed younger siblings. In short, they desperately needed the money and joined up for a steady income.

Standing on the memorial above the sunken battleship *Arizona* at Pearl Harbor while writing *The Admirals*, I had only a vague awareness that thirty-eight sets of brothers served aboard the ship on December 7, 1941. Whenever I mentioned that to others, I was met with almost universal disbelief but also a certain measure of fascination. Thirty-eight sets of brothers? Eighty or so men? How could that be?

The Pearl Harbor story has never been told through the eyes of the many brothers serving together aboard the *Arizona* that fateful day. The bigger story is inexorably wrapped around those of the individual men who fought there, but it is never more poignant than the family stories of these brothers. Among the 2,403 American servicemen who died on December 7, 1941, 1,177 were crew members of the *Arizona*. In an era when family members serving together was an accepted, even encouraged practice, sixty-three of the *Arizona*'s dead were brothers, a staggering 80 percent casualty rate among those brothers assigned to the ship.

In gathering their stories, there were some surprises: I simply was not prepared for the outpouring of information and support that came from the families of those brothers who served together on the *Arizona*. As they shared with me treasured letters, faded photographs, and family reminiscences, two things struck me most deeply: their willingness to recount what in many instances were very private personal stories, and the continuing sorrow these family members feel—at least a generation or sometimes two or three generations removed from that day.

It may have been a youngster's fleeting memory of an

uncle as he left a family gathering for the last time or the admonishments decades later to grandchildren told to "play quietly because of grandpa's nerves." And who were the girlfriends these brothers left behind? Was there really an engagement ring for one of them secretly tucked in a sailor's locker on the ship? What a privilege it has been to get to know their family members and be entrusted with their stories.

All aboard the *Arizona* were figurative brothers in arms, but these men were literal brothers in blood—brothers who paid the ultimate price or lived with enormous personal grief and, sometimes, profound guilt. They were all brothers who, in the words of British poet John Masefield, went "down to the seas." Their stories cast a profound light on one of America's darkest days of infamy.

Silvis, Illinois;
Christmas Eve, 1941

FOR ONE FAMILY, in a working-class neighborhood nestled along the Mississippi River in northwestern Illinois, the smattering of Christmas lights brought no holiday cheer. Inside the modest home of George and Concetta Giovenazzo on Fifteenth Street, everyone milled around with a pit in the hollow of their stomachs. Stockings were still hung and presents wrapped. The younger of the Giovenazzo children could sense but not understand the gloom that filled the air. Photos of their older brothers, quite handsome and confident in their sailors' uniforms, smiled down at them from across the living room floor.

Only a few weeks earlier, the surprise attack at Pearl Harbor had shaken the country to its core. The bulk of the Pacific battleship fleet lay in ruins. Thousands of American servicemen—no one yet knew the exact number—lay dead. But George and Concetta Giovenazzo had very personal concerns: of their eleven surviving children, they had two sons serving with the United States Navy in Hawaii.

A few days after the attack, their oldest son, Joe, got word to his parents that he was safe and unhurt. George and Concetta exhaled with some measure of relief, but what, they wondered, of his brother, Mike? The younger

Giovenazzo was a watertender on the battleship *Arizona*. Mike's job was to tend to the oil-fed fires and boilers in the engine room.

Three years earlier, much to their chagrin, big brother Joe had encouraged Mike to enlist and join him on the battleship just before the baseball-loving seventeen-year-old was to begin his senior year of high school. Their parents simply could not understand the lure. After all, wasn't their hometown of Silvis, three thousand strong in the heartland of the good old USA, the best place to be?

Throughout the dark days of December, the Giovenazzo family waited and prayed. An eerie quiet fell across town as tiny Silvis and all of America adjusted to wartime realities. Neighborhood baseball diamonds where Joe and Mike had spent many a hot summer evening lay still under freezing rain. Every crunch of footsteps on the icy sidewalk outside George and Concetta's small, wooden-framed house brought a new rush of anxiety. Was this a messenger with news?

Finally, on December 22, a telegram arrived reporting what George and Concetta had feared: Mike was missing. By all reports, he had been on the *Arizona* that morning and had not been seen since the attack. It promised to be a bleak and bitter Christmas.

On Christmas Eve, the Giovenazzo family, minus two, gathered for an evening meal, when icy footsteps and a knock were heard at the front door. Even the youngest among them fell silent as George greeted a uniformed Western Union delivery boy with another telegram.

George took the envelope, glanced at Concetta, and unfolded the message inside. It didn't take long to read its contents. George looked again toward Concetta with misty eyes. Their boy was alive! Mike was alive! As the youngest of the Giovenazzo children, five-year-old Dorothy, remembered the moment, "I knew there was sadness in the air," but then "suddenly, everyone was so happy. Everyone was hugging and saying, 'He's alive! He's alive!'"

The Giovenazzos celebrated what proved to be a very happy holiday. Teresa Giovenazzo Ickes, Mike's older sister by two years and herself married with two youngsters of her own, remembered years later, "We had that beautiful Christmas." It truly seemed to be a Christmas miracle.

George and Concetta breathed sighs of relief and took their brood to give thanks at mass at Our Lady of Guadalupe Catholic Church a few blocks away. No one could know what the war would bring or what dangers their boys might face in the days ahead, but for now George and Concetta knew that both Joe and Mike were safe. Their lives began to return to normal. Mike was due to be discharged on January 3 and be home soon afterward. Given the wartime disruptions across the country, they were not particularly alarmed when he did not arrive as scheduled.

But then a few days later, a third telegram arrived. There had been a gut-wrenching mistake.

Charles Luther (left) and Melvin Elijah Murdock. Murdock Family Papers.

Brothers
Down

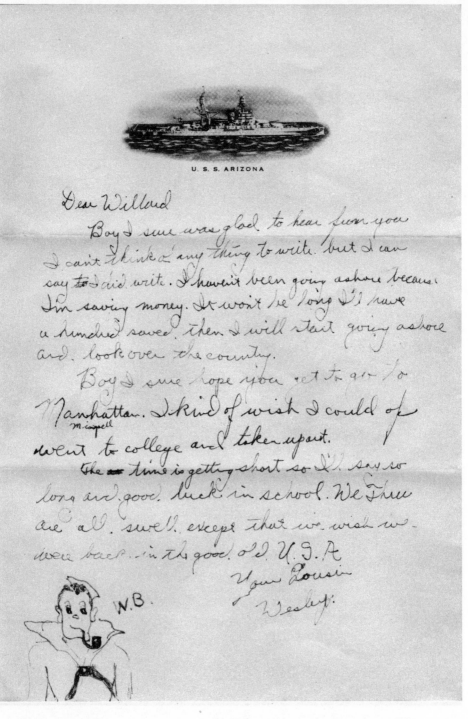

U. S. S. ARIZONA

Dear Willard

Boy I sure was glad to hear from you
I can't think of any thing to write. but I can
say to I did write. I haven't been going ashore because
I'm saving money. It won't be long I'll have
a hundred saved. then I will start going ashore
and. look over the country.

Boy I sure hope you get to go to
Manhattan. I kind of wish I could of
went to college and taken up art.

The time is getting short so I'll say so
long and good. luck in school. We three
are all swell. except that we wish we
were back. in the good old U.S.A.

Your Cousin
Wesley

W.B.

Wesley Becker to his cousin, Willard Hansen, postmarked USS
Arizona, *September 14, 1941.* Becker and Hansen Family Papers

PART I

"Time Is Getting Short So I'll Say 'So Long...'"

CHAPTER 1

"At 'em Arizona"

In a world at peace, there did not seem to be any particular danger to brothers serving together on warships. Family ties were judged a good thing. An older brother sending a photo home of himself in a handsome uniform was better than any recruiting poster the US Navy could devise. For young men during the Great Depression, this was particularly true when in addition to the uniform, the Navy offered a steady paycheck and a chance to see the world—or at least more of it than the county where one had grown up.

Recalling why he joined the Navy in the fall of 1940 at the age of eighteen and reported to the battleship *Arizona*, John Willard Evans, one of six children from a poor farm family in the hills of northwestern Alabama, was blunt: "Most of the boys that I went in with were school dropouts. I was a school dropout. And most of 'em were hungry. Most of their families were hungry. It was very, very tough times, after having come through that Great Depression. No job, no place to go, no homes. And we found a home in the Navy."

Like so many enlistees, Evans saved every penny from his meager pay and sent it home to help his family. His enlistment wasn't motivated by patriotic pride or an impending threat of war, but rather by the need to put food on his family's poverty-ridden table. As Donald Stratton from Kansas, another eighteen-year-old in similar straits who arrived aboard *Arizona* about the same time put it, "The Navy offered us a way out of that, and we took it."[1]

The decision to enlist was even easier when an older brother led the way. Thomas Daniel Murdock stuck it out in the farmland of northern Alabama until he was twenty-one and then took a hundred-mile bus ride to Birmingham to enlist in the spring of 1930. A year later, Thomas reported to the *Arizona* and was soon on his way to becoming one of its old hands. When the mid-1930s gave no promise of improving economic conditions, his younger brothers joined up, too. Charles Luther Murdock enlisted in the fall of 1934, and kid brother Melvin Elijah Murdock followed in the spring of 1938. After their respective basic training, Charles and Melvin joined their big brother on the *Arizona*.

There was certainly no guarantee of serving alongside one's kin, but recognizing the positive impact on morale, the Navy made an effort to accommodate such requests. There had to be an opening aboard the desired ship, of course, as well as the need for the rating held by the requester, but that wasn't much of an issue with newly minted apprentice seamen. There was almost always a need for them on battleships where the complement of about fifteen hundred men was sometimes two or three, or even four or five times the population of a new sailor's hometown. And battleships seemed plenty safe. As one sailor wrote home to his mother, "I am safer on this battleboat than I would be driving back and forth to work if I was home."

*   *   *

Eighteen-year-old Esther Ross of Prescott, Arizona, could hardly contain herself. It was Saturday, June 19, 1915. Dressed completely in white—from wide-brimmed hat and shapely tailored jacket to a dress ending just above her shoes—Miss Ross was not a bride, but on this glorious sunny day she was nonetheless about to occupy the undivided attention of a crowd of seventy-five thousand onlookers.

Esther's America was flexing its muscles. The country was young and decidedly rural. About half its population of one hundred million people was under twenty-five years of age; half lived in farming and ranching areas or small towns. World War I had been raging in Europe for almost a year, but the United States remained on the periphery.

Industrialization was surging, but the chief business of America was still farming. Sputtering automobiles were novelties, about one for every fifty people. Most Americans walked or hopped trolleys to get around cities or rode horses and trains across wide-open spaces. Tractors only gradually replaced horse-drawn farm equipment.

There were no antibiotics, fear of polio was rampant, and childbirth—most deliveries were made at home even in large cities—was not to be taken lightly. Only 30 percent of homes had a telephone. Bestseller lists included *The Lone Star Ranger* by Zane Grey, while at theaters audiences sat through three hours of *Birth of a Nation,* a silent film about the Civil War. News spread chiefly by word of mouth, telegraph, or multiple editions of big-city newspapers and the weekly pages of small-town papers.

On this very spot along New York's East River just fifteen months earlier, Franklin D. Roosevelt, the thirty-two-year-old assistant secretary of the Navy, standing tall and looking natty in a derby hat, had presided over the laying of the keel of an as yet unnamed battleship, designated only as number 39. Now, it was Esther's honor to give the mammoth ship a name.

Like the battleship Esther Ross was about to christen, her state was brand new. Arizona had become the forty-eighth state only three years earlier. Esther's parents were among its pioneers. Her father, William Ross, was a pharmacist in Prescott. Responding to an informal competition for a suitable representative to christen the namesake of their state, Ross prevailed upon Governor George Hunt to select his daughter for the honor.

A gentle breeze blowing from the river kept those assembled at the Brooklyn Navy Yard from getting too hot under a cloudless cobalt-blue sky. As attentive Marine escorts ushered dignitaries holding white tickets to special seats near the front, a repetitive chorus of "bang, bang, bang" reverberated from the massive hull towering above.

At 608 feet in length, the ship was not much to look at yet. Inside the hull, between the bottom of the keel and the main deck, there were four lower decks running the length of the ship, each level filled with a honeycomb of compartments and passageways. Above the main deck, the superstructure and four turrets for the main fourteen-inch guns would take more than a year to complete once the ship was safely afloat.

The banging sounds came from workers knocking away supports that had held the ship in place since its keel laying. Other workers greased skids that sloped downward from the construction bay to the East River. They applied some twenty-five thousand pounds of tallow and lard, which at this stage of construction amounted to about one pound of lubricant per ton of vessel. Next came the order "Saw off!" and large blades whined through the last of the holding blocks.

A hush fell over the crowd as a billowing red flag flut-
tered downward from a construction crane to signal that the
awaited moment was at hand. At precisely 1:00 p.m., to
take advantage of a high tide, hydraulic levers gave the flag-
bedecked mass a gentle nudge. For what seemed like long
minutes, nothing happened. Then, quite suddenly, and very
quietly, the big ship began to move.

Esther Ross's moment was at hand. Despite the time-
honored tradition of christening ships with champagne, Esther swung two bottles suspended from the vessel by a
long cord and wrapped in red, white, and blue ribbons. One
was indeed the traditional bottle of champagne—described
by the *New York Times* as "American champagne from
Ohio"—but the other was "a quart of the first water that
flowed over Roosevelt Dam in Arizona." As the bottles
broke against the starboard bow, Esther cried out, "I name
thee *Arizona!*"

The crowd erupted into cheers. Sirens throughout the
Navy Yard and whistles from nearby ships joined in and
drowned out the strains of "The Star-Spangled Banner," as
it was played in unison by bands from ships of the Atlantic
Fleet. Later, with the benefit of hindsight, some would con-
tend that this unusual use of water damned the ship, but
at the time, Arizona was a dry state and, according to the
Times, "the 'teetotalers' and the rest of the Arizonians demanded that the *Arizona* be named with water as well as
wine." As the ship slid faster and faster down the ways, one
estimate claimed it bested fifteen knots by the time it hit the
water of the East River and floated off in the direction of
the Williamsburg Bridge. A flotilla of tugs swarmed around
the hull and shepherded it to a dock in the Navy Yard for
completion.[2]

Afterward, before an invited luncheon crowd of nine

hundred guests, Secretary of the Navy Josephus Daniels expounded at length on the role of the United States Navy on the global stage. When it was her turn to say a few words, Esther Ross came right to the point: "Mr. Secretary, friends," she told Daniels and those seated before her, "this is the proudest day of my life, because I have christened the largest battleship in the world with the name of the greatest state in the union."[3]

Few could dispute Esther Ross's claim that the *Arizona* was a cutting-edge weapon of its day. The behemoth was built to project American power and counter any aggressor on the high seas. Battleships made completely of steel were themselves relatively new. America's earliest were the *Texas* and the *Maine,* commissioned within a month of each other in 1895. Barely over three hundred feet in length and displacing only sixty-seven hundred tons, they in retrospect have been termed coastal defense battleships or, in the case of the *Maine,* a mere armored cruiser.

The *Maine* blew up under mysterious circumstances in Havana Harbor, Cuba, in February 1898, and its sinking became a rallying cry during the subsequent Spanish-American War. Short-lived though the war was, it underscored the importance of a battleship Navy. In one storied episode, the two-year-old battleship *Oregon* raced from the Pacific coast of California all the way around Cape Horn and into the Atlantic to take part in the Battle of Santiago off Cuba. It was a bold display of sea power, but the roundabout nature of the voyage set thirty-nine-year-old Assistant Secretary of the Navy Theodore Roosevelt to thinking about the need for a canal across the Isthmus of Panama.

By 1900, the United States Navy floated five battleships and had seven more under construction. Beginning with the

Indiana (BB-1), commissioned at the end of 1895, they were each given the designation "BB" for battleship and a number, usually in chronological order from the date when their keels were laid down. Save for the anomaly of the *Kearsarge* (BB-5), all bore the names of states.

During the first decade of the twentieth century, the United States built battleships at a frantic pace. The battleship had become the ultimate measure of national pride and power—one, historian Michael Howard argues, "even more appropriate to the industrial age than armies." The battleship "was a status symbol of universal validity, one which no nation conscious of its destiny could afford to do without."[4]

The prescient assistant secretary of the Navy was now president of the United States, and in December 1907, Theodore Roosevelt dispatched a fleet of sixteen battleships, painted white for peace and dubbed the Great White Fleet, on a multiyear voyage around the world to underscore America's international interests and demonstrate its global reach. Most of these battleships were more than four hundred feet in length and displaced at least twice the tonnage of the *Maine*.

Many of the men who would command ships and fleets in years to come gained experience serving as young officers aboard the giants of the Great White Fleet. Among these newly minted lieutenants and ensigns were Husband E. Kimmel on *Georgia* (BB-15), Isaac C. Kidd on *New Jersey* (BB-16), William F. Halsey, Jr., on *Kansas* (BB-21), and Harold R. Stark and Raymond A. Spruance on *Minnesota* (BB-22).

Even as this impressive armada returned to Hampton Roads, Virginia, in February 1909, its battleships were being surpassed by increasingly larger and heavier dreadnoughts packing ever more firepower. In 1916 alone, the United States Navy commissioned four newcomers: *Nevada* (BB-36) and *Oklahoma* (BB-37), measuring 583 feet in length and carrying ten fourteen-inch guns in two triple and two twin turrets, and *Pennsylvania* (BB-38) and *Arizona* (BB-39), 608 feet in length and mounting twelve fourteen-inch guns in four turrets of three each.

Ships are usually built in classes of comparable specifications named after the lead ship, even if there are only two ships in the class. Hence, the *Arizona* was a *Pennsylvania*-class battleship. While there were small differences among the classes, pre–World War II battleships, beginning with *Nevada,* were "standard-type," with generally the same top speed (21 knots), turning radius (700 yards), and armor, to facilitate steaming together.

Arizona's commissioning—its official acceptance into active service—occurred in the Brooklyn Navy Yard on October 17, 1916. Europe had been at war for two years, and it looked as if the United States would soon enter the conflict. The new ship and its sister, *Pennsylvania,* were, the *New York Times* reported, the "most powerful fighting craft afloat." From keel laying to commissioning, *Arizona*'s construction had taken two and one-half years and cost $16 million (comparable to $369,000,000 in 2017 purchasing power). An initial complement of 1,034 officers and men took up their stations onboard.[5]

The *Arizona* spent the ensuing years of World War I deployed along the Atlantic coast, mostly on training missions. After the Armistice in November 1918, *Arizona* crossed the Atlantic to England and then joined the flotilla of warships escorting President Woodrow Wilson to peace talks in France. A second Atlantic voyage to France and across the Mediterranean followed. By 1921, *Arizona* had made its first transit of the Panama Canal and first crossing of the equator, and came to be home-ported in San Pedro, California, not yet engulfed by greater Los Angeles.

High morale and esprit de corps are essential components in any military command, but particularly so aboard ships at sea. BB-39's can-do motto quickly became "At 'em *Arizona*" and a newsletter with that name—at first crudely typed but increasingly polished as the years went by—was, as its masthead proudly proclaimed, "Published daily aboard the U.S.S. *Arizona* wherever she may be."[6]

Meanwhile, ever more battleships, most laid down amid the fury of World War I, were commissioned into active service. The *Tennessee*-class of *Tennessee* (BB-43) and *California* (BB-44) joined the fleet by the end of 1921, as did the *Maryland* (BB-46), which managed to be completed before the lead ship of her *Colorado*-class, the first class to mount sixteen-inch guns. *Colorado* (BB-45) and *West Virginia* (BB-48) were commissioned during 1923. Eight of these battleships, *Nevada* and *Oklahoma, Pennsylvania* and *Arizona, Tennessee* and *California, Maryland* and *West Virginia*—all built within a decade of one another—would forever be linked by the events of December 7, 1941. *Colorado* escaped the date only because it was undergoing an overhaul in the Bremerton Navy Yard in Washington State.

The fourth member of the *Colorado*-class was never completed because the Washington Naval Treaty of 1922 brought new battleship construction worldwide to a halt. The World War I victors agreed to limit capital ship construction and scrap certain existing vessels to result in a 5:5:3 ratio among the three major naval powers of the United States, Great Britain, and Japan. Signatories pledged to honor a ten-year moratorium on capital ship construction and guarantee ships would not exceed thirty-five thousand tons or carry armaments larger than sixteen-inch guns.

The treaty also contained a non-fortification clause aimed at American and Japanese intentions across the broad reaches of the Pacific. Beyond what the United States might undertake in Hawaii or what Japan might do in its home islands, the signatories agreed not to fortify bases on their island possessions, including Japan's Caroline and Marshall Islands, recently won from Germany, and such American outposts as Wake, Guam, and most important, the Philippines.

Whether Japan would honor this commitment was a matter of considerable debate. Franklin Roosevelt, out of the public eye while recovering from polio, asked in an article, "Shall We Trust Japan?" Citing Japan's participation in the Washington Naval Treaty and noting there was "enough commercial room" in the Pacific "for both Japan and us well into the indefinite future," Roosevelt answered with an optimistic yes.[7]

The end result was that America honored its treaty commitment and built no new battleships between commissioning the *West Virginia* in 1923 and the *North Carolina* (BB-55) in 1941. This left the *Arizona* and its sisters the undisputed, though aging, queens of the seas on the American side during the latter 1920s and throughout the 1930s. But even queens require an occasional facelift, and from May 1929 to March 1931, *Arizona* underwent a twenty-two-month modernization at the Norfolk Navy Yard.

Sleek, three-legged tripod masts replaced the heavy cage support of the fore and main masts. Fire control stations topped each mast and were stacked one atop the other. The main battery director was on top, spotting positions for the main battery in the level below, and directors for the ship's five-inch secondary armaments were in the bottom level. These independently directed the fire of the fourteen-inch guns in the four turrets and the five-inch broadside guns.

The thickness of the armor decking was increased by 1.75 inches, and giant torpedo bulges, or blisters, were added below the waterline on the exterior of each side of the hull. In theory, these bulges provided some measure of protection from torpedoes or near-miss bombs. They were filled with air in the outer half and water in the half next to the hull, and were designed to absorb the shock of an explosion and dissipate potential damage to the ship. Bulkheads bisecting the bulge limited flooding and damage to a particular section. All this meant more weight and new boilers and turbines were also installed to keep up *Arizona*'s speed, which peaked at 20.7 knots (23.8 mph) during post-overhaul sea trials.

Returned to full commission on March 1, 1931, *Arizona* embarked President Herbert Hoover from Hampton Roads, Virginia, for a ten-day tour of the Caribbean, calling at Puerto Rico and the Virgin Islands. It was the sort of low-key inspection of naval operations combined with a warm respite from wintry Washington that American presidents happily undertook in those years. Franklin Roosevelt would soon become a master of it.

Early the following year, *Arizona* steamed from its home port at San Pedro to Hawaii to participate in Army-Navy Grand Joint Exercise No. 4. It was a mouthful of a name for a round of war games that simulated an attack on Oahu from "enemy" aircraft carriers lurking to the north. Near sunrise on February 7, 1932, the first strike of carrier planes caught Army Air Corps bases by surprise. A second wave achieved similar results after slow-to-respond Army pilots landed for refueling and breakfast. In the after-action critique, the Army protested that the Navy's attack at daybreak on a *Sunday* morning, while technically permitted under the rules, was a dirty trick.[8]

A few weeks later, on March 2, *Arizona* entered Pearl Harbor for the first time. Pearl Harbor in the early 1930s was minuscule compared to the massive installation it would become just one decade later. Despite wide inner lochs— bays of water spreading out from the main channel—its entrance was historically shallow. Nineteenth-century visitors had anchored off Honolulu a few miles to the east instead.

In 1887, Hawaii's King Kalākaua granted the United States the exclusive right to establish a coaling and repair station in Pearl Harbor and improve the entrance as it saw fit. No facilities were built, but the United States annexed the Hawaiian Islands in 1898. When the American Navy built its first installations within months of annexation, they were at Honolulu, not Pearl Harbor, because of the difficult channel access.

Finally, in 1908, Congress authorized dredging the channel entrance and constructing a dry dock, as well as adding accompanying shops and supply buildings. Naval Station Pearl Harbor was officially dedicated in August 1919. The Army and Navy jointly acquired Ford Island in the harbor's center for shared airfield facilities that same year.[9]

On its 1932 visit, *Arizona* took on the obligatory pilot to enter Pearl Harbor and made its way to the dry-dock facility on the South Channel between Ford Island and the mainland. The shipyard performed routine maintenance, and *Arizona* rejoined the fleet in time for Fleet Problem XIII. Between 1923 and 1940, the United States Navy conducted twenty-one large-scale fleet maneuvers, essentially war games, designed to bolster readiness and tactical proficiency. Fleet Problem XIII featured an "enemy" force attacking eastward from Hawaii to establish beachheads on the West Coast.

The most significant aspect of both Fleet Problem XIII and the earlier Army-Navy Grand Joint Exercise No. 4 was the growing dominance of naval aviation delivered by aircraft carriers. *Arizona* and its battleship consorts were still a key part of the fleet, but during the maneuvers, nimble aircraft deployments proved increasingly effective against both land and sea targets. How quickly the United States Navy would embrace this glimpse of the future, only time would tell.[10]

Overshadowing these annual war games were the color-coded war plans against potential foes that had been developed and routinely revised since before World War I. These included Plan Black against Germany, Plan Green against Mexico, and Plan Red against Great Britain—however unlikely the latter. Plan Orange anticipated a war against Japan and decreed that in that event the US fleet would sail west to relieve the Philippines—judged a likely target—and engage the Japanese fleet en route in a pivotal battle, just as Admiral George Dewey had done in Manila Bay during the Spanish-American War.

While this played the old saw about planning to fight the latest war, revisions of Plan Orange during the 1930s reflected the realization that a rapid mobilization and deployment across the breadth of the Pacific was unrealistic, particularly as Japan had come to fortify the Mariana, Caroline, and Marshall Islands without regard for the Washington Naval Conference treaties.

By 1937, with Japan gaining military strength and using

it to invade China, American war planners devised a worst-case scenario in the event of an attack on the Philippines. It called for a withdrawal to a defensive Alaska–Oahu–Panama line in the eastern Pacific—a strategic triangle—and an economic boycott to constrain Japan while sufficient forces were mobilized. As war clouds again loomed in Europe, Plan Orange and other singular-foe plans evolved into "Rainbow" war plans that anticipated simultaneous operations against multiple foes. In effect, this meant a two-ocean war and operations in both the Atlantic and Pacific.[11]

For much of the 1930s, the crew of the *Arizona* was blissfully unaware of the details of these strategic and diplomatic factors. Life aboard ship was good and, particularly for enlisted rates (akin to ranks in the Army), offered something that was at a premium during the hardship years of the Great Depression—a steady paycheck and three square meals a day. Never mind that new seamen made barely thirty dollars a month and ate plenty of potatoes.

For some, the Navy experience became a matter of lifestyle. Clem House hailed from Missouri and joined the Navy when he was still shy of eighteen. (While it accepted seventeen-year-olds, the Navy required parents' signed permission to do so.) House first reported aboard *Arizona* in 1921. He left briefly for other duty, but returned to the ship four years later to stay. Considered an old hand by the time he made chief watertender, House was nicknamed "Maw" because he took a sympathetic interest in newly assigned seamen and patiently indoctrinated them into the ways of the *Arizona*. On a quiet Sunday morning twenty years after first reporting aboard, Chief House was still among the *Arizona*'s crew.[12]

The US Navy into which young men enlisted during

the late 1930s and early 1940s was decidedly white. This had not always been the case. During the latter half of the nineteenth century, African Americans served in a largely integrated American Navy and made up about 25 percent of its enlisted strength. Some thirty thousand African Americans manned Union vessels during the Civil War, with little discrimination as to duties. After segregation was legalized in 1896, African American enlistments declined and black men were increasingly relegated to the galley or engine room.

After World War I, African American enlisted personnel declined further as the Navy recruited Filipino stewards for mess duties. By June 1940, African Americans accounted for only 2.3 percent of the Navy's 170,000 total manpower. The fleet had mostly converted from coal to oil, and the vast majority of African Americans performed mess duties. Black reenlistments in technical specialties were never barred, however, and a few African American gunner's mates, torpedo men, and machinist mates continued to serve.

Amendments to the Selective Training and Service Act of 1940 guaranteed the right to enlist regardless of race or color, but in practice, "separate but equal" prejudices consigned most blacks to the Steward's Branch. Its personnel held ratings up to chief petty officer, but members wore different uniforms and insignia, and even chief stewards never exercised command over rated grades outside the Steward's Branch. The only measure of equality came when, just as with everyone else aboard ship, African American and Filipino stewards were assigned battle stations. Only then could they stand shoulder to shoulder with their white brothers in arms.[13]

*　　*　　*

During these years between the wars, the *Arizona* was "neither the best nor the worst among the fleet's battleships."
According to historian Paul Stillwell, "She generally fit in
around the middle in gunnery practice, overall battle efficiency, sports, and the rest of the contests" but earned an
occasional E for excellence painted on her smokestack. Her
mission was twofold: to be a force in readiness should hos-
tilities break out against some color-coded opponent and to
train men for what by the end of the 1930s had become the
increasingly inevitable prospect of another war.[14]

But in many respects, as long as there was peace, serving
aboard a battleship was a bit like belonging to a college fraternity. Each vessel fielded a complement of sports teams.
Rowing, football, and baseball were high on the list of team
sports, but wrestling and boxing were also popular. Like
college teams, there were perquisites that went with team
membership, not the least of which were excused absences
from other duties to practice and special food. And as with
college, when a team was winning or a boat-crew rowing its
way past competitors, the cheers from shipmates were loud
and prolonged. Mediocre performances, on the other hand,
were apt to breed resentment toward those missing regular
duties.[15]

In the spring of 1937, the "Wildcat Nine," as the "At 'em
Arizona" newsletter called the ship's baseball team, were
hot. "The Arizona's slugging ball team registered eight
wins and one defeat since we last went to press," the "At
'em" reported, "bringing us up to third place in the Battle
Force standings." Behind three-hit pitching, the Wildcats
started the run by knocking off the *West Virginia*'s team 5-0.
Brothers Andy and Al Konnick from Wilkes-Barre, Pennsylvania, delivered good work "with the willow," as the
reporter termed it, "Andy connecting three times out of five,

and Al poling a home run." On a December morning four years later, Albert Joseph Konnick was still aboard the *Arizona* as a carpenter's mate.[16]

Exceptionally good teams were not above slipping in a "ringer" from another ship from time to time. Ship captains also went out of their way to recruit young officers to their staffs who just happened to have been exceptional college athletes. After assuming command of the *Arizona* in 1938, Captain Isaac C. Kidd found the ship highly spirited but its athletic teams in somewhat of a slump. Kidd, a physical fitness guru, made a few inquiries among his Annapolis friends and soon Ulmont "Monty" Whitehead, Jr., USNA class of 1940 and captain of its baseball team, and Gordon Chung-Hoon, USNA class of 1941 and a standout football player, were among the *Arizona*'s crew.[17]

Beyond seeking a competitive sports advantage, Captain Kidd cared deeply about the welfare of the men serving under his command. Born in Cleveland, Ohio, in 1884, Kidd graduated from the United States Naval Academy in the class of 1906. He was definitely a battleship officer, having done multiple tours in between staff assignments at Annapolis and the Naval War College. Kidd made it a point to know as many of his enlisted men as possible on a ship of more than a thousand souls.[18]

On one occasion Captain Kidd was strolling the *Arizona*'s deck while the ship lay at anchor in Seattle. "Everett," the captain asked a young enlisted man he encountered on the quarterdeck, "what are you doing in your dress blues?" The nearby officer of the deck quickly responded that Fireman, Second Class, Everett Reid had just come off duty and was supposed to be going ashore to get married, but in his rush to get cleaned up he had missed the liberty boat.

Captain Kidd chatted with Reid for a few moments and then instructed the officer of the deck, "Call away my gig." The bugler standing watch sounded the call for the captain's gig, and presently it came smartly alongside the captain's gangway—usually reserved only for the captain. With a smile, Kidd said to Reid, "Everett, be my guest" and motioned him into the gig all alone. The captain's boat then delivered Reid to the pier in style in time for his wedding. Needless to say, the story quickly made the rounds below decks on the *Arizona* and stood the captain aces high.[19]

Isaac Kidd served his first months on the *Arizona* with another officer cut from the same cloth. On the very day that Kidd reported aboard as *Arizona*'s captain—September 17, 1938—Rear Admiral Chester W. Nimitz raised his flag on the ship as commander of Battleship Division One (COMBATDIV One). Each battleship division comprised three battleships and was usually commanded by a rear admiral. Kidd was indeed the captain of the *Arizona,* but Nimitz gave operational orders to the division as a whole.

Nimitz graduated from Annapolis one year ahead of Kidd. Born in the sand hills of Texas in 1885, Nimitz tried for an appointment to West Point before making the Navy his career. Always an innovator, he went to sea in submarines and helped make the transition from deadly gasoline-fired boats to diesels. After building the submarine base at Pearl Harbor in the early 1920s, Nimitz attended the Naval War College, taught Naval ROTC, and commanded the cruiser *Augusta* (CA-31). Along the way, he war-gamed with aircraft carriers at the center of the battle force instead of battleships and experimented with refueling ships at sea.

Nimitz's tenure as COMBATDIV One aboard *Arizona* lasted only eight months. He returned to Washington to become chief of the Bureau of Navigation, essentially the Navy's personnel office. Kidd remained the *Arizona*'s captain until February 3, 1940, when Captain Harold C. Train relieved him. Nicknamed "Choo-choo" by the crew, Train commanded *Arizona* during Fleet Problem XXI maneuvers in the spring of 1940. This war game featured a prolonged defense of Hawaii after a series of simulated attacks. The fact that it lasted more than two months showed how serious the US military was about training for war. When it was finally over, there was a big change in the wind.[20]

Rather than return to home ports on the West Coast, American battleships and aircraft carriers, along with escorting cruisers, destroyers, and support ships, stayed in Hawaiian waters, mostly mooring within the confines of Pearl Harbor when not at sea. Former assistant secretary of the Navy Franklin Roosevelt, now president of the United States, ordered the move as a show of force to Japan, signaling that America would not condone its further aggression in the western Pacific. The results were not encouraging. Japan did not so much as pause in its drive into China. Almost everyone else, from the commander in chief of the US Fleet, Admiral James O. Richardson, down to the greenest seaman on the *Arizona,* thought the Hawaiian deployment was a bad idea.

In October 1940, Admiral Richardson met with President Roosevelt at the White House to voice his objections firsthand. In the presence of Roosevelt's favorite sailor, former chief of naval operations Admiral William D. Leahy, Richardson minced no words that the fleet could be better prepared for war in West Coast shipyards instead of the cramped facilities of Pearl Harbor. In addition, Richardson cited the logistical problems of hauling men and munitions halfway across the Pacific to support the deployment.

Leahy listened in silence as Richardson pressed his point home: "The senior officers of the Navy," Richardson told the president, "do not have the trust and confidence in the civilian leadership of this country that is essential for the successful prosecution of a war in the Pacific." Leahy watched Roosevelt's impassive face. No one spoke to the president that way.[21]

Three months later, the election of 1940 behind him, Roosevelt removed Richardson from command, reorganized the US Fleet into three separate fleets—Atlantic, Pacific, and Asiatic—and appointed a commander in chief for each. Admiral Husband E. Kimmel became commander in chief of the Pacific Fleet. There would be no more talk of withdrawing the fleet from Pearl Harbor.

Among the *Arizona*'s crew, there were mixed feelings. Once the ballyhooed glamor of Honolulu wore off—and it did so rather quickly—most sailors preferred to be nearer their wives and sweethearts in their home port of San Pedro. The truth of the matter was that unless one chose to visit the red-light district, there wasn't much to do in Honolulu except bar hop—and either recreation was tough on the limited pay of enlisted sailors. The reputable single girls in town were easily captured by hordes of young officers who usually had a few more dollars in their pockets.

The good news for the *Arizona*'s crew was that although the fleet was assigned to Pearl Harbor, there were reasons for the ship to return to the West Coast. In September 1940, after a summer of maneuvers, the *Arizona* steamed from Hawaiian waters to Long Beach, adjacent to San Pedro, and the crew enjoyed several weeks of leave. Then, it was up the coast to Bremerton Navy Yard for the ship's annual overhaul. The work lasted almost three months and again afforded opportunities for leave among its officers and crew when they were not engaged in scraping, painting, and other jobs.

The most ominous part of this overhaul was that the *Arizona* was clearly being readied for war. Four .50-caliber machine guns were installed atop the main mast in a gun enclosure popularly known as the birdbath. It afforded antiaircraft protection from the highest vantage point without interference from the ship's superstructure. The shipyard also constructed metal shields to protect the crews of the antiaircraft guns. Other things were removed. Radios for the crew were deemed unnecessary luxuries and left ashore, as was the ship's elaborate silver service. Formal dinners were not on the agenda.

By the time *Arizona* completed post-overhaul sea trials and again headed south for San Pedro in January 1941, a new rear admiral awaited the ship. He was a familiar face. Isaac Kidd returned to the *Arizona* with his admiral's stars and this time stowed his gear in flag quarters, making the ship his flagship as commander, Battleship Division One.[22]

Just before he did so, Admiral Kidd gave a recruiting talk in Tucson, Arizona. James Randolf Van Horn, a sophomore at Tucson High School, listened intently and right then and there decided to quit school and join up. "James never said anything about the Navy until he heard the admiral talk," his mother later recalled. "Then nothing would hold him. He was inspired. He wanted to go." Young Van Horn — barely seventeen — enlisted, completed basic training, and reported onboard the *Arizona* later that year at Pearl Harbor.[23]

As the *Arizona* returned to Hawaiian waters after a five-month absence, a new captain also reported for duty. Franklin B. Van Valkenburgh, a 1909 graduate of Annapolis and an old hand in battleships as well as destroyers, took command on February 5, 1941. Van Valkenburgh was content with his thirty-year-plus naval service and at ease with the fact that command of a battleship would be the capstone of his career. As Chief Watertender Joseph Karb, a sixteen-year veteran, remembered Van Valkenburgh, "It didn't take an act of Congress to make him a gentleman" because he already was one.[24]

And if the captain was a gentleman, his ship was indeed a lady. After twenty-five years in commission, the *Arizona* had long since developed a character all its own. As war clouds gathered over the Pacific, its motto remained, "At 'em *Arizona*." The captain and his officers might set the tone for a happy ship or a disgruntled one, but it was the men who served below decks who gave the *Arizona* its special mystique and pride. This was especially true among the many brothers who had chosen to do their service with one another aboard the same ship. While all crew members were figurative brothers in arms, these men were literal brothers in blood.

By December 1941, there were thirty-eight sets of brothers serving on the *Arizona*, including the trio of Murdock brothers. As the year 1941 ticked toward a close, one thing was certain: all the brothers held forebodings of war, sometime, somewhere. None, however, had any idea how dramatically and tragically it was about to descend upon them.

CHAPTER 2

"My Brother Joined Up..."

Before Dust Bowl winds roared across the Great Plains, Nekoma, Kansas, in Rush County, was an idyllic place to grow up. Walnut Creek coursed its way eastward to join the Arkansas River near Great Bend, and miles and miles of farmland spread toward all points of the compass. In 1885, one year after the Atchison, Topeka, and Santa Fe Railway platted a site for a depot and stockyard, William Anton Becker, a twenty-nine-year-old immigrant from Germany, built a sod house and homesteaded 160 acres about six miles south of town. He also became one of the founding members of Hope Lutheran Church in nearby rural Rush Center. Faith would always be an important part of the Becker family and sustain them through the darkest of times.

Anton, as he was known, and his bride of one year, Johanna "Ricka" Neumann, soon welcomed six children. They named their third-born and first son William Fredrick Becker. Young William, called Bill, grew up helping his parents on the farm as Anton and Ricka acquired more acreage and also ran horses and cattle. At twenty-four, Bill did what many immigrants and first-generation Americans did—he married a recent arrival from the "old country," a girl he met in church.

Freda Paulsen and her sisters, Christina and Mary, had grown up in Schleswig-Holstein, Germany, and immigrated through Ellis Island, New York, in July 1909. They soon stepped off a Santa Fe train onto the wide-open plains of Kansas. The locals who met the train were dressed in bib overalls. Freda and her sisters laughed at the farmers' fashions, but as Freda later recalled, the joke was on them because she and her sister Christina both ended up marrying farm boys.

Bill and Freda married in Hope Lutheran Church in 1913 when Freda was nineteen. Anton and Ricka moved into Great Bend with their younger children, and Bill and Freda set up housekeeping on the expanding Becker farm. Over the next eighteen years, Bill and Freda had seven children. Four boys and a girl were born in rapid order: Walter William (1914), Harvey Herman (1916), Marvin Otto (1918), Wesley Paulsen (1922), and Theresa Wilma (1924). Bobbie, known by most as Bob, followed in 1927, before Mary Ann rounded out the Becker clan in 1932. They were all born at home, and Freda recounted years later that she "never had any trouble."

Despite the increasing gloom of the Great Depression, these were still good years for rural Kansas. The wheat crop of 1931 set a record. Farmers optimistically planted more acreage in 1932 and 1933, but declining exports and huge surpluses soon drove prices below the cost of production. Then, the rains failed and the winds began to blow. By the following year, the Dust Bowl had a death grip on western Kansas and gave no indication of letting go.

On May 27, 1934, a few weeks shy of his twentieth birthday, the oldest Becker boy, Walter, married Charlotte Blattner, six months his junior, who had grown up in Rozel, just south of Nekoma. Charlotte's father was a blacksmith, and her mother owned and operated a grocery store in Rozel. The young couple lived with Bill and Freda for a time, and Walter worked on the family farm. Later, they moved to Rozel, where Walter worked at the grain elevator, drove a gasoline truck to deliver fuel, and hired out as a laborer. Charlotte was well known for her angel food cakes, sometimes baking as many as six in a day to sell. She also worked in her mother's grocery store.

Newlywed bliss for the oldest Becker brother aside, over the next few years both the Great Depression and the Dust Bowl darkened many a door in western Kansas. These were hard times with no jobs and no money for college. It was a fight just to put food on the table. And Mother Nature gave no reprieve. Dust storms blackened the skies so that one couldn't see ten feet. Grasshoppers descended in droves, and by the time farmers figured out how to poison them, they lay in piles three feet deep. What the winds didn't take or the grasshoppers didn't eat, hundreds of thousands of jackrabbits finished off, gnawing the ground bare.

By the summer of 1938, something had to change. After graduating from La Crosse High School and a few years of working on the family farm, Bill and Freda's second son, Harvey, took the Santa Fe train east to Kansas City. On July 12, he enlisted in the Navy and reported to Naval Station Great Lakes, north of Chicago, for basic training.

But just because a young man wanted to join up did not mean that the US Navy necessarily wanted him. In 1938, of the 129,610 men who tried to enlist only 15,094, slightly less than 12 percent, were accepted. During that year, there were only about 105,000 enlisted sailors in the entire American Navy. That number, as well as the number of enlistees, would triple by 1941.[1]

Naval Station Great Lakes was one of several naval training stations around the country, but during the buildup to World War II, it would become the largest. While Harvey Becker mingled with only a few thousand sailors undergoing boot camp or enrolled in specialty schools, that number soon mushroomed to over one hundred thousand being trained at the same time.

For recruits like Harvey, it was well understood that his twelve weeks at Great Lakes were merely the beginning. His training as a seaman would continue and accelerate once he reported aboard a ship. Some men would join the engine room force for duty as firemen, the next step to becoming boilermakers, machinist's mates, watertenders, metalsmiths, and electrician's mates. The rest would remain in the seaman branch and develop into coxswains, boatswain's mates, gunner's mates, carpenter's mates, and quartermasters. According to *The Bluejackets' Manual*, the bible of every enlisted man, in every case such training was "for the sole purpose of making you a useful man, a trained man, and a leader of men."[2] After three months at Great Lakes, Harvey Becker reported aboard the *Arizona* as it lay at anchor off San Pedro.

Harvey left behind a girl with whom he had an understanding. Marie Maresch was two years younger than Harvey and had grown up on her parents' farm about one mile west of the Becker homestead. For reasons not entirely clear, Marie attended high school in Manhattan, Kansas, graduating in 1936. Afterward, she enrolled in nursing school—likely at the St. Rose School of Nursing in Great

Bend, Kansas—got her degree, and went to work at the hospital in nearby Larned.

Meanwhile, Harvey Becker had risen through the enlisted rates and gotten his rating as a gunner's mate. As such, he was responsible for a wide range of duties associated with the *Arizona*'s armaments. These included everything from maintaining small arms—pistols, rifles, and shotguns—to know-how with .50-caliber machine guns and the five-inch and fourteen-inch deck guns. For the deck guns, gunner's mates were responsible for the hydraulic and electrical systems necessary for tracking, aiming, loading, and firing the gun. At general quarters, a gunner's mate might be inside the gun mounts or the turrets of the big fourteen-inch guns or below in the ammunition bays.

With Harvey as their example and economic conditions on the farm not improving, Bill and Freda's next two boys decided to follow suit. Marvin Becker enlisted at Kansas City on December 19, 1939, at the age of twenty-one. People who remembered him described Marvin as a quiet, kind, and gentle young man. After basic training at Great Lakes, there wasn't much question where he wanted to serve. Marvin reported aboard the *Arizona* and joined his older brother on March 15, 1940, at San Pedro.

Seven months after joining the *Arizona*, Marvin wrote his cousin, Willard Hansen, who was serving in a Civilian Conservation Corps camp in the Black Hills of South Dakota, that he hoped to be promoted to Seaman, First Class, because his pay would jump from thirty-six to fifty-four dollars per month—a tidy sum of eighteen extra dollars in those Depression days. Marvin was assigned to Turret No. 2 along with Harvey and told Willard that he liked it much better than the deck force. "All you do on the deck," Marvin wrote, "is scrub it and scrub it some more."[3]

The following year, it was Wesley's turn to follow his brothers. Eighteen-year-old Wesley had an artistic streak as well as a special affinity for food—family stories remember him taking a bite or two out of a hot dog and then saving the rest in a pocket to savor later. Wesley enlisted on January 28, 1941, and reported to the *Arizona* on April 27, just as the ship returned to Pearl Harbor from training exercises.

Leaving home back then was a big adjustment for small-town farm boys. Wesley's departure was particularly hard on his younger brother, Bob. The two had always been close, but an incident when Bob was about eight or nine years old forged an unbreakable bond between them. Wesley had organized a camping trip for Bob and their three cousins. The boys rode bikes and camped along Walnut Creek about ten miles from the Becker farm. A heavy rainfall overnight sent a tangled logjam down the creek, and in the morning the boys couldn't resist exploring it. They found big sticks and climbed through the maze, trying to push the mass along.

Bob's stick broke and he fell into the water among the logs and got trapped. He managed to thrash his way out the downstream side, but he couldn't climb out of the rushing creek because of its steep, muddy banks. Wesley took charge and had his cousins form a human chain so that he could reach Bob and pull him to safety. Bob always figured that Wesley had saved his life and from then on considered him his "best bud."

Wesley worried—just as Marvin had—about making Seaman, First Class, in a "Dear Bud" letter he mailed to Bob on October 13, 1941, while the *Arizona* was moored at Pearl Harbor. Wesley had had temporary duty as a relief mess cook in the chief petty officers' mess, and he told Bob that he didn't like it. But it did have its benefits. Wesley assured Bob that he had gotten "all the good ham I wanted and all the strawberry ice cream."[4]

Normally, Wesley ate his meals with his division in the same compartment where hammocks were hung and cots unfolded at night. The least senior men in each division served as mess cooks and set up tables and benches for each meal. They retrieved food from the main galley in pots and on platters, and it was passed around family-style. The place settings were heavy white porcelain plates and mugs and stainless-steel utensils. The senior rated man at each table was responsible for the conduct of the men at his table. It was quite permissible to ask for seconds if there was food left—usually a rarity—but anyone who attempted to help himself before all had been initially served was apt to get more than his hand slapped. Afterward, the mess cooks hauled everything back to the galley for washing to make it ready for the next meal.[5]

"I sure am glad that you are enjoying yourself," Wesley continued in his letter to Bob, "but remember Bobbie that when you have dad's car that one little accident will probably stop the use of it. So remember there is always a chance of something turning up that you do not know how to handle—that's one thing that I've learned in the good old US Navy. Be alert and attentive." Wesley signed off with "Well that's about all I know so I'll say so long Bud," before turning the page over to jot a few lines to his mother.

Saying that he didn't know anything more than what Freda could read in his letter to Bob, Wesley assured her, "We three are all <u>OK.</u>" He signed it "Your son Wesley," but added in parentheses what may have been his shipmates' way of keeping the three Becker brothers straight: "(Big Becker, Little Becker, & Little Little Becker.)" Then, Wesley added a P.S. sure to bring a smile to any mother's face.

"Boy you ought to see my locker now [that] I really have it fixed up," he wrote Freda. "It's a good thing I learned how to keep my drawers and things straitened out at home."[6]

It was indeed a lot of comfort for Wesley, as well as for Bob and the folks he left back home, that he would be serving with his older brothers. They had always taken care of one another growing up, and there was little reason to believe they would not do the same on the *Arizona*. By the fall of 1941, Harvey was a Gunner's Mate, Second Class, and Marvin was a Gunner's Mate, Third Class. Wesley, his worrying to the contrary, received his promotion to Seaman, First Class, effective on November 1. Having been assigned to Turret No. 2 along with Harvey and Marvin, Wesley was eyeing a gunner's mate rating just like his older brothers. For the Becker brothers, it really was a family affair.

CHAPTER 3

Unsettled Seas

T HROUGHOUT 1941, THE officers and crew of the *Arizona* were caught up in an ever-escalating whirlwind. The air was filled with war tension that everyone from admirals to raw recruits could feel. Most traced the origins to the day Adolf Hitler invaded Poland in September 1939, but Japan had been at war in the Pacific since its efforts to subjugate China in 1937. At the heart of the matter were natural resources. What Japan's home islands lacked, Japan needed to find elsewhere. After France surrendered to Germany and Great Britain stood alone against the Axis threat, Japan took advantage of the collapse of French authority in Indochina to move south, seize more territory, and threaten the natural resources of the Netherlands East Indies.

While Japan's brazenness and duplicity on the morning of December 7, 1941, would come as a shock to the American psyche, President Franklin Roosevelt had slowly but steadily been preparing the country for war from the start of his presidency. He began in 1933 by diverting dollars from a public works bill to build two aircraft carriers. A year later,

Congress voted to increase naval strength to the limits of existing treaties. The 1938 Naval Expansion Act boosted tonnages further, and additional legislation in 1940—including one bill called the Two-Ocean Navy Act—authorized the construction of seven battleships, eighteen aircraft carriers, and an assortment of smaller ships.

Weapons, tanks, and aircraft, including B-17 bombers and P-40 fighters, rolled off assembly lines in increasing numbers. Armed forces recruiters and full-color advertisements encouraged young men to enlist in their chosen branch of service, but just in case patriotism or three squares a day weren't enough inducement, Roosevelt signed the Selective Training and Service Act of 1940 into law. The nation's first peacetime draft required all males between twenty-one and thirty-five to register and be chosen by lottery for twelve months of military service.

By the spring of 1941, there was no longer any doubt that America was gearing up for war. In March, Roosevelt announced Lend-Lease aid to Great Britain, and in May, he declared a state of "unlimited national emergency." Such support for Great Britain did nothing to ease American relations with Japan.

In July, determined to stop further Japanese expansion beyond Indochina, the United States, Great Britain, and the Netherlands acted in concert to shut off the flow of raw materials upon which the Japanese war machine relied. The three countries instituted an embargo against Japan of oil, steel, and other strategic imports. Roosevelt froze Japanese assets in the United States, closed the Panama Canal to Japanese shipping, and recalled Major General Douglas MacArthur to active duty to defend the Philippines. Far from slowing Japan's war-making capabilities, these actions, particularly the oil embargo, served only to increase the urgency Japan felt to subjugate China and gobble up oil and rubber from the East Indies.

By September, after a German U-boat fired a torpedo at the American destroyer *Greer* (DD-145) while it was on convoy duty in the North Atlantic, Roosevelt authorized a shoot-on-sight policy against U-boats. A month later, the destroyer *Reuben James* (DD-245) spotted a periscope too late and caught a torpedo that blew off its bow. The ship sank in five minutes. Out of a complement of 143 officers and men, only 44 enlisted men survived.

Folksinger Woody Guthrie began to write a song about the ill-fated destroyer and the men who perished aboard it. Initially, Guthrie planned to memorialize each of the dead with his own line or two in the song. Convinced by fellow musicians that this would make the tribute unbearably lengthy, Guthrie and others rewrote the verses and added a haunting chorus to demand that listeners "tell me, what were their names" and ask if anyone had "a friend on that good *Reuben James*?" The final verse proclaimed that mighty battleships would "steam the bounding main" and remember its name.[1]

One of those mighty battleships anchored off San Pedro on June 17, 1941, having arrived from Pearl Harbor in a task force that conducted short-range gunnery practice en route. Among those eager to depart *Arizona* were members of its band. All looked forward to seven-day leaves before reporting to new assignments. In their place, the *Arizona* welcomed a new band, twenty-one toe-tapping musicians who had just graduated together from the US Navy School of Music in Washington, DC. Temporarily known as US Navy Band Number 22, they arrived on the West Coast aboard the ammunition ship *Lassen* (AE-3) after a transit of the Panama Canal.

At thirty-one years old, their bandmaster, Musician, First Class, Frederick W. Kinney, was the old man of the group. About half his charges were still in their teens; the oldest, hulking, six-foot-tall Neal Radford, loved football almost as much as he did playing baritone and tuba. He had just turned twenty-six.

But the youth of this group proved a good thing. *Arizona*'s departing band comprised mostly older and—let's face it—somewhat staid musicians. Kinney's younger talents were ready to boogie and belt out the current big band hits. Scarcely had his men dropped their sea bags below decks when Kinney had them back topside for an impromptu concert.

At the first few notes, crewmen not on duty stood open-mouthed and stared. Their personal radios had been ordered ashore six months earlier during the Bremerton overhaul and they were starved for the latest sounds. Kinney and his young musicians—the new USS *Arizona* Band—did not disappoint. Admiral Kidd sent Kinney his compliments and gave hearty approval of this first concert, but the crew went wild. According to Gunner's Mate, Third Class, John W. Doucett, they clapped long and hard that first day and could never get enough of the music.[2]

A week after coming aboard, the *Arizona* band showed its diversity by playing a concert of marches and classical music, including "Entry of the Gladiators," the traditional march of the circus, and selections from Verdi, Rachmaninoff, and Dvořák, while the ship was still anchored off San Pedro.

Once *Arizona* got underway for Pearl Harbor, however, the bandsmen also got an indoctrination into what it meant to be a *Navy* band aboard a warship. Among a full complement of 1,512 men, the musicians were assigned duty stations in sick bay and trained to administer injections of morphine. They were also introduced to their battle stations. As a unit, they were to man the hoists that carried gunpowder charges from the ammunition hold up to the fourteen-inch guns in Turret No. 2.[3]

But there was plenty of time for practice, and the guys belted out the big band sounds of "Boogie Woogie Bugle Boy," "Chattanooga Choo Choo," and "Take the A Train." Curtis Haas, a Seaman, Second Class, from North Kansas City, Missouri, played woodwinds, but also wrote arrangements and doubled as a singer. Haas performed the moody "Dolores," then hitting the charts thanks to a rendition by a young crooner named Frank Sinatra who sang with the Tommy Dorsey Orchestra.[4]

Arizona arrived in Pearl Harbor from San Pedro on July 8, 1941. For the remainder of the summer, the ship spent two weeks at a time moored along Battleship Row adjacent to Ford Island, interspersed by a week of training exercises. These exercises included everything from range-finder calibration on the big fourteen-inch guns to antiaircraft practice. Sometimes *Arizona* operated independently, escorted by several destroyers, and at other times the battleship steamed in concert with *Nevada* and *Oklahoma,* the other ships of Battleship Division One.[5]

These schedules made friendly athletic contests ashore a matter of hit-and-miss, but *Arizona* was moored off Ford Island on Saturday night, September 13, when one of its more famous musical competitions occurred. That fall, there were seventeen Navy bands and one Marine Corps band stationed on Oahu. All were proficient, and just as in athletic competitions, there were healthy rivalries among groups of young men representing their respective ships.[6]

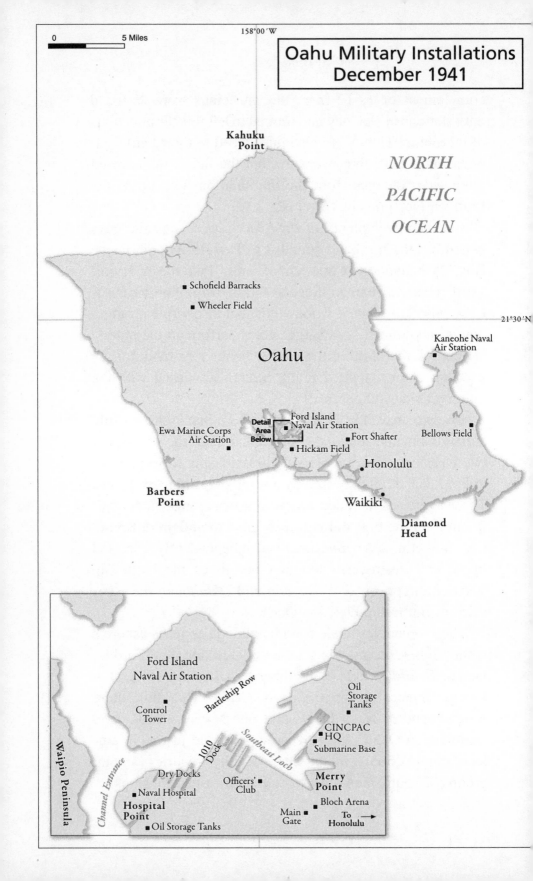

On a Saturday night, if you were an enlisted man and didn't have money for a fancy dinner in Honolulu or the urge for a three-minute tryst in one of the Hotel Street brothels, Bloch Arena was the place to be. Located only a few minutes' walk from the fleet landing, where boats from the battleships moored along Battleship Row disgorged their liberty-hungry crews, Bloch Arena was a multipurpose recreation center that hosted everything from concerts and dances to basketball games and boxing matches.

Beginning on September 13 and every other subsequent Saturday night, four bands competed in three categories of swing, sweet, and specialty, the latter a catch-all encompassing everything from rousing marches to classical. Judges awarded points in each category based on the applause level of the audience. The bands finished by taking turns pounding out the notes for a jitterbug contest in which guys lucky enough to have dates swarmed the dance floor with them.

The winning dance couple got a loving cup, and the two top bands advanced to the next round of competition to determine the best band in the Pacific Fleet. That first night, from among the bands from *Arizona, West Virginia, California*, and the submarine base, Kinney's *Arizona* charges came in first and the *California* band, another group of relative youngsters, placed second. Both bands became eligible to play in the semifinals scheduled for November and early December.

These Saturday Battles of Music, as they were called, were broadcast by radio to the fleet in the harbor, and they were a big deal—both for the entertainment and for the esprit de corps they encouraged for one's ship. Because audience reaction was the main criteria for winning, the more crew that a ship had present to hoot, holler, and applaud, the better its band's chances of winning. As a ship's band advanced through the contest, there was pressure among enlisted personnel to attend and cheer just as if it had been a championship football game. The Battles of Music contests always ended with the four competing bands joining en masse to play the National Anthem.[7]

While Kinney and his bandsmen savored their victory and looked forward to the semifinal round, *Arizona* spent a few days in dry dock fixing a bent propeller shaft and then put to sea. Captain Van Valkenburgh led the ship through a series of short-range gunnery practices and antiaircraft drills. After a few days back in port, *Arizona* sortied again for two days to conduct night operations with the *Nevada*.[8]

During the ten-day respite in Pearl Harbor that followed, a real old salt reported aboard. His name was Thomas Augusta Free, but shipmates had long called him "Gussie," as had his family. Born in Alabama in 1891, Gussie moved with his family, including his older sister, Lillie Mae, to Plantersville, Texas, southeast of College Station, a year later. After working on the family farm, he registered for the World War I draft—noting that his parents were old and partially dependent on him and that he was married but separated. Gussie and Beatrice Anderson later divorced.

Gussie entered the Navy in December 1917 and took his basic training at Hampton Roads, Virginia. Despite being relatively old—twenty-six at the time—he had spent most of his life in Brazos County, Texas. His thoughts turned to home and particularly to his aging mother, Mary. Finding a book of postcards showing photos of the training site, Gussie promised to "write some verses in it for you, Mother." And he did. He filled the backs of the cards with heartfelt sentiments. "Mother," Gussie scrawled in pencil on one, "while I am far far from you my faith looks up to thee but my thoughts are of you."

On another, his expansive script promised, "When I am gloomy and blue, I know I have friends but none like you, dear Mother." And in a hint of his life to come, he wrote, "I am all over the world both land and sea, but there is a beautiful time that's awaiting for me." His nickname aside, Gussie signed them all, "Thomas."[9]

Completing his basic training and joining the fleet, Gussie crossed the Atlantic as far as Bermuda. Tense times on U-boat-filled waters aside, there were lighter moments, too. A photo of Gussie from the family album shows him standing in the doorway of an ice cream shop with the caption, "I didn't know he was going to take my picture." He referred to Bermuda as "Great Britain," which as a matter of ownership, it was.

Mustered out on August 1, 1919, Gussie returned home to Texas and on December 21 married Myrtle Bice, who was thirteen years his junior and not quite sixteen. The Free and Bice families were well acquainted, as two of Gussie's brothers had already married older sisters of Myrtle. But whatever "beautiful time that's awaiting" Gussie longed for, this did not seem to be it. For whatever reason— perhaps economic, perhaps marital, it is unclear—he rejoined the Navy in July 1923 and determined to make it a career. His other option was likely farming, but that did not seem to fit his roving spirit that had been awakened by his first tour at sea. Myrtle was a few months pregnant with their firstborn.

Myrtle followed Gussie to Portsmouth, Virginia, and William Thomas Free was born there on January 9, 1924. A daughter, Myrtle Marie Free, called Marie to distinguish her from her mother, was born almost two years later in San

Diego. But Myrtle had evidently had enough of Navy life with Gussie away so much, and she filed for divorce soon afterward. She chose not to keep custody of their two young children, and Gussie sent them home to Texas to live with his sister, Lillie, and her husband, Frank Meads, in College Station. William and Marie grew up with the Meads family, but William in particular idolized his father and his Navy life.

Gussie visited when he had leave, but a seafaring life made parenting difficult. Over the years, Gussie served on half a dozen ships throughout the Pacific, including the oiler *Ramapo* (AO-12), the transport *Wharton* (AP-7), and the destroyer *Parrott* (DD-218). Along the way, he dispatched letters from many ports, including a greeting from the fictitious *Neptune Rex* postmarked Manila after the *Parrott* crossed the equator during duty with the Asiatic Squadron in November 1936.

Now a Machinist's Mate, First Class, Gussie Free was fifty years old and looking for one more good ship before retiring with twenty years of service. But Gussie also had a very personal reason for transferring to the *Arizona*. One of the green seamen aboard was his son. Uncle Frank and Aunt Lillie had been skeptical, but William Thomas Free enlisted shortly after his seventeenth birthday—with Gussie's parental permission to do so—during his junior year of high school. William reported to the *Arizona* on April 27, 1941, after basic training at San Diego. Gussie threw his seabag on deck six months later, on October 10.

Getting underway again, *Arizona* cleared the Pearl Harbor entrance and steamed off for night battle practice. On the evening of October 22, *Arizona*, as part of Battleship Division One along with *Nevada* and *Oklahoma*, was still at sea conducting maneuvers. As darkness fell, Admiral Kidd, as COMBATDIV One on *Arizona* leading the way, ordered the three ships out of column and into a line abreast.

As the lead ship, *Arizona* occasionally flashed a searchlight off low-hanging clouds as a reference point. Nonetheless, the distance between *Arizona* and *Oklahoma* to port decreased until it became uncomfortably close. Aboard *Arizona*, Captain Van Valkenburgh ordered hard right rudder and signaled for flank speed. On *Oklahoma,* its captain ordered full astern as his ship was constrained from turning left by the proximity of the *Nevada* on his port beam. Both ships sounded collision sirens, but it was too late.

Oklahoma, having a reinforced bow meant for ramming, struck the *Arizona,* a glancing blow on the port quarter. The portside torpedo blister meant to absorb torpedo attacks took the brunt of the blow. It resulted in a V-shaped gash in the blister four feet wide and twelve feet high. The structural integrity of the *Arizona*'s hull was not compromised, but this damage necessitated the ship's return to Pearl Harbor for a week in dry dock. The *Oklahoma* got off easy with only the jack staff on its bow bent out of shape from the force of the impact.[10]

While the *Arizona* was in dry dock, nineteen-year-old Seaman, Second Class, Harlan Carl Christiansen reported for duty. He was eager to join his older brother, twenty-year-old Edward, who served aboard as a baker. The boys had been born only fifteen months apart in Jewell County, Kansas, on the Nebraska line in the north-central part of the state. Their family moved to Columbus, a railroad junction of about three thousand residents in the extreme southeastern corner of Kansas, a few years later. Eventually, the Christiansen family numbered four boys and five girls.

Always close growing up, the boys attended Cherokee

County Community High School together. As teenagers they worked as curb-hops at an all-night café and learned to be short-order cooks. Edward, called "Sonny," enlisted in January 1940 and reported to the *Arizona* two months later. He had wanted to go to college, but with nine kids in the family, money was more than tight. In joining the Navy, Sonny figured that he could save up and go to college when he got out.

Sonny's brother, Harlan, called "Carl" but nicknamed "Buddy," spent a year at a Civilian Conservation Corps camp in Nebraska after high school and then found himself back home in Columbus working for his father. Buddy also dug gas pipelines by hand with a pick and shovel to, as he remembered it, "earn some money to help the folks."[11]

Buddy hadn't seen Sonny since he'd enlisted. One day, their mother, Winona, became distraught after her father, the boys' grandfather, told Winona that she would never see Sonny again. Determined that *he* would, Buddy promptly told his father he was quitting and drove to Joplin, Missouri, to enlist. Less than three months later, when Buddy walked up the gangway and presented his orders to the officer of the deck on the *Arizona,* Sonny was there to greet him. Buddy and Sonny Christiansen became the thirty-eighth set of brothers to be currently serving together on the *Arizona.*

During that same week, Captain Van Valkenburgh wrote a letter to his aunt in Milwaukee. He provided her a glimpse of the rigorous training he and his men were undergoing amid a great deal of uncertainty. "We are training, preparing, maneuvering, doing everything we can do to be ready," the captain wrote. "The work is intensive, continuous, and carefully planned." Then, in an acknowledgment of the decades-long thinking of Plan Orange, Van Valkenburgh professed, "We never go to sea without being completely ready to move on to Singapore if need be, without further preparation." Indeed, he concluded, "Our eyes are constantly trained westward and we keep the guns ready for instant use against aircraft or submarines whenever we are at sea. We have no intention of being caught napping."[12]

When *Arizona* emerged from dry dock with new steel plates welded into place on the portside blister to close the gash from the collision, there was a far more noticeable and ominous change in the ship's appearance. The Navy's peacetime color scheme of light gray had given way to a dark bluish-gray applied to the hull and superstructure up to the level of the bridge. Only the foretop and maintop enclosures on the two tripod masts and the tops of the masts themselves were still light gray. This was a form of wartime camouflage that supposedly made the ship less likely to stand out against the horizon.[13]

On November 13, the day after leaving dry dock, *Arizona* put to sea for a short four-day stint to fire antiaircraft guns and exercise its main batteries. According to Neal Radford, the ship's baritone and tuba player, it was quite a sight to see a broadside fired at night from all twelve of the fourteen-inch guns. Radford wrote his mother that one could follow the glow of the projectiles as they left the muzzles and streaked toward their target.[14]

Arizona returned to Pearl Harbor on Sunday, November 16, but did not stay in port very long. The battleship was at sea on Thursday, November 27, when the fleet and all of America celebrated Thanksgiving. Thoughts of home flooded the *Arizona*'s mess amid turkey, stuffing, and mounds of mashed potatoes. Back home, as families gathered around other Thanksgiving tables, their thoughts also turned to loved ones—sons, brothers, husbands, and sweethearts—serving on the *Arizona*. In Columbus, Kansas, Winona Christiansen reserved a special place for the Thanksgiving cards from Sonny and Buddy. Her boys were together again and seemed to be doing just fine.

Whatever anxiety crew members on the *Arizona* and through-out the Pacific Fleet felt about the future would have been heightened had they known that on this same Thanksgiving day, the War and Navy departments in Washington issued what came to be called their "war warning" to all commands: "negotiations with Japan looking toward stabilization of conditions in the Pacific have ceased and an aggressive move by Japan is expected within the next few days."

At Pearl Harbor, Admiral Husband E. Kimmel, commander in chief of the Pacific Fleet, met with Vice Admiral William F. Halsey, Jr., the commander of his carrier forces, and Army Lieutenant General Walter C. Short, commander of land forces in Hawaii. Kimmel and Halsey had already organized task forces of cruisers and destroyers around the three aircraft carriers then operating in the Pacific: *Lexington* (CV-2), *Saratoga* (CV-3), and *Enterprise* (CV-6).

To guard against a concerted attack or sabotage, they adopted a general protocol that only one carrier task force would be in Pearl Harbor at any one time. At the moment, this meant alternating between *Lexington* and *Enterprise* because *Saratoga* had yet to return to Hawaiian waters after a lengthy overhaul at Bremerton. A similar alternating routine was supposed to be in place among the three battleship divisions. Of the nine battleships in those three-ship divisions, *Colorado* was currently in Bremerton undergoing its own overhaul.

With the war warning in hand, Admiral Kimmel and General Short concerned themselves primarily with the outer boundaries of their commands and not with Hawaii itself. The chief topic they discussed with Halsey was the delivery of aircraft to reinforce garrisons on Wake and Midway islands. Short wanted to deploy Army squadrons of new P-40s, but Halsey quoted an arcane regulation that Army pilots were required to stay within fifteen miles of land and asked what good they would be in protecting an island.

Kimmel turned to Marine pilots instead and ordered Halsey to deliver a squadron of twelve Grumman F4F Wildcats aboard *Enterprise* to the more distant and potentially dangerous destination of Wake, about 2,300 miles west of Pearl Harbor. After Short left, Kimmel and Halsey talked alone about possible scenarios. The two had been close friends since their days at Annapolis. In fact, Kimmel had been a groomsman in Halsey's wedding. It was likely that Halsey would encounter elements of the Japanese Navy en route—even if only to be overflown by reconnaissance planes or spotted by snooping submarines.

Both men knew that one false move might light the fuse to the Pacific powder keg. "How far do you want me to go?" Halsey bluntly asked his friend. Kimmel frowned and snapped back, "Goddammit, use your common sense!" Halsey and *Enterprise* sailed from Pearl Harbor the next day.[15]

The absence of battleships in the task force that steamed with *Enterprise* toward Wake had little to do with the growing importance of the aircraft carrier as a strategic weapon. There were many officers in the Navy—"black shoes," as opposed to those upstart aviators who wore brown shoes—who clung stubbornly to the doctrine of battleship might. But hurling fourteen-inch shells a dozen miles at one's opponent was about to change.

47

For *Arizona* or other battleships that might have accompanied *Enterprise,* it was a simple matter of math. The top speed of the *Arizona* and the standard classes of battleships built before the Washington Treaty was 21 knots (24 mph). *Enterprise,* the slowest of the three carriers then in the Pacific, could move along at 32 knots (37 mph). When it came to covering distances and getting the job done, *Enterprise* and its consorts were high-speed delivery machines. The plodding battleships simply could not keep up. Had they been along, the trip to Wake would have taken 50 percent longer, exposing the force to enemy submarines that much longer.

The day Halsey and *Enterprise* sailed from Pearl Harbor bound for Wake, President Roosevelt was trying to make his own departure from Washington. He had wanted to spend Thanksgiving with polio patients in Warm Springs, Georgia, one of his favorite respites. The trip kept being delayed, however, and at a morning press conference on the day after Thanksgiving, Friday, November 28, Roosevelt told reporters that he still hoped to get off by three o'clock that afternoon. Asked when he would be back in Washington, the president replied that he was uncertain and gave as the reason "the Japanese situation."

Roosevelt then read a press release: despite the undeclared U-boat war in the North Atlantic, American merchant vessels sailing between the United States and Spain and Portugal, North and South America, and throughout the Pacific would not be armed "under existing circumstances." Questioned how long "existing circumstances" might prevail, Roosevelt responded, "I think I would ask that question in Tokyo and not in Washington."

When questioned by a reporter if there was anything

Roosevelt could add "about these Japanese situations—I mean negotiations," the president replied, "I think it's better not." But then, having initially declined to comment, Roosevelt launched into lengthy "background"—under the rules of the day not to be attributed to him directly but to the "best information obtainable in Washington."

Roosevelt condemned Japanese expansion into French Indochina and noted that American territory in the Philippines was caught in "a sort of a horseshoe, open at the southern end" but surrounded by Japanese control of Indochina to the west and the Japanese-controlled mandates of the Caroline and Mariana Islands to the east. Fearing what Japanese domination across the whole of the Pacific might mean to America, the president concluded, "We are"—Roosevelt paused looking for the right word. "We are waiting."[16]

Roosevelt's "waiting" was for a response to a message Secretary of State Cordell Hull had handed Japanese Ambassador Kichisaburō Nomura on November 26. Marked "Strictly Confidential, Tentative and Without Commitment," it was an attempt to keep negotiations alive between the two powers. Under certain conditions, the United States suggested lifting the freeze on Japanese assets and resuming some measure of trade, but it also asked Japan to "withdraw all military, naval, air and police forces from China and from Indochina."[17]

However unlikely Japan was to do the latter, the presidential special left Washington on Friday afternoon. As it steamed south toward Warm Springs, Roosevelt held some glimmer of hope that the November 26 note might at least stave off military confrontation in the near-term. He had barely arrived and settled into the cottage dubbed "the little

White House" midday on Saturday, however, when Secretary Hull telephoned to report the likelihood of the Japanese breaking off negotiations. Hull implored the president to return to Washington.

Early the next morning, the president's train pulled out of Warm Springs and hurried back north. It arrived in the capital shortly before noon on Monday, December 1. "That means the president is here," Eleanor Roosevelt commented to reporters covering her press conference, as Fala, her husband's faithful Scottish terrier, trooped into the room for a welcome-home pat. Mrs. Roosevelt was in the process of announcing an invitation asking her to tour Latin America.[18]

The news the president soon received from Admiral Harold R. Stark, chief of naval operations, was grimmer. Code breakers deciphering Imperial Japanese Navy messages were at a loss to account for the location of its aircraft carriers. More ominously to some, the call signs for its ships afloat had been changed for the second time in a month. As Admiral Kimmel's intelligence briefing at Pearl Harbor put it, "The fact that service calls lasted only one month indicates an additional progressive step preparing for active operations on a large scale." Most evidence suggested a major thrust southward.[19]

By the time Roosevelt faced reporters the following morning, December 2, the focus was indeed on the buildup of Japanese forces in Indochina. Their naval, air, and land forces far exceeded the numbers that the Vichy French government had approved under extreme duress only months earlier, and now many more appeared to be en route. Attacks against China from the south or on Thailand were considered possibilities. Roosevelt reported to the press that he had directed Secretary Hull to query the

Japanese government "very politely," in his words, what its purpose was in doing so.

Asked if there was a time limit put on the question, the president replied, "No, no. That's a silly question. One doesn't put a time limit on things anymore. That's the last century. We are at peace with Japan. We are asking a perfectly polite question. I think that's all."[20]

That same day in Long Beach, California, Clara May Morse sat down and wrote letters to her sons, Francis and Norman. Despite their service on the same ship, she always penned separate messages to them. May had last seen "her boys" the previous June when the *Arizona* anchored at San Pedro for two weeks. Like many anxious parents, wives, and sweethearts, May rented a place near their ship's home port in anticipation of seeing them whenever *Arizona* was in town. She shared a little cottage with another Navy mother and waited less than patiently. With the Pacific Fleet assigned to Pearl Harbor indefinitely, there were no guarantees when *Arizona* might again drop anchor there.

This December, twenty-two-year-old Francis was about to celebrate five years with the Navy. May was proud that her son had just been promoted to Boatswain's Mate, First Class, but this was to be, she painfully told him, "the second Christmas I have been without you boys." She admitted to being "a bit worried over this old war"—as if fighting had actually begun in the Pacific—but then added that she was worrying "foolishly I guess, for I am sure we know how to handle it."

"Francis," his mother continued, "I am talking to you like you were here, anyway, I can just about see you all, how big powerful a scene the ships are, I would give a lot to see things like they used to be." Part of that wish may or may not have extended to Francis's wife of two years. May thought Dorothy was "hiding" from her, and the record is incomplete as to whether Francis and Dorothy had become a case of a Navy marriage frayed by time at sea or perhaps an overly protective mother-in-law. "I don't know where Dorothy is," May told Francis, adding, "of course she is ok."

In closing, May relayed her hope that "something can be figured out to keep us out of war." She signed off, encouraging him, "Now dear son, take care of your health and Mama is thinking of her boy every minute, let me hear from you often, and love and kisses to the sweetest boy in the world."[21]

To Norman, who had turned twenty a few weeks after *Arizona* sailed from San Pedro that summer, May confessed similar anxiety over the prospect of war. She wrote that she had had Norman's suit and "both the shirts" cleaned so that "they will be nice and clean for you." She asked if Norman had seen Francis lately and guessed "you boys got your Christmas package early as I was told we should mail early." But in her rush, May had forgotten to write, "not to open until Xmas." She assured Norman that it was all right if they had.

May thanked Norman for the *Our Navy* magazine she had been receiving and told him, "It's sure nice." Her only big news was the recent Torrance earthquake a few miles to the west of Long Beach. "Well, my dear son," May concluded, "you be careful, drop me a line as often as you can, and don't worry about me. I am fine, and thinking of both of my dear sons." Then, Clara May Morse put a three-cent stamp on each of the envelopes and pushed them through the slot of the Long Beach Post Office.[22]

*　　*　　*

As December 2 drew to a close over the waters of Pearl Harbor, Admiral Kimmel added his fourth postscript to an already lengthy letter addressed to Chief of Naval Operations Harold Stark, a graduate of Annapolis one year prior to Kimmel. They were old friends, and Stark would have felt slighted had Kimmel addressed him any way other than "Dear Betty," Stark's academy nickname.

With Halsey and *Enterprise* en route to Wake with their delivery of twelve Marine fighter planes and *Saratoga* still on the West Coast after its overhaul at Bremerton, Kimmel was nervous that the naval situation in the Pacific was stretching thinner. He recounted for Stark the status of defenses at Wake and Midway and noted that Halsey's advance was being covered by patrol aircraft flying out of those locations as well as out of Johnston Island, about 800 miles southwest of Pearl Harbor.

Despite years of war-gaming otherwise, there was a mindset that any threat to Hawaii was likely to come out of the west or southwest from the general direction of Japanese bases in the Marshall Islands. Submarines were judged a significant threat, and Kimmel told Stark that he had "issued orders to the Pacific Fleet to depth bomb all submarine contacts in the Oahu operating area."

Unknown to either Kimmel or Stark, ten Japanese submarines had left Yokosuka Naval Base in Japan on November 11 with instructions to rendezvous at Kwajalein in the Marshall Islands and then proceed toward Hawaii. Within a few days, the number of enemy submarines operating in Hawaiian waters would approach thirty.

Kimmel's final postscript to Stark showed that he still envisioned the long-held Plan Orange concept of advancing across the Pacific with a battle line for one decisive encounter with the enemy fleet. All these defensive actions were getting in the way of that. "I fear we may become so much concerned with defensive roles," Kimmel concluded, "that we may become unable to take the offensive."[23]

The following morning, December 3, Admiral Kimmel's morning intelligence briefing still contained no information on the whereabouts of the Japanese carriers. That afternoon, military and diplomatic circles in Washington, as well as the naval intelligence office at Pearl Harbor, learned from code intercepts that Japanese embassies around the world had been instructed to destroy code machines, ciphers, and important documents. Kimmel soon learned that these locations included the Japanese consulate in Honolulu.

In Washington, Roosevelt's naval aide, Captain John R. Beardall, advised the president that this was "very significant" and a clear sign that war was going to break out. "When do you think it will happen?" Roosevelt asked after reading the message.

"Most any time," Beardall replied.[24]

CHAPTER 4

Chasing Ghosts

Thursday, December 4

SEAMAN, FIRST CLASS, Edwin Chandler and Radioman, Third Class, Malcolm Shive each had brothers who were not in the United States Navy serving with them aboard the *Arizona*. How could that be? Civilians were not permitted aboard warships. Donald Chandler and Gordon Shive were present on the *Arizona* because—as they were *very* quick to tell anyone and everyone—they were proud members of the United States Marine Corps assigned to the *Arizona*'s Marine Detachment, known as its MARDET.

The Marine Corps was formed in the early days of the American Revolution. The Continental Congress initially authorized two battalions of experienced seamen who were also well acquainted with a musket. From this beginning, the Corps developed a specialty in seaborne operations that found Marines on the shores of Tripoli fighting the Barbary pirates in 1805, in China protecting American lives and property in the 1930s, and at a hundred places in between.

Marine detachments long served special duty aboard major ships of the US fleet. It was up to each vessel's captain to determine the specifics of the service based on need, but duties generally included serving as guards and orderlies for the captain and any embarked admiral, staffing the ship's brig and guarding prisoners, providing security for the ship while in port, and delivering messages and running errands ashore. But just as during the Revolution, the most crucial duty involved the defense of the ship at sea. When battle stations sounded, Marines could be found manning guns fore and aft right alongside their sailor shipmates.

The Marine Detachment aboard *Arizona* totaled eighty-eight men, five officers and eighty-three enlisted personnel, including First Sergeant John Duveene, a grizzled veteran, six months shy of twenty years in the service, who had the habit of calling his younger charges "champions." The ranking Marine aboard, Lieutenant Colonel Daniel Russell Fox, was assigned to Admiral Kidd's staff as the division Marine officer. This meant Fox had overall responsibility for the three Marine Detachments assigned to each of the three battleships in Kidd's Battleship Division One.

A tour at sea in a MARDET frequently gave a Marine officer a leg up for promotion, particularly if that service was aboard a ship with an admiral embarked. "The best of the best went to sea," recalled one of Fox's subordinates, "and the best of them went to the flagship."[1]

"Danny" Fox joined the Marines just days after his eighteenth birthday during the buildup to World War I. He survived the meat-grinder at Belleau Wood in France and emerged from the war with a Distinguished Service Cross (second only to the Medal of Honor) and a commission as a second lieutenant. By 1939, Fox had achieved the rank of major and begun a year of study at the Naval War College.

Upon graduation, he reported to the *Arizona* at Pearl Harbor to serve under Admiral Kidd.

Fox's wife, Elsie, and their three-year-old son, Daniel, Jr., followed as far as Long Beach. Like so many families, they took up residence there to be as close as possible should the *Arizona* return to the West Coast. According to Fox family lore, on one occasion when the ship did so—likely the two blissful weeks anchored at San Pedro at the end of June 1941 remembered by so many—Admiral Kidd invited by-then Lieutenant Colonel Fox and his wife to dinner aboard ship. The parents tried to hire a babysitter for little Daniel, but when none could be found, they took the youngster along to the formal affair. Admiral Kidd, his own son about to graduate from Annapolis, did not seem to mind.[2]

While the *Arizona* was at sea in early December 1941, its Marine Detachment prepared to undergo a change of command. Major Alan Shapley, a well-liked 1927 graduate of Annapolis, had a new assignment in San Diego as the personnel officer for the Amphibious Corps, Pacific Fleet. He would be turning over command of the *Arizona*'s MARDET to Captain John H. Earle, Jr., who was transferring from the detachment on the *Tennessee*. Except for perhaps an extra inspection and a brief change-of-command ceremony, none of this had much impact on Private, First Class, Gordon Shive. He was happy that his younger brother had just joined the *Arizona*'s crew.

Radioman, Third Class, Malcolm Shive was indeed a newbie on the ship. He came aboard on October 27, the day *Arizona* returned to Pearl Harbor after its collision with the *Oklahoma*. Malcolm reported from the hospital ship *Solace*

(AH-5), on which he had gotten a transit to Pearl Harbor from San Diego. He was eager to join his big brother, the Marine. The Shive boys had experienced their share of turmoil in recent years and to be serving together on a great battleship was a dream come true.

Marine Gordon Shive was a month shy of turning twenty-one. Malcolm was not quite two years his junior. The boys grew up in Laguna Beach, California, during the 1920s, when the town was a coastal enclave of barely two thousand souls. Their father, Grover, was a gardener, and their mother, Lois, worked as a laundress doing washing and ironing for a local cleaners. Gordon and Malcolm ran around as barefooted beach bums, and their world seemed good. But shortly after a third brother, Robert, joined the family, Grover developed a brain tumor and died in the spring of 1935 at the age of fifty.

Soon afterward, Lois Shive remarried—or at least took up with a man named Westgate—likely, in part, out of economic necessity.[3] By then, Gordon and Malcolm were well into their teens. They clashed with this new male in the household and quickly came to refer to him as "the mean son-of-a-bitch."

Gordon escaped first. After graduating from Laguna High School in 1939 with respectable grades, he enrolled in Fullerton Junior College, but dropped out during the spring of his freshman year to join the Marines. Throughout, he remained devoted to his mother. "Dearest Mother," Gordon cabled from boot camp on Mother's Day 1940, "Just remember this. That wherever I am and whatever I do you are always foremost in my thoughts."[4]

Having lettered in football during high school, Gordon was hard and lean and took to the Marine lifestyle right away. Putting his shoulders into a commonality of purpose as a member of a Marine rowing team helped to put some of the bad memories of home behind him. Gordon and his teammates won the right to represent the *Arizona* in the Pacific Fleet Whaleboat Rowing Championships and placed second. Of the MARDET on the *Arizona*, Gordon reported to his mother that they were "all swell fellows."

Malcolm Shive lacked Gordon's physique as well as any semblance of academic achievement. Malcolm's report card from his sophomore year at Laguna High during the 1938–39 term boasted a high grade of C- in wood shop along with a D- in English and an F in auto shop. But Malcolm, too, had specific interests, and he found his own escape by initially attending radio school. A month after he turned seventeen, Lois signed the papers for him to join the Navy. Malcolm, a slight lad, enlisted on November 18, 1940, and after basic training found that his radio experience gave him a leg up in getting his rating as a Radioman, Third Class.

Gordon and Malcolm's kid brother, Robert, could not remember the last time he saw Gordon, but his memory of Malcolm's final appearance at the family home was vivid. Sometime before shipping out to the fleet in the summer of 1941, Malcolm came home after a late night of drinking with his Navy buddies. Predictably, he got into an argument with his stepfather. Heated words were exchanged and probably a fist or two. Malcolm picked up his seabag and headed out the door. Robert never saw him again.[5]

The good news for Malcolm was that he was headed for a reunion with Gordon aboard the *Arizona*. While Malcolm was still in training, Gordon had written him that if he got the chance to pick a good ship, he should "try a cruise on the good old At 'Em, which would mean *Arizona*. We would have a swell time together."[6]

Still, Gordon expressed complete surprise one day when he came back from liberty and the first person he saw as he came over the gangway was Malcolm. "It sure does seem good to have him around again," Gordon wrote their mother. A few days later, Gordon and Malcolm headed into Honolulu to celebrate Malcolm's eighteenth birthday.

The other set of Navy-Marine brothers on the *Arizona* were the Chandlers. They grew up all the way across the country from the Shives along the creek bottoms of western Alabama. Originally called Lick Skillet, the town of Millport had about two hundred people and a collection of water-powered mills when the Georgia Pacific Railroad built through the area in the 1880s.

John Carl Chandler and his wife, Pearl, had eight children, the oldest of whom was Edwin Ray Chandler, born April 23, 1916, in Millport. Ray, as he was usually called, finished high school there and for reasons not entirely clear, made his way to Washington State, where he enlisted in the Navy at Seattle on March 13, 1939. Prior to leaving for basic training at San Diego, he met Mary Louise McCary, who was about four years Ray's junior. Ray reported to the *Arizona* while it was anchored off San Pedro on May 14, and then married Mary Louise on July 29, when the ship was at Seattle. They set up housekeeping in Long Beach, but Ray was to spend most of the next year either at sea or in Pearl Harbor.

The number four son of the Chandler clan, Donald, soon got roving feet of his own. After Donald turned eighteen in the spring of 1940, he enlisted in the Marine Corps and headed for basic training at Parris Island, South Carolina.

Why Don chose the Marines over the Navy is uncertain, but he seemed well suited for duty with a MARDET when his request for assignment to the *Arizona* was approved. He arrived aboard to join his big brother Ray on November 6, 1940, while the ship was undergoing its last major overhaul at Bremerton.

Meanwhile, twenty-year-old Mary Louise Chandler had spent most of the first two years of her marriage alone in Long Beach. After the *Arizona* called at San Pedro for two weeks at the end of June 1941, Ray and Mary decided that they couldn't bear to be apart any longer. Despite Ray's meager salary of fifty-four dollars per month, the couple hatched a plan that Mary would move to Honolulu and hope that Ray might be able to spend plenty of nights ashore when the *Arizona* was in port at Pearl Harbor.

Mary sailed from San Francisco on August 1 and arrived in Honolulu on August 6. Housing was tight, but she managed to find a small apartment, and she and Ray could finally enjoy brief interludes of marital bliss. The other beneficiary of this arrangement, of course, was Marine Private Don Chandler, who managed to wrangle a few home-cooked meals from his sister-in-law when both brothers were ashore.[7]

On the evening of Wednesday, December 3, the Shive and Chandler brothers were among those in the *Arizona*'s crew looking forward to another stint in port. The *Arizona* had been at sea for more than a week, since before Thanksgiving. Along with *Oklahoma* and *Nevada,* the other battleships of Admiral Kidd's Battleship Division One, the ship was momentarily anchored in Lahaina Roadstead, the deep and relatively protected anchorage between the western end of Maui and the island of Lanai. The US Fleet had used this area as a regular anchorage before the channel into Pearl Harbor was deepened. Given the threat of war late in 1941, Lahaina Roadstead offered a handy place to position ships without them being underway or constricted to the confines of Pearl Harbor.

Japanese submarines lurking in Hawaiian waters were well aware of the Lahaina anchorage and under orders to report the comings and goings of vessels there just as Japanese spies were doing from the heights above Pearl Harbor. "Maneuvers usually beat painting," recalled Seaman, First Class, Don Stratton about the *Arizona*'s current time at sea, "but we all felt uneasy about *this* maneuver." Two things happened to underscore those feelings of unease.

Around 1:00 a.m. on the morning of December 4, the general quarters alarm blared throughout the ship, and those men in their hammocks rolled out in their skivvies and raced to join their comrades who had the night watch. Destroyers stationed around the outskirts of the Lahaina anchorage had detected sonar images that could only be Japanese submarines. As every sailor manned his battle station, lookouts scoured the surrounding seas under a full moon for any sign of the telltale wake of a torpedo. "We weren't at war," Don Stratton remembered, but "it was starting to feel that way."[8]

Admiral Kidd was taking no chances. He ordered Battleship Division One to weigh anchor and steam for the open sea to conduct live-fire gunnery exercises long planned for that day. The early morning disruption and subsequent early departure left the *Arizona*'s crew with little rest, however, and made for a particularly long day for the Anderson twins. John "Andy" Anderson was assigned as a gunner in Turret No. 4, aft. His brother, Jake, had a battle station on one of the antiaircraft guns out on deck.

The Anderson twins hailed from Minnesota, but had been born in Verona, North Dakota, a speck of a place some seventy miles southwest of Fargo. There isn't much there today, although the town boasted 250 residents in the 1920 census. Sometime on August 26, 1917, nineteen-year-old Laura Anderson gave birth, and she and her husband, Edwin, named their twins John Delmar Anderson and Delbert Jake Anderson. In time, their family would include ten children: the twins, four other boys, and four girls.

Two years after the twins were born, Laura and Edwin moved about one hundred miles east to Dilworth, Minnesota, in the Red River Valley just east of Moorhead. John and Jake—the latter was rarely Delbert—graduated from high school together in Dilworth and pondered their future. They had dreams of college—John, in particular, was interested in the University of Minnesota—but money was a problem.

Life in Dilworth had been relatively good—their father had become a judge—but with a family of ten children, Edwin Anderson told the twins that they would have to work to help pay their way. Their mother's brother, uncle Ray Stokes, had always spun tall tales of his time in the US Navy, and the Anderson twins decided to give it a try. They had done everything together growing up, but this time John got the jump on Jake. He took the Great Northern Railway to Minneapolis and enlisted on March 16, 1937, a few months before his twentieth birthday. Jake, having briefly flirted with joining the Marines, followed him two months later.

After basic training at Great Lakes, John Anderson reported to the aircraft carrier *Saratoga* at Puget Sound

Navy Yard in Bremerton, Washington. There were too many new seamen assigned to the ship, however, and he was ordered to the nearby *Arizona* as it sat in dry dock. John "rode the Arizona," as he put it, for five months and then transferred to a destroyer in the Asiatic Squadron.

Twin brother Jake Anderson reported to the *Arizona* on September 19, 1937, at San Pedro and stayed aboard. John, who was increasingly nicknamed "Andy" by his shipmates, saw duty in the South China Sea and became familiar with the Japanese aircraft then engaged in operations against Chiang Kai-shek's Nationalist Chinese forces. Jake wanted his twin on the *Arizona,* and as the brothers wrote letters back and forth, Jake kept urging John to rejoin him on BB-39. Finally, after a stint on the destroyer *Ellet* (DD-398) operating out of Pearl Harbor, John reported back aboard the *Arizona* on December 6, 1940.

By the following December, the Anderson boys were twenty-four and held the rating of Boatswain's Mate, Second Class. As such, they were at the heart of the *Arizona*'s operations. A boatswain's mate might well be called a sailor's sailor. Not only did he have to know how to handle lines, anchor chains, and equipment for loading general stores, fuel, and ammunition, but he also had to train and supervise work parties of seamen in those duties as well as the maintenance of the ship's exterior structure, deck equipment, and small boats. If there was a problem, boatswain's mates were front and center in damage-control parties. All that changed, of course, when battle stations sounded. Then, John Anderson's position was below decks in Turret No. 4 and brother Jake manned an antiaircraft gun above decks.

* * *

It was one thing to be assigned to the deck crew, but slots in the gun turrets were highly coveted. This was an extra special fraternity. The men worked and slept in extremely close quarters, and there was also a bit of smug pride that they were the ones responsible for the "big guns."

One didn't ask to join a gun crew so much as he was recruited. According to Gunner's Mate, Third Class, John Watson Rampley, "A man's name was presented by the senior petty officer to the whole gun crew. If any of them didn't like him or thought he wouldn't be compatible, you didn't get in. So, if you did make it, you felt that you were part of a select crew."[9]

Turret men lived on the base or bottom deck of the turret. "Lived" frequently overstated actual conditions. Here, as in other parts of the ship, each sailor had an assigned sleeping space, and it was his job to set it up the last thing at night and break it down the first thing in the morning. Enlisted men either hung hammocks from hooks that were attached to overhead deck supports or set up foldable cots. Big rings at each end of the hammock slipped over the hooks, and lines running through the sides of the hammock were then cinched tight. It required a hefty pull and a solid knot to keep its occupant from falling out and onto hammocks below. Newbies forced to set up and climb into upper hammocks took a good deal of guff from those below to make sure their knot held.

Old salts swore by hammocks on rough seas—claiming they were more forgiving of the roll of the ship. Still, it was considered a promotion when one was assigned to a cot. Younger hands took some time getting used to the notched dowels—1 inch by 1 inch by 16 inch "spreaders"—that held the outside lines of hammocks apart at each end. These kept the canvas from engulfing its occupant like a hungry caterpillar. One's hammock or cot—rolled neatly or folded and stowed away during the day—along with a personal locker about 14 inches wide by 20 inches high by 14 inches deep in which to stow uniforms, toiletries, books and magazines, and minimal personal gear, constituted one's personal space.[10]

Each of the four main turrets had four or five levels (turrets No. 2 and No. 3 were a level taller so they could maneuver and fire over turrets No. 1 and No. 4.) The telephone talker in each turret received orders from the fire control director on the bridge who was in contact with the main battery directors atop the tripod masts. The turret talker communicated between the levels of the turret as fifteen-hundred-pound shells and one-hundred-pound bags of gunpowder—made of silk to avoid an errant static electricity charge—were hoisted from the ammunition holds to the gun deck level and loaded into the breech of each gun.

Because the deck log of the *Arizona* for November and early December was destroyed, there is some question as to which guns were fired on December 4 and what happened when the officer of the deck reported a periscope in an area where no American submarines were known to be operating. Scuttlebutt later spread throughout the ship that Captain Van Valkenburgh suggested to Admiral Kidd that the *Arizona* remain at sea as a decoy while its escorting destroyers ferreted out the intruder.

By one account, Kidd proposed the idea of a decoy operation to Admiral Kimmel, but Kimmel, growing increasingly worried about submarines, rejected it. Kimmel ordered Kidd to return his entire division to Pearl Harbor as scheduled. Kleber S. Masterson, a 1930 graduate of Annapolis who would become a vice admiral, was then a lieutenant on the *Arizona* serving as a gunnery officer. Masterson later speculated that Kimmel ended up with eight battleships in Pearl Harbor all at once—something that had not happened since before the announcement of the oil embargo in July—because of his fear of submarine attacks.[11]

Regardless of what did or did not happen that day when it came to chasing the ghosts of Japanese submarines, after the day's live-fire exercises, a second event occurred—the first being the hasty departure from tranquil Lahaina Roadstead—that underscored the unease among the crew. In some respects, it was far less serious than the threat of a torpedo attack, but to a nineteen-year-old seaman it was perhaps even more ominous, certainly more personal, because it served warning that the entire fabric of life aboard ship was changing.

Athletics had long been a source of recreation, camaraderie, and morale among the crew, and few things were more important than the football game scheduled for that Sunday against an Army team from Schofield Barracks. After the morning's gunnery practice, the football team assembled on deck for a much-needed practice. The big game was only three days away.

Barely had the drills begun, however, when an officer strode up to the players, returned their hurried salutes, and informed them that practice was cancelled. Moans and groans gave way to disbelief as the officer continued. Not only was practice at sea cancelled, but also the Sunday game. In fact, he unceremfconiously informed the team that the entire season was over. Gear was to be stored in the athletic locker after returning to port. In the meantime, players who bunked in the fourteen-inch turrets were told to stack their equipment in the turrets.[12]

*   *   *

Meanwhile, a few time zones to the east, the headlines on the final edition of the *Chicago Daily Tribune* were concerned with war, but not against Japan. Robert R. McCormick's newspaper, which unabashedly proclaimed on its masthead to be "the world's greatest," was as anti-Roosevelt as a media mouthpiece could be in those years. "Colonel" McCormick, a title from his service in World War I, and his publishing cousins, Joseph Medill Patterson, founder of the *New York Daily News,* and Eleanor "Cissy" Patterson of the *Washington Times-Herald,* were staunch Republicans certain that Roosevelt's New Deal was inexorably changing the American fabric at home just as his internationalism was leading the United States into another conflict in Europe. Now, thanks to a Washington leak, McCormick had damning evidence that Roosevelt was laying the groundwork for a massive intervention in Europe.

"F.D.R.'s War Plans!" announced the *Tribune*'s headline of December 4. Their reported goal was ten million armed men, half of whom were to embark for Europe and "smash" the Nazis by the summer of 1943. Calling this news an "astounding document, which represents decisions and commitments affecting the destinies of peoples throughout the civilized world," the *Tribune* characterized the report as "a blueprint for total war on a scale unprecedented in at least two oceans and three continents."

As for Japan, "F.D.R.'s War Plans" recommended assisting the Soviet Union with the defense of Siberia, making a defensive stand in Malaysia, continuing an economic blockade, and countering Japanese military power directly with a coordinated Chinese offensive against Japanese occupation forces. Japan's interests in Siberia had long been a matter of debate in Tokyo given that crucial natural resources lay to the south. Counteroffensives by China against Japan had met with only limited success since 1937. That tended to focus on Japan's intentions in Southeast Asia. A separate article reported the massing of Japanese troops in Saigon and included a large map highlighting possible Japanese advances from there.[13]

While Colonel McCormick's newspaper took on Franklin Roosevelt yet again, the America First Committee opened its campaign to champion candidates in the upcoming midterm elections. Founded in September 1940 to oppose *any* American involvement in the war in Europe, America First pledged to support isolationist candidates for Congress regardless of party. Republican senator Gerald P. Nye of North Dakota and hero Charles Lindbergh headed the list of speakers slated to tour the country during December. Other notables on the America First circuit included Republican congresswoman Jeannette Rankin of Montana, the first woman elected to national office in the United States. One month into her first term in 1917, Rankin had cast one of fifty votes in the House of Representatives against the United States entering World War I. Senator Nye was scheduled to keynote the week's signature event before some twenty-five hundred people in Pittsburgh on Sunday afternoon, December 7.[14]

In the shadow of the Brooklyn Navy Yard, where the *Arizona* slid down the ways a quarter of a century earlier, there was a decidedly different tone. New York Mayor Fiorello La Guardia dedicated the city's first defense-related housing project and assured 750 onlookers that the United States was not bluffing in its preparations for the present national emergency. Called Wallabout Houses, the 207-unit apartment complex was built for married enlisted men and their families from the Coast Guard, Navy, and Marines. "This beautiful structure means more than providing housing for a small percentage of enlisted men," La Guardia told the crowd. "It indicates that Uncle Sam means business." The thirteen-story building had been erected in just over six months and was already filling with tenants. "We do not know what will happen tomorrow, next week, or next month," the mayor concluded, "but the United States Navy stands ready."[15]

On the economic front, under the caption "The Siege of Japan," editors of the *New York Times* offered pointed thoughts on the impact of the July 1941 embargo on Japan's economy. Before the embargo, Japan had relied chiefly upon the United States, the British Empire, and the Netherlands Indies "for such industrial and military necessities as petroleum, iron, steel, aluminum, lead, zinc, copper, tin, machine tools, wool and cotton." The embargo cut off an estimated 75 percent of Japan's normal imports. Since freezing Japanese assets, United States exports to Japan had dwindled to practically nothing—$500 in September 1941 compared to $18 million in September 1940 ($310 million in 2017 dollars). Whether this had encouraged Japan to reform its expansionist foreign policy or simply made it more desperate remained to be seen. "Japan is facing international economic siege and she is very vulnerable," the *Times* noted. "If there was ever a country that needed to live on terms of peaceful trade with the rest of the world, it is Japan."[16]

Perhaps it would, but Admiral Kimmel's morning intelligence summary still offered no hint about the location of Japan's aircraft carriers. In yet another sign pointing to major operations south from Japan, the powerful radio transmitter at Takao on Formosa had adopted Radio Tokyo's call sign and was handling a flurry of radio traffic to major commands throughout the Japanese fleet.

That evening, Kimmel learned that the US Navy was preparing its own destruction of secret and classified material. The naval station on Guam, part of Admiral Thomas Hart's Asiatic Fleet and not under Kimmel's command, received orders from Washington to "destroy all secret and confidential publications and other classified matter" and "be prepared to destroy instantly all classified matter you retain in event of emergency."

Just what that emergency might be went without saying. Guam was thirty-eight hundred miles distant from Pearl Harbor, well beyond the outpost of Wake currently in the process of being reinforced, but it was only 600 miles from the Japanese-controlled Caroline Islands and Japan's major naval base at Truk. If Japan wanted to disrupt sea lanes between Wake and the Philippines, Guam looked vulnerable.[17]

As the *Arizona* steamed on through the night of December 4, the Czarnecki brothers from Michigan listened to the sounds of the ship. Tony and Stanley Czarnecki were particularly attuned to its mechanical workings because they had to be—that was their job. Their father, Martin, had immigrated to the United States from Poland in 1903 when he was a teenager. He met Varonaca Pettyka, a first-generation American, whose parents had also emigrated from Poland to Michigan. "Veronica," as her name became Anglicized, was seven years Martin's junior and the two married in Michigan. They set up housekeeping in Rogers City on the shores of Lake Huron just east of the Straits of Mackinac and welcomed their firstborn, Anthony Francis "Tony" Czarnecki, on February 7, 1915.

Martin worked as a laborer in a stone quarry, and Veronica gave birth to six more children—five boys and a girl—over the next dozen years. Their fourth child, a boy born in 1919, was named Stanislaus, which soon became "Stanley." By 1930, the youngest of their brood had arrived and the family of nine had moved to Blackman Township, in Jackson County between Battle Creek and Ann Arbor. Martin worked in an auto parts factory, and in addition to tending to seven children, Veronica worked as domestic help for another family.

Tony left home first. He enlisted in the Navy on October 14, 1935, at Detroit and headed west to Naval Station Great Lakes for his basic training. He marched up the gangplank of the *Arizona* as it was moored at Bremerton on February 8 of the following year and stayed there. When Tony seemed content and signed up for another hitch four years later, Stanley followed his lead and made the trip to Detroit to enlist on December 18, 1939. Stanley also did his basic training at Great Lakes. He spent time aboard the former battleship *Utah* (BB-31, re-designated AG-16), which had been converted to a target ship and was used as a platform for antiaircraft gunnery practice, and reported to the *Arizona* on May 21, 1940.

By then, older brother Tony was a Machinist's Mate, First Class, well up the ladder of petty officer rates. His responsibilities included operating the main engines and making whatever adjustments and repairs might be required on the open seas. Machinist mates also had to be familiar with the ship's distilling plant that produced potable water for the crew's consumption and the evaporators that removed salt from briny seawater and turned it into suitable boiler feedwater. If it worked with a clang or a whir, chances were that a machinist's mate might be required to put a wrench to it.

Younger brother Stanley had duty with the engine room force, a part of the broader mechanical branch that was responsible for tending the boilers. After almost seventeen months on the *Arizona*, Stanley was a Fireman, First Class. To the uninitiated, that sounded like a much higher rank than it actually was. Because of the more strenuous work in the engine room, the engine room force was organized slightly differently than the deck force. Engine room men received more money than their deck counterparts, and a Fireman, First Class, got paid at the same pay grade as third-class petty officers in other branches.

Stanley Czarnecki had been promoted to Fireman, First Class, as of September 1, 1941, and this was one grade above Seaman, First Class. His job was not to put out fires—aboard ship everyone had fire responsibilities should one break out—but rather to tend to the fires that heated the water in the boilers that produced the steam to turn the turbines that connected to the four propeller shafts. With so much water involved in the boiler system, operating, adjusting, and repairing pumps was a routine part of the job. Drifting off to sleep in close quarters surrounded by the sounds of machinery was something one got used to.

Two thousand miles to the west, Vice Admiral Bill Halsey watched as the *Enterprise* turned into the wind to launch the planes of Marine Fighting Squadron 211 toward Wake. Mission accomplished, the carrier and its escorts turned eastward. If all went well, *Enterprise* was scheduled to enter Pearl Harbor late on December 6. The crew of the *Arizona* expected their ship to be moored along Battleship Row awaiting the carrier's arrival in anticipation of a high-stakes baseball game between the two ships still scheduled for the next day despite the abrupt curtailment of the football season.

Halsey's orders had been for the task force to operate under wartime conditions, but it had yet to sight any Japanese planes or submarines. Halsey remained suspicious nonetheless. As he scrutinized the building seas, he did not know that hundreds of miles to the north of his position a fleet of six aircraft carriers was roughly paralleling his eastward course.

CHAPTER 5

Weekend Dreaming

Friday, December 5

T HE ACRONYM TGIF, "Thank God It's Friday," had not
yet become widely popularized in American culture, but
that did not mean sailors on the *Arizona* were not dreaming of the weekend. For some, there would be continued
duty aboard ship and no break, but for others, a few hours
of liberty ashore on Saturday or Sunday meant time to
unwind with a beer or two, do some last-minute Christmas shopping for the folks back home, or maybe take in
a movie if the one showing on the deck of the *Arizona*
Saturday night did not appeal. A lucky few, mostly married officers and senior enlisted men, would be granted
regular liberty ashore to spend Saturday night with their
wives.

There was a big difference between liberty and leave.
"Liberty" was short-term, an authorized absence from duty
for less than forty-eight hours. Generally, when ships were
in port, no sailor could be deprived of liberty on shore for
more than twelve days unless — in the words of the venera-
ble *Bluejackets' Manual* — "the exigencies of the service or
the unhealthfulness of the port prevent." Liberty could also

be denied to those whose prior conduct on shore had proven "discreditable to the service."

"Leave" was the authorized absence from duty for more than forty-eight hours. At the discretion of their commanding officer, enlisted men whose services could be spared were granted up to thirty days leave in any one calendar year, exclusive of travel time. A month's paid vacation per year was a major perk. Because leaves had to be distributed throughout the year to maintain the efficiency of the ship, it behooved one to make requests early.[1]

Sonny Christiansen, one of the *Arizona*'s bakers, and his younger brother, Buddy, who was still green to the ship after only one month aboard, had big plans. They each had liberty on Sunday and were going into Honolulu to take photographs together in uniform to send home to their mother. With the *Arizona* at sea so much during the past month, they had not had the opportunity to do so sooner, but they figured they still stood a good chance of getting a package to her by Christmas. Dress whites would be their order of the day.

The routine at sea Friday morning was relatively unhurried. The three battleships of Admiral Kidd's Battleship Division One, along with their escorting destroyers, plowed their way through calm seas inbound to Pearl Harbor. Any thought of using the *Arizona* as a decoy to flush out snooping Japanese submarines had not come to pass. According to Lieutenant Commander Edward T. Layton, Admiral Kimmel's intelligence officer, "Our attention that Friday morning at Pacific Fleet headquarters was focused on the western side of the Pacific." The flurry of Japanese radio messages radiating from Takao continued.[2]

As Pearl Harbor prepared to welcome the return of Admiral Kidd's battleships, there were also hectic departures as two task forces put to sea on different missions. With *Enterprise* at sea with Bill Halsey ferrying Marine fighters to Wake Island, the *Lexington* was the only aircraft carrier remaining in Pearl Harbor. Her crew liked it that way and most had their own plans for the weekend. These were rudely shattered at the last minute, however, when Admiral Kimmel ordered Rear Admiral John H. Newton to deliver eighteen Marine Vought SB2U-3 Vindicators, single-engine, carrier-based dive-bombers, to reinforce air defenses at Midway.

Newton gathered three heavy cruisers and five destroyers around *Lexington* and headed west-northwest toward Midway, thirteen hundred miles distant. Given that American ships had not frequented that general area for some time, Newton later testified that he was convinced that "there might be more danger from submarines than we had considered in the past" and, accordingly, "set a speed of 17 knots in day light and zig-zagged." He also ordered scout planes from the cruisers to cover their advance.[3]

Aboard *Lexington,* the crew swallowed their disappointment over a lost weekend and settled into the routine at sea, which included the usual rounds of training exercises. Electrician's Mate, Third Class, Bill Dye, a newly minted nineteen-year-old from Petaluma, California, six months out of high school, was one of those still dreaming of the weekend that might have been. Dye had to cancel what he called "a top notch" dinner invitation with friends in Honolulu on Saturday night. He would have to settle for the Saturday night movie on the *Lexington*'s hangar deck instead.[4]

Admiral Newton's immediate superior also left Pearl Harbor this Friday. Vice Admiral Wilson Brown, commander of the Scouting Force, took his flagship, the heavy cruiser *Indianapolis,* and five destroyers converted to double as high-speed minesweepers and sailed for Johnston Island. This atoll was nine hundred miles southwest of Pearl Harbor and roughly halfway to the Japanese-controlled Marshall Islands.

Brown planned to reconnoiter the area because of reports of Japanese submarines converging there. He was on record as asserting a few weeks earlier, "Japanese fliers were not capable of executing [an aerial attack on Hawaii] successfully, and that if they did, we should certainly be able to follow their planes back to their carriers and destroy the carriers so that it would be a very expensive experiment."[5]

With the three task forces led by Halsey, Newton, and Brown at sea and other ships scattered along the West Coast of the United States, Admiral Kimmel's Pacific Fleet was relatively dispersed. Of the ships under his command—not counting PT boats, harbor tugs, barges, patrol craft, and similar types or those ships assigned to the various coastal naval districts—101 vessels were someplace other than Pearl Harbor. Spread across the Pacific were three aircraft carriers, one battleship, ten heavy cruisers, three light cruisers, twenty-four destroyers, nine destroyer-minesweepers, three minesweepers, nine oilers, eighteen submarines, seven seaplane tenders, and fourteen transports, cargo vessels, ocean-going tugs, and auxiliary ships.

Almost uncannily, the number of ships inside Pearl Harbor or in waters immediately adjacent to Oahu also numbered 101. Despite this balance, it was highly unusual for eight battleships to be moored in Pearl Harbor at the same time, but with Battleship Division One inbound to Pearl Harbor that was exactly what was about to happen. Indeed, the only absent member of the Pacific battleship divisions was *Colorado*, still undergoing an overhaul at Bremerton.

Once *Arizona*, *Nevada*, and *Oklahoma* tied up along Battleship Row later in the day on Friday, Kimmel's ships present at Pearl Harbor numbered eight battleships, two heavy cruisers, six light cruisers, thirty destroyers, fourteen minesweepers, nine minelayers, two oilers, four submarines, six seaplane tenders, one hospital ship, and nineteen assorted vessels, including the aging target ship *Utah* and the repair ship *Vestal*. No aircraft carriers were present.[6]

As far as the crews were concerned, this clustering of battleships would provide the opportunity for some overdue socializing among friends as well as some postponed athletic contests. Kimmel's rationale for marshaling his battleships in such a fashion was more problematic and continues to be debated three quarters of a century later.

Worrying about the Japanese submarines that were increasingly prowling Hawaiian waters—witness the recent alert at Lahaina Roadstead—Kimmel may well have judged Pearl Harbor to be the safest place for the battleships. He may also have been thinking of the offensive—just as he had told Admiral Stark the day before. Should the Japanese attack the Philippines en route to their conquest of Southeast Asia, sailing the fleet westward to the relief of the islands was long-standing Plan Orange doctrine. Japanese land-based air in the Marshall and Caroline islands had recently made this prospect less likely, but Kimmel still thought that he might be called upon to conduct combined fleet operations westward.

Back in Washington, President Roosevelt concluded a late Friday morning press conference. Asked if there had been any response from Japan to his query about its intentions in Indochina, Roosevelt replied that he wouldn't know until he lunched with his secretary of state. The reporters who crowded into the Oval Office were well aware that the president had met with congressional leaders the day before and passed the word "that it would be advisable for Congress to remain in session and forego more than perhaps two three-day recesses during the Christmas holiday period because of the Japanese situation."[7]

When Secretary of State Hull arrived at the White House for lunch at 1:00 p.m., he had no positive news to report and was particularly glum. His mood continued into the regular cabinet meeting Roosevelt held later that afternoon. Hull said little except to express his frustration over the ongoing conversations with Japan's envoys.

According to Secretary of Labor Frances Perkins, the only woman in the cabinet, Hull felt certain that Japan was not serious about reaching any sort of a rapprochement. "I'm convinced that they don't intend to make any honorable agreement with us about anything, or to come to any understandings," Hull told the president. "I think this is useless and futile." Nonetheless, Roosevelt turned to him and admonished, "Don't let [the negotiations] deteriorate and break up if you can possibly help it."

But there did not seem to be any thought that Japan would directly attack the United States. Instead, the cabinet speculated about Japan's continued moves into Indochina and whether or not it would attack the British at Singapore. Roosevelt went around the table and asked each cabinet member what the American response should be if that occurred. The consensus—perhaps, as Perkins put it, more in the form of "moral advice" to the president than an intimate knowledge of the situation—was that the United States would have to go to Britain's aid. There was no mention of the Philippines as a possible target. Hawaii? That was definitely out of the question.

As the meeting ended, Secretary of the Navy Frank Knox, whom Perkins described as unusually agitated, assured the group that the Navy's sources of communication were "in pretty good shape" and that he expected to be able to report "within the next week" the whereabouts of the Japanese fleet. "So," concluded Perkins, "we went off to our various activities planned for the weekend."[8]

Meanwhile, in the far-off Philippines, Lieutenant General Douglas MacArthur told a visiting British admiral that he expected war with Japan, but not until the following spring. Vice Admiral Sir Tom Phillips of the Royal Navy had flown from Singapore to Manila to meet with MacArthur and the commander of the US Asiatic Fleet, Admiral Thomas Hart. Phillips brought with him the encouraging news that the British admiralty had deployed the battle cruiser *Repulse* and the battleship *Prince of Wales* to strengthen its fleet off Southeast Asia.

Across the International Date Line, it was already Saturday, December 6, in Manila, and an urgent communiqué soon interrupted the second day of Phillips's visit. It reported that Japanese amphibious forces were indeed bound to the Malay Peninsula. Phillips hurriedly returned to Singapore, telling MacArthur and Hart that he intended to gather what ships he could around the *Repulse* and *Prince of Wales* and sail north to meet the threat. MacArthur reminded his own field commanders that any Japanese invasion of the Philippines was to be repulsed on the beaches and the territory held at all costs.[9]

As the *Arizona* passed through the Pearl Harbor entrance and into the harbor's inner lochs, the ships of the Pacific Fleet on hand made for an impressive sight. Rounding Hospital Point, the *Arizona* entered the channel between Ford

Island to port (left) and the mainland to starboard (right). Beyond the hospital, the first major installations on the mainland were the dry dock facilities and a series of oil storage tanks that spread across the hillside above the docks.

The destroyer *Shaw* (DD-373) rested in the floating dry dock undergoing repairs. Dry Dock No. 2 and No. 3 were unoccupied, but No. 1 was crowded with two destroyers, *Downes* (DD-375) and *Cassin* (DD-372), ahead of the battleship *Pennsylvania*. Aging veteran though it was, *Pennsylvania* was the flagship of the Pacific Fleet and sitting high and dry with three of its four propeller shafts removed. Its normal berth, because of its flagship status, was B-2, just beyond Dry Dock No. 1 along 1010 Dock, so named for its length in feet. In the battleship's absence, the cruiser *Helena* (CL-50) sat in its place with the minelayer *Oglala* (CM-4) moored alongside and separated from it by eight-foot-wide floats.[10]

Beyond 1010 Dock, the Southeast Loch extended inland from the main channel directly opposite Ford Island. Its waters housed the submarine base, but more important to sailors, the fleet landings near Merry Point at its far end were the usual gateways to liberty ashore. Bloch Arena and the main gate to the base sat just inland from the landings. On the hill above the sub base another tank farm sprouted before the crest along Makalapa Drive, which was adorned with officer quarters, including Admiral Kimmel's residence.

Clusters of destroyers were tied up together at the far end of the East Loch beyond Ford Island, but it was the moorings along the island's eastern side that commanded the most attention. These were home to the backbone of the Pacific battleship fleet. Numbered F-1, or Fox-1, to

F-8 from southwest to northeast, the moorings, or quays, spread out almost three quarters of a mile. With good reason, everyone called it Battleship Row.

By the evening of December 5, Battleship Row was home to the following ships: A small seaplane tender, the *Avocet* (AVP-4), tied up at F-1 for the weekend. F-2, which normally berthed an aircraft carrier was empty, *Lexington* and *Enterprise* both being at sea. Northeastward, *California*, the flagship of the Battle Force, moored at F-3. The oiler *Neosho* (AO-23), which was unloading a cargo of aviation gas and scheduled to depart for the states Sunday morning, occupied F-4. Then, things got a bit crowded.

At F-5 and F-6, moored side by side in pairs, with fenders between them, sat *Maryland* on the inboard (Ford Island side) with *Oklahoma* outboard, and *Tennessee* inboard with *West Virginia* outboard. Astern of *Tennessee* lay the *Arizona* at F-7. All of these battleships were moored with their bows pointed down the channel to facilitate a rapid departure to sea.

Astern of the *Arizona,* the third member of Admiral Kidd's Battleship Division One moored alongside quay F-8. The *Nevada* was the only battleship whose numerical designation, BB-36, matched the number of its namesake state when admitted to the Union. Aboard *Nevada* this day, there was a band of blood brothers double the number of the Becker clan aboard *Arizona*. They were the Pattens, and all six of them hailed from Lake City, Iowa, about seventy-five miles northwest of Des Moines.

The Patten patriarch was Clarence Floyd Patten. In 1909, he married Anna Billotte and moved to a farm just south of Lake City. A daughter, Martha, soon arrived, followed at two-year intervals by seven sons: Gilbert, Marvin,

Clarence "Bick," Allen, Myrne "Ted," Ray "Bub," and Bruce. In 1923, Floyd and Anna moved their family to tiny Lamar in Chase County in the extreme southwestern corner of Nebraska and continued farming. An eighth son, Wayne, joined the family there, but Anna died suddenly in 1927, perhaps in part heartbroken over the death of an infant daughter. Floyd moved his motherless flock back to Iowa to live with their grandparents, and oldest daughter Martha became a surrogate mother to the eight growing boys.

During 1934, the four oldest Patten sons, Gilbert, Marvin, Bick, and Allen, enlisted in the Navy within months of one another and after basic training reported to the *Nevada*. Floyd soon moved the rest of his family, except Martha, who had married, twenty-five miles west of Lake City to Odebolt and ran a sawmill there. While in Odebolt, Ted and Bub watched their older brothers reenlist after initial four-year hitches and decided to follow them. Sixteen-year-old Bruce professed to be waiting his turn, but fourteen-year-old Wayne declared his intention to become an aviator instead.

In May 1940, Floyd moved with the two boys who were still at home from Odebolt to Ridgefield, just north of Vancouver, Washington. Bruce made good on his promise that December and marched after his six older brothers. When he did, there was no question that he wanted to join them in what was almost a family business aboard the *Nevada*. Wayne hunkered down in high school and still dreamed of flying, but Papa Patten was about to get into the act himself.

In September 1941, at the age of fifty-two, Floyd Patten volunteered to follow his sons into the Navy. With seven brothers in uniform, the Patten clan made for good press. The Navy gave Floyd a waiver for his age and made him a recruiter. With seven boys of his own sailing the seas, if Floyd couldn't persuade young men to volunteer, who could? A month later, Ted Patten's enlistment was up, and he opted to leave his brothers and take a civilian job in Long Beach. Thus, as the *Nevada* eased to its moorings off Ford Island on Friday, December 5, the count of Patten brothers serving together in its engine room was six: Gilbert, Marvin, Bick, Allen, Bub, and Bruce.[11]

Over on the *Arizona,* twenty-year-old Michael James Giovenazzo watched as another ship tied up alongside to port. Launched in 1908 as a collier, the *Vestal* (AR-4) was converted into a repair ship a few years later as oil replaced coal as the Navy's principal fuel. At 465 feet in length, about three-quarters the size of the *Arizona, Vestal* boasted one-stop service. It was a floating repair shop and fully stocked hardware store capable of performing just about every type of maintenance and construction that could be done short of dry-docking.

Aboard the *Vestal* there were shops for welding, pipe and copper fitting, carpentry, and electrical work, as well as a blacksmith shop, machine shop, and equipment to facilitate ship fitting and boiler overhauls. Scheduled maintenance to the *Arizona* included constructing a new compartment aft of the signal bridge to house radar equipment, which was due to be installed on the ship's next visit to Bremerton; re-bricking its boilers; and replacing countertops in the galley. As Seaman, First Class, Don Stratton recalled of the *Vestal,* "The men on that ship were old salts, many of them, and they had been around so long they had fixed most everything on the Pacific Fleet at one time or another."[12]

But it wasn't the *Vestal* itself that interested Mike Giovenazzo. Among the *Vestal's* crew was his older brother, Joe. The Giovenazzo brothers had grown up in Silvis, Illinois, a small community just east of East Moline. Joseph Raymond Giovenazzo, born April 28, 1916, was the oldest of twelve children of George and Concetta Giovenazzo. After two girls, Mike followed on January 4, 1921.

Big brother Joe led the way and joined the Navy on December 17, 1935. While many young men enlisted solely for a steady paycheck, Joe Giovenazzo was among those who were looking for something else. He had a bit of wanderlust about him, and as his son later recalled, he "knew more was out there than Silvis." George and Concetta were not happy that their eldest was going off in such a fashion, but they acquiesced in Joe's decision.

After basic training at Great Lakes, Joe reported to the *Arizona* and worked his way up as a watertender. A generation or two earlier, watertenders had been called firemen or stokers and were responsible for firing and maintaining the coal furnaces that heated the water in the boilers to produce steam. Fuel oil now powered most surface ships, and watertenders saw to the oil-fed fires and boilers in the engine room. These engines produced steam for propulsion and generated electrical power for the ship's lights and equipment.

Among Joe Giovenazzo's pastimes was baseball. Joe wasn't a particularly accomplished player, but he brought hustle to the game and was among those crew members glad to be on a team because of the perks of better food and time ashore. Joe later recalled one game while the *Arizona* was moored at San Pedro. He stepped into the batter's box and received the signal to lay down a bunt. Joe gave it his best but bunted foul for a third strike. No less a star than veteran Yankee pitching ace Red Ruffing, who lived in Long Beach during the off-season, trotted over afterward to offer some advice for the next time.[13]

Joe's younger brother, Mike, also liked baseball. Mike played a lot of it on the sandlots in his Silvis neighborhood while growing up, especially with Zeke Weltzer, one of his best friends. Mike was ruggedly handsome, with dark, wavy hair and a big winning smile. He had earned an American Legion medal for outstanding scholarship while attending East Moline High School. But just before the start of his senior year, Mike dropped out and enlisted in the Navy on August 2, 1938.

Joe Giovenazzo seems to have played a big role in encouraging Mike to follow in his footsteps. This time, their parents, George and Concetta, were really unhappy. Their large brood was scattering well beyond Silvis, and they didn't like it. The following December, Mike graduated from basic training at Great Lakes and reported for duty on the *Arizona*. Mike requested duty on the *Arizona* because of Joe's presence there, and Joe encouraged him to do so.

But in May 1940, after about eighteen months of service together, Joe was ordered to the *Zane* (DD-337), a *Clemson*-class destroyer commissioned shortly after World War I. Most of Joe's first six months aboard were spent at Pearl Harbor working on the *Zane*'s conversion to a high-speed minesweeper (new classification DMS-14). Meanwhile, Mike made Seaman, First Class, and again followed Joe's footsteps to get his rating as a watertender on the *Arizona*.

Joe's duty on the *Zane* was fortunate because he was married with a wife and baby daughter. He and his little family—wife, Helen, and fourteen-month old daughter, Janean—had a tiny apartment in Honolulu, and Joe spent weekend liberty ashore with them. He remained assigned to the *Zane* until he reported aboard the *Vestal* on August 31, 1941. While *Vestal* might be ordered to sea to sail with the fleet in the event of major operations, in all likelihood the floating repair ship would stay in Pearl Harbor and service the growing number of ships coming in and out. That made Joe and his wife smile because it seemed to assure them time together, especially as Helen was about four months pregnant with their second child.

As the *Vestal* tied up next to the *Arizona* on December 5, Mike Giovenazzo, having been at sea so much recently, looked forward to a reunion with Joe and a home-cooked meal on Saturday night. The brothers had plans to attend the University of Hawaii football game Saturday afternoon and watch the Rainbow Warriors take on the Bearcats of Willamette University. Mike traded some duties around so that he would be able to spend the entire weekend with Joe and his family. Their agreement was that they would stand Saturday morning inspections aboard their respective ships and then head into Honolulu together.[14]

Besides the Shive and Chandler brothers, there was another special pair of Navy-Marine shipmates aboard the *Arizona*; they were not brothers, but they shared a special bond as former rivals on the basketball court. Russell John Durio was born in the tiny town of Sunset in St. Landry Parish, Louisiana, in 1922. Sunset was so small that Russell—he was never "Russ"—wrote his folks from the *Arizona* that "this ship is as long as the whole main street of Sunset."

Russell's father, Simon Durio, was a blacksmith and mechanic whose brother had been killed in the trenches of France during World War I. Simon and his wife, Marie, had five children, four sons, Howard, John, Russell, and Aristide Daniel—always "A. D."—and a daughter, Charlsey, named for her father's lost sibling. Marie was recognized throughout the parish as a great cook but also a firm disciplinarian who made certain that homework was done and her children accounted for even on long summer evenings. As A. D. recalled, "Momma never went to bed until everyone came home."

Oldest son Howard joined the Navy and served an enlistment in submarines during the 1930s. John died very young. Russell grew up strumming a guitar, pitching softball, and playing on the Sunset High School basketball team. His biggest rival in basketball was a tall kid named Achilles "Archie" Arnaud, who led the team from nearby Arnaudville, a town named after Archie's forebears. Russell and Archie were tough competitors and had no way of knowing that a few years later they would end up on the same side thousands of miles away.

Younger brother A. D. revered Russell and shared a bed with him growing up. One night after Russell had had some minor surgery, Russell awoke hollering and screaming. Marie rushed to his bedside thinking it was related to his surgery. Russell, however, had been having a horrible dream. He was drowning, he told his mother, and there was water all around.

Shortly after turning sixteen in 1938, Russell graduated from Sunset High School, which like many rural schools of that era had only eleven grades. With his best friend, Willie Lee Sibille, Russell enrolled in Southwestern Louisiana Institute in nearby Lafayette. Russell and Willie spent two years together there, but both young men wanted desperately to join the Marines.

According to family lore, Russell Durio told his father that he was going to enlist on his eighteenth birthday with or without Simon's permission, so Simon might as well sign the required papers after Russell turned seventeen. Simon did so, but Russell and Willie finished their sophomore year before reporting for basic training in San Diego in the fall of 1940. Three months later, recognizing good candidates for their top-flight Marine Detachments, the Marines assigned Russell to the *Arizona* and Willie to the *Saratoga*.

Life aboard ship wasn't anything like Sunset, but Russell took to it and found pride in his work. "I certainly would like a piece of pie and fried chicken the way Mama used to cook it," Russell wrote home to his folks after some time at sea. "The food here is good, but they don't know how to cook."

As for pride, "Sure we're good. The best there is," Russell wrote in another letter home. "But we worked to get that way and we are still working. Working to make America safe and safe she'll be as long as there are sailors and Marines. This is America's first line of defense. It's a great thing to see."

Russell boxed on the *Arizona*'s Marine boxing team and continued to play softball, telling his folks that he pitched a full nine innings for the Marine team in one game against the *Arizona*'s aviation section. When he got a promotion and sewed on the one stripe of a Private, First Class, Russell told his family, "Ranks are pretty slow in the Marine Corps, and when you do make one you know darn well you're a good man." He was also an assistant section leader in charge of a twelve-man antiaircraft gun crew. "Not bad," Russell told the folks in Sunset proudly, "for an old country hick who's been in the Marines a little over a year."

Meanwhile, Archie Arnaud, Russell Durio's archrival in high school basketball, had enlisted in the Navy in the spring of 1941. After basic training, Archie reported to the oiler *Platte* (AO-24) as a Fireman, Third Class. He, too, was a long way from the sugar cane fields of southwest Louisiana. Archie stayed on the *Platte* only until November 18, 1941, when he was transferred to the *Arizona*. Among fifteen hundred-plus crew members—especially with Russell being in the Marine Detachment and Archie below decks as a fireman—neither man realized that the other from St. Landry Parish was aboard until each got a letter from his parents back home, who had compared notes about their boys. Past basketball rivalries aside, Russell and Archie made plans to meet on deck on Sunday morning, December 7, at 7:30 a.m.[15]

Postcard from Marine PFC Gordon Shive to his mother, Lois
Shive Westgate, postmarked aboard Arizona November 12, 1941.
Censorship required Gordon to draw a squiggle line where "Wess
has left for --." Shive Family Papers.

PART II

"Got to Find My Brother..."

CHAPTER 6

"By This Time Next Week..."

Saturday, December 6

Iₙ THE NATION'S capital this Saturday, all of official Washington—both military commanders and political leaders—were occupied with what continued to be called "the Japanese situation." Westerly winds rattled barren tree branches as they blew up Pennsylvania Avenue, and it seemed much colder than the 33 degrees recorded. In reporting the latest on President Roosevelt's concerns about Japanese forces en route to Indochina, the front-page headline in the *New York Times* read: "Army Sent South Only to Check China, Tokyo Replies to Roosevelt Inquiry."

Tomokazu Hori, a spokesman for the Cabinet Information Board in Tokyo, expressed confidence that talks with Secretary of State Cordell Hull would go on. "Both sides will continue to negotiate with sincerity to find a common formula to ease the situation in the Pacific," Hori was quoted as saying. "If there were no sincerity there would be no need to continue the negotiations."[1]

But the American public was skeptical. Asked by a nationwide survey during the week ending December 1, "Do you think the United States will go to war against Japan

95

sometime in the near future?" two-thirds of those offering an opinion answered in the affirmative.[2]

Despite Japan's offhand response to Roosevelt's query about its intentions in Indochina, Japan had yet to reply formally to the American proposal of November 26—essentially, that the United States might be willing to unfreeze Japanese assets and resume some measure of trade in exchange for Japan withdrawing military forces from China as well as Indochina.

At about 8:00 a.m. Washington time, a fourteen-part message with Japan's response finally began to make its way from Tokyo to the Japanese embassy a dozen or so blocks from the White House. The parts were not transmitted in sequential order. Instead, sections 4 and 9 were sent together, as were sections 5 and 10. Sections 6 and 11 dribbled in several hours later, and sections 7 and 8 followed later still.

It was almost as if Tokyo was sending its own embassy a puzzle. The pieces were to be decoded by embassy staff, formatted into a typed document, and delivered to the American secretary of state upon further instructions. Preliminary dispatches emphasized utmost secrecy, and Ambassador Kichisaburō Nomura was ordered to prepare the presentation document with his senior staff and not use a typist from the secretarial pool. Unbeknownst to the Japanese, as their embassy settled in for a long Saturday of decoding and hunt-and-peck typing by the only member of Nomura's inner circle with neophyte typing skills, the United States military had intercepted these same disjointed message parts and was doing its own decoding.[3]

Meanwhile, President Roosevelt had been considering sending a personal message directly to Japanese emperor Hirohito in the hope of easing the tension between their two countries. At the president's request, Secretary of State Hull provided Roosevelt with a suggested draft, but as was frequently the case, FDR subsequently opted to produce his own version. While the State Department draft reprised the salient goals of the November 26 communication and proposed a ninety-day ceasefire between Japan and China, Roosevelt's version focused on Japanese advances into Indochina.

"Almost a century ago," Roosevelt's letter began, "the President of the United States addressed to the Emperor of Japan a message extending an offer of friendship." The president went on to catalog the large numbers of Japanese military in Indochina that far exceeded the agreement with the Vichy French government. Reports of more and more forces en route were disturbing the equilibrium of all of Southeast Asia. "It is clear," concluded Roosevelt, "that a continuation of such a situation is unthinkable."

Then, donning the persona of the squire of Hyde Park addressing squabbling neighbors, Roosevelt suggested to Hirohito that the countries of the region, including the American Philippines, could not "sit either indefinitely or permanently on a keg of dynamite." He assured the emperor there was "absolutely no thought on the part of the United States of invading Indo-China" and offered, if Japanese forces were withdrawn, to obtain similar assurances from other governments in Southeast Asia and "even undertake to ask for the same assurance on the part of the Government of China." It was vintage Roosevelt, but was it too late?

"I am confident," Roosevelt told the Japanese emperor, "that both of us, for the sake of the peoples not only of our own great countries but for the sake of humanity in neighboring territories, have a sacred duty to restore traditional amity and prevent further death and destruction in the world."

Then, well aware of public opinion as well as the exigencies of the situation, Roosevelt handwrote a cover note to Secretary of State Hull and ordered him to send the plea on its way: "Dear Cordell: Shoot this to Grew [the American ambassador to Japan]—I think can go in gray code—saves time—I don't mind if it gets picked up. FDR."[4]

In Honolulu, after an overnight low of 71 degrees, the temperature was headed to a balmy high of 84. Joseph C. Harsch, foreign correspondent for the *Christian Science Monitor,* and his wife, Anne, had arrived in Honolulu aboard the steamship *Lurline* a few days earlier along with the Willamette and San Jose State football teams. This Saturday morning, however, Harsch's mind was not on football. He had scored a difficult-to-arrange interview with the top sailor in the Pacific.

Admiral Kimmel eschewed most interviews and was not known to be chatty with the press, but thirty-six-year-old Harsch had a huge following and had spent considerable time in Berlin. Indeed, at the outset of their meeting in Kimmel's office overlooking the harbor, it was Kimmel who peppered Harsch with questions about Germany's war plans. Harsch finally protested politely that it was his turn to ask a question or two.

Professing to know little about the situation in the Pacific, Harsch got right to the point. "Is there going to be a war out here?" he asked the admiral. Kimmel gave a one-word answer, "No," but Harsch wanted to know more. Why was Kimmel so confident of that?

Kimmel focused on the global situation and noted that

recent German setbacks on the Eastern Front meant that they were not going to capture Moscow that winter and that the Russians—nominal British and American allies—would still be in the war in the spring. Kimmel claimed that the Japanese would not attack the United States in the Pacific and chance a two-front war with it and Russia. "The Japanese are too intelligent to run the risk of a two-front war unnecessarily," Kimmel explained. "They will want to wait until they are sure that the Russians have been defeated." The admiral's public relations officer, Lieutenant Commander Waldo Drake, remembered the admiral's conclusion a little more pointedly: "I don't think they'd be such damned fools."[5]

If Saturday evening meant liberty and relaxation for many on the *Arizona*'s crew, Saturday morning meant a rigorous inspection for one and all. Captain Van Valkenburgh's formal rounds throughout the ship were a weekly staple whether the *Arizona* was at sea or in port. Van Valkenburgh was well liked and had a deserved reputation of caring for his men, but that did not mean they could expect leniency. Anything found amiss was likely to cancel much-desired liberty ashore for those responsible.

Seaman, Second Class, Oree Weller, just six months out of boot camp, applied a special dose of spit and polish to the navigator's station on the *Arizona*'s bridge in anticipation of the captain's scrutiny. Suddenly, Weller heard a racket overhead and looked up to see a drill bit boring through the ceiling. It was quickly withdrawn, but no sooner had it been than a steady *drip, drip, drip* of red-lead primer paint fell from the hole and splattered onto the navigator's desk below.

Weller was beside himself. It had to be those maintenance guys from the *Vestal*. He mouthed some choice words up at the overhead and the signal bridge, beyond where workers from the repair ship had begun to build housing for the radar equipment scheduled for installation at Bremerton. Fortunately, Captain Van Valkenburgh was not yet making his rounds, and Weller had time to use a dose of elbow grease to clean up the mess.[6]

At that moment Captain Van Valkenburgh was in his cabin conferring with Lieutenant Commander Samuel G. Fuqua, the *Arizona*'s first lieutenant and damage control officer. Born in Laddonia, Missouri, in 1899, Fuqua had served a brief stint in the Army during World War I and then spent a year at the University of Missouri before his appointment to the Naval Academy in 1919. Upon graduation four years later, Fuqua reported to the *Arizona* as its newest ensign. He was aboard for about a year before receiving other assignments, including sea duty on a destroyer and another battleship and, eventually, command of the minesweeper *Bittern* (AM-36) with the Asiatic Squadron. After a stint ashore at Naval Station Great Lakes, Fuqua reported back aboard *Arizona* in 1941.

"First lieutenant" was a position title, not a rank, held by the officer in command of the Deck Department, which comprised those junior officers and crew charged with the general handling and maintenance of the ship. While other departments, such as gunnery, had their specialties, Fuqua and his men were the go-to team for just about every shipboard function from dockside replenishment to waste disposal. It was Fuqua's job to keep the *Arizona* in tip-top shape and ensure that Captain Van Valkenburgh's weekly inspections met with his approval.

Van Valkenburgh used his time with Fuqua prior to his rounds to confirm the rumors running rampant through the ship's grapevine. Upon the *Arizona*'s return to Pearl Harbor on Friday, Admiral Kidd had met with Van Valkenburgh and given the captain the official word: after the repair work by the *Vestal* was complete, the *Arizona* would depart Pearl Harbor on Saturday, December 13, for a port call and liberty in Long Beach before proceeding up the coast to Bremerton for its scheduled overhaul. Knowing what that would mean to his crew, Van Valkenburgh couldn't help flashing a smile as he told Fuqua, "By this time next week, we will be on our way home for Christmas."

Fuqua wasn't so sure. "Don't you think the Japanese situation will cancel the trip to Long Beach?" he asked the captain. Van Valkenburgh shook his head and assured him that it wouldn't.[7]

Waiting out a mother's vigil in Long Beach, Clara May Morse had already resigned herself to another Christmas without her boys, but now, Captain Van Valkenburgh had put the matter squarely to Commander Fuqua. While May Morse had no way of knowing it, it seemed that Francis and Norman Morse, along with their shipmates, would be stateside for Christmas.

Below on the quarterdeck, the *Arizona*'s band had gone through its usual morning routine. Arriving topside at 7:45 a.m., Bandmaster Kinney gave the command to march as a unit to the fantail to play the National Anthem for the colors ceremony. It went off without a hitch as the Marine honor guard hoisted the Stars and Stripes to the top of the ensign staff at the stern of the ship. Band members then returned below decks to stand at attention for inspection.

Captain Van Valkenburgh's inspection met with his approval, and as sailors finished their respective duties, those with liberty spruced up for their time ashore. Commander Fuqua's Deck Department had one major task to complete, however, before it could relax. Having been at sea, *Arizona* needed to replenish its fuel tanks. In expectation of the upcoming voyage to Long Beach—some 2,500 miles—a full load of 1.5 million gallons of fuel oil was pumped aboard. Despite the trade winds blowing across Pearl Harbor that December morning, an oily smell lingered and lay heavy in the air.

Elsewhere aboard the *Arizona*, storage tanks contained 180,000 gallons of aviation fuel for the three Vought Kingfisher scouting planes, and ammunition lockers brimmed with more than a million pounds of gunpowder. Crew members had long learned to take such explosive cargo as a matter of course, but each of the seven battleships moored along Battleship Row—and *Pennsylvania* momentarily on blocks in Dry Dock No. 1—carried the ingredients to readily become floating bombs.[8]

For those who found time to peruse the Saturday morning edition of the *Honolulu Advertiser,* its headline was not reassuring. "America Expected to Reject Japan's Reply on Indo-China," it read. "Japan, however, denied [its] troops were there for aggressive purposes," the newspaper went on to report, optimistically characterizing the Japanese response as "an attitude indicating a desire to keep the situation from boiling over, if possible."[9]

Down under, it was already Sunday, December 7, and to the Australian government the possibility of keeping the lid on tensions seemed remote. A United Press story, datelined Melbourne, confirmed the southward movement of the Japanese navy and reported that the Australian cabinet had "met twice in Melbourne instead of at Canberra in order to maintain closest contact with the armed forces." The cabinet had cancelled its normal weekend adjournment due to late information that seemed "to indicate an immediate break in Japanese-American relations."[10]

Given what was about to occur and the ramifications it would have throughout the United States in the months ahead, an editorial in the *Honolulu Advertiser* would, in retrospect, become particularly poignant. "Let's Drop the Word 'Nisei,'" the *Advertiser* urged, in an unqualified statement of what it meant to be an American:

"The time is long past when the term 'nisei' should have been dropped from the American language, written or spoken. In translation from the Japanese, it is 'second generation.' It came into being with the first of the American-born of Japanese parents. It was a meaningless expression, except from the point in which it sought to designate between alien and American.

"We have, slowly but surely, accustomed ourselves to a new type of American so that 'nisei' becomes outmoded in Hawaii.... Americans are not to be classified by anything other than just plain Americans. They are not to be labeled with words stolen from the ancestors' tongues or to be this or that kind of a hyphenated American. As it is with Caucasians, the trend is to melt them from birth thoroughly and solidly into this great nation."[11] That principle was about to be put to the test.

At least for this afternoon, there were plenty of college football games to distract the country. Mississippi State, sitting atop the SEC standings with a 7-1-1 overall record, was in San Francisco taking on the University of San Francisco Dons. Rice and SMU had comparable records in the Southwest Conference, but were playing only for pride as conference champion Texas A&M, ranked ninth in the country with an 8-2 record, arrived in Pullman, Washington, to take on nineteenth-ranked Washington State.

Proving that national standings have always been controversial, the University of Texas was ranked ahead of the Aggies of A&M in the AP poll, but the Longhorns were in second place in the Southwest Conference behind A&M because of a tie at Baylor. The number twelve ranked Oregon State Beavers (7-2) had the weekend off, but were gearing up to play number two Duke in the Rose Bowl on January 1. Ohio State and Michigan, having battled to a 20-20 tie two weeks earlier, settled for a second-place tie in the Big Ten behind the undefeated conference champs, the Golden Gophers of Minnesota.

The big game in Honolulu Saturday afternoon that the Giovenazzo brothers, along with a crowd of twenty-four thousand others, were planning to attend was the first in a mini series among the Rainbow Warriors of the University of Hawaii and teams from Willamette University and San Jose State. Both of the visitors' contingents had arrived in Honolulu aboard the passenger liner *Lurline* a few days earlier. Sponsored by the Aloha Chapter of the Shriners as a benefit for local police and firemen, the Shrine Bowl Classic, as it was billed, promised three games over ten days.

The Rainbow Warriors had finished a dismal 2-5 in 1940, but were looking strong at 7-1 by the end of the 1941 season. They would host the Willamette University Bearcats, the Northwest Conference champs, who were 8-1 going into the first game at Honolulu Stadium. Hawaii and the San Jose State Spartans were scheduled to play the following Saturday, with San Jose State and Willamette playing the third game of the series on December 16. Whichever team won two games would be the champion.[12]

Meanwhile, New York Giants baseball fans looked

ahead to the spring season in no small measure because veteran homerun slugger Mel Ott had just been designated the team's manager. "Marvelous Melvin Ott" or the "boy wonder" of the Polo Grounds, as the *New York Times* variously described him, was both to manage the team and continue to lend his bat to the lineup while playing right field. In a snub to the cross-town Dodgers, Ott claimed that the St. Louis Cardinals were the team to beat for the National League pennant. Reportedly, thirty-two-year-old Ott would receive the princely salary of twenty-five thousand dollars a year.[13]

Over on the *Vestal,* those crew members not detailed to work parties on the *Arizona* mustered for their own Saturday-morning inspection. Watertender, First Class, Joe Giovenazzo had the luxury of a minuscule apartment on Kapahulu Avenue in Honolulu with his wife and young daughter, but that didn't excuse him from Saturday-morning inspections. Once Joe was dismissed, he met up with younger brother Mike, and together they took the crew boat to the fleet landing.

They stopped first at Joe's apartment, where Joe suddenly felt feverish and chilled, perhaps the result of a series of recent vaccinations. Joe decided to forgo the football game, and Helen, Mike's sister-in-law, went with Mike instead. It was a great day for football at Honolulu Stadium, even if the weather was hardly what most teams on the mainland had come to expect in December.

Mike and Helen watched the University of Hawaii Rainbow Warriors claim a 20-6 win over Willamette's Bearcats. Willamette fans looking for excuses were quick to note that after leaving Oregon in near-freezing conditions and spending a week aboard ship en route, the double whammy of

Honolulu's 80-degree temperature and high humidity were enough to do in their team.

Mike was supposed to return with Helen to the Giovenazzo apartment, but sometime during the football game, he ran into his old baseball pal from his hometown of Silvis, Lucien Marius "Zeke" Weltzer, who was now in the Marine Corps. Mike decided to join Zeke for a while and then return to the *Arizona* to write letters home instead of spending the night with Joe and Helen. Mike was scheduled to be discharged on January 3, 1942 and planned to be married shortly afterward. There was a lot to say to his many family members before the big day. He could hardly wait.[14]

Harvey Becker's wife, Marie, was also in Hawaii with him. They had been married at her parents' residence in Nekoma, Kansas, on December 22, 1940, while Harvey was home on leave. Marvin was able to get leave for the occasion, too. (Wesley has not yet enlisted.) It was the last time Bill and Freda's entire family would be together. With her nursing degree, Marie had gotten a job at a hospital in Honolulu and arrived in town only six weeks earlier after sailing from Los Angeles on the *Lurline*. The extra income from her job allowed Harvey and Marie to rent a modest house in town with a small yard.

Harvey's brothers Marvin and Wesley were at the house with Harvey just before the *Arizona* put to sea the week of Thanksgiving. Marie took a photo of the trio, their arms draped around one another's necks, which would become a treasured family keepsake. Harvey, who because of his wife's presence in Hawaii could enjoy regular liberty when the *Arizona* was in port, stood in the center in civilian clothes; Marvin and Wesley flanked him in their whites.

Happy though the three brothers appeared, they all had

thoughts of home. "Boy, how I would love to be back on the farm for a few weeks," Marvin wrote to their cousin, Willard Hansen. "I guess I'll do well if I ever see it again," Marvin continued. "I am still looking forward to it, if I ever get to the state again. That is just back to the coast again it will be like getting home. I guess we will be back sometime in the near future. How near I don't know. Well that's enough of that." Then, wistfully commenting on Willard's attendance as a freshman at Kansas State, Marvin concluded, "I wish I was there with you...."[15]

Marvin and Wesley had been granted liberty for this weekend, too, but they both opted to stay on the *Arizona*. Marvin was busy packing for a scheduled leave home around Christmastime regardless of the *Arizona*'s schedule. Always frugal, Wesley was watching his money and determined not to spend even a nickel ashore until he had saved one hundred dollars. But the main reason Marvin and Wesley didn't visit their big brother and his wife was because they had decided that they should give Harvey and Marie some time alone.

It was somewhat ironic, but if Captain Van Valkenburgh's news about departing for San Pedro in a few days held true, Marie—recently arrived in the islands though she was—might be left alone on Oahu for Christmas while the three Becker brothers steamed east. There were indeed marital benefits to be had if one's wife lived in Honolulu, but if one's ship sailed, she would be left behind.

For Marvin, his scheduled leave home to Kansas meant that he would have a chance to see the girl he was sweet on. Marvin had spent considerable time with her when home on leave for Harvey's wedding, and he was eager to see her again. He could also receive his Christmas presents in person. When asked what he wanted from his family, Marvin mentioned only one thing: a jar of his mother's canned pickles. Weeks before, Freda Becker had taken care to label a jar for Marvin and place it in the cellar awaiting his arrival home in Nekoma.

While Marvin packed and daydreamed of his mother's pickles, his father, Bill, and fourteen-year-old Bob were hard at work building a sheep barn three hundred miles from Nekoma. The Beckers had recently purchased a farm near Savonburg, in the southeastern part of the state, that promised a more fertile environment than the windswept plains. Bill and Freda fell in love with the place and thought it quite beautiful, especially the stand of timber along what they called Big Creek. There was so much to do to prepare for the move that Bill and Freda kept Bob and his older sister, Theresa, out of high school that year so they could help. Late into the evening on Saturday night, Bill and Bob hammered away on the sheep barn.

In the depths of the *Arizona,* Edward "Bud" Heidt and his brother, Wesley, were used to lots of racket. The Heidt brothers served aboard the *Arizona* as firemen. Like Stanley Czarnecki from Michigan, this meant that they were assigned to the engine room force, tending to the boilers and operating the pumps.

Bud and Wesley had been born to George and Genevieve "Jennie" Heidt less than a year apart in the Lawndale area of greater Los Angeles. Their big sister, Julia, was two years older than Bud. Lawndale in those years was a classic 1920s bedroom community of about three thousand. The boys attended Leuzinger High School, playing on the football team and graduating together in the class of 1936. Bud was a handsome guy with an award-winning grin. Wesley sported a pencil-thin, Errol Flynn–type mustache. After high school, they signed up with the Civilian Conservation Corps.

By then, George and Jennie Heidt had gotten a divorce and both remarried. George worked as a typesetter for the *Los Angeles Times*. His new wife, Hazel, was a decade his junior and had a brother, Harold Flanders, who had joined the Navy at sixteen. Harold, now thirty-five and a Boatswain's Mate, First Class, had made a career of it and been on the battleship *West Virginia* since 1935. Their step-uncle's career may have influenced Bud and Wesley to enlist, which they did together—as they usually did things—on September 13, 1939. Bud reported to the *Arizona* immediately after completing basic training, and Wesley followed on February 16, 1940.

According to the *Arizona*'s muster roll, sometime during the first week of December 1941, Wesley Heidt was promoted to Machinist's Mate, Second Class, making him a junior petty officer. What older brother Bud thought of being outranked by his younger sibling has gone unrecorded, but Bud was preoccupied with a girl back home.

Her name was Donna Streur and she had four sisters, including little four-year-old Fran. A year earlier, Bud had been home on leave and brought Fran a giant stuffed panda bear as a Christmas present. As for Bud's present for Donna this year, her family felt certain that she and Bud were "unofficially engaged." Whether or not Bud had a ring for Donna safely tucked into his gear on the *Arizona,* only Bud knew for sure.[16]

"When I get my next leave and we're back together," Bud had written Donna only a week earlier, "let's not waste a minute of it because it may be the last time we get together." Maybe he shouldn't have said that, Bud continued, "but you know as well as I do that we may be at war any day now. It will be hard for those we love and those that love us.... All my love, Bud."[17]

As for Wesley Heidt, he had recently written to his mother, Jennie, trying to ease her angst over both his dearth of correspondence and his safety. "Hello Mom, this is your bad son again," Wesley's letter of November 22 began. "Boy have I been catching hell for not writing. I don't know why you worry about us so much, if anything happened to us you would hear from the Navy first thing.... I am safer on this battleboat than I would be driving back and forth to work if I was home."[18]

Two days later, Bud Heidt wrote their big sister, Julia, and apologized for taking two weeks to answer her latest letter. The next time he received one, Bud promised, "I will answer it the same day." Then, he got to the heart of the matter: "God! I sure wish that I could have been home to get a piece of that butterscotch pie you made," Bud wrote, before pleading, "you will have to bake another one when I get home."[19]

Two of the Heidt brothers' shipmates also assigned to the engine room were Fireman, First Class, Masten Andrew Ball, and his younger brother, Seaman, First Class, William V. Ball. Masten was twenty-two, and Bill had recently turned twenty-one. The Ball brothers hailed from Iowa, having been born in the little hamlet of Linn Grove, in the northwestern corner of the state. They were the sons of Wiley and Rebecca Ball, who by 1940 were farming near Fredericksburg, Iowa, about thirty miles north of Waterloo.

Masten Ball enlisted in December 1937 and reported to the *Arizona* six months later. He seemed willing to make the Navy his career, but brother Bill definitely had other plans. Bill Ball had played a lot of baseball growing up and was good at it. The minor-league Seattle Rainiers of the Pacific Coast League were interested in him once his Navy stint was up. Bill enlisted about a year after Masten and reported aboard *Arizona* on New Year's Day, 1939.

There was also a girl. How serious the relationship was changes with the telling. Despite moving from Waterloo to Fredericksburg late in his sophomore year of high school, Bill Ball was reportedly sweet on Genevieve Sullivan. She was several years his senior and lived in Waterloo. Genevieve was the only girl in a family of five brothers, two older and three younger than she. But they didn't intimidate Bill Ball. He spent a lot of time at the Sullivan house whenever he was in Waterloo.

The two older Sullivan brothers, George and Frank, left home in May 1937 to serve their own hitches in the Navy. As family friends, they may have had some influence on Masten Ball's decision to join up later that year. George and Frank Sullivan had duty together on the destroyer *Hovey* (DD-208), a World War I four-piper, for much of their four-year enlistment. Then, they both mustered out and returned home to Waterloo in May 1941, just as the sinking of the *Bismarck* was front-page news. Nonetheless, they thought their military service was over.

Throughout Saturday afternoon, launches from the *Arizona* and the six other battleships moored along Battleship Row ferried sailors to the fleet landing in the harbor's Southeast Loch. Leaving one's ship was a formal affair. Those answering liberty call lined up on the quarterdeck in two rows. The officer of the deck inspected those assembled to make certain that uniforms were clean and pressed and shoes polished. Receiving his liberty card, each man saluted the officer of the deck and asked for permission to leave the ship. As his salute was returned, the man's name was checked off the liberty list. He then saluted the American flag above the quarterdeck and climbed down the gangway to the waiting launch.

Arriving at the fleet landing, the sailors showed their liberty cards and in tight-knit groups of buddies streamed to the buses waiting to take them into Honolulu. By and large, they watched each other's backs, and heaven help anyone they encountered who spoke rudely about their ship.

There were indeed a few brawls broken up by the shore patrol and a few wayward souls stumbling dead drunk back to their ships, but generally, liberty was a well-ordered affair, particularly when one considered that thousands of sailors descended on Honolulu on a Saturday night. In fact, each ship had men assigned to shore patrol to watch out for their own—to make certain their shipmates did not get into trouble or find it coming their way unprovoked.

The happy respite of liberty ashore aside, most sailors had family back home who worried about them. In Tucson, Arizona, the mother of Seaman, Second Class, James Randolf Van Horn, re-read her son's most recent letter and couldn't help fretting. Having felt compelled to drop out of high school and join the Navy after hearing Admiral Kidd speak the previous spring, Van Horn told his mother that he was considering asking for a transfer to the Atlantic Fleet. That's where the action was, he wrote; that's where he wanted to be. His mother shook her head and sighed for the umpteenth time. "I begged him not to," she remembered. "There had just been two sinkings on the East Coast and I was afraid."[20]

CHAPTER 7

Luck of the Draw

Saturday, December 6

T HE RAINS CLAN was almost as old as the Alabama hill country they called home. Thomas Rains married Synthia McLeaird in 1879 in DeKalb County. Synthia's reported occupation of "keeping house" was an understatement, as the couple proceeded to have thirteen children. Mary, the seventh child and fourth girl, married Charles Wesley Murdock, a boy from across the Georgia line, on Christmas Eve 1905, when he was twenty-two and she was fifteen.

C. W., as Charles was called, was a blacksmith by trade, but also rode the circuit on Sundays as a Baptist pastor. C. W. and Mary, who was nicknamed "Sleatie," in turn had seven children: Vada Rebecca (1907), Thomas Daniel (1908), Lythonia (1914), Charles Luther, called "Luther" (1916), Melvin Elijah (1918), Verlon Aaron (1923), and Kenneth Dewayne (1927). The five Murdock brothers would all become Navy men.

Vada married young and left home at fifteen. Thomas finally left home and joined the Navy in the spring of 1930 at the age of twenty-one. He rose through the ranks and got his rating as a yeoman after reporting to the *Arizona* in the summer of 1931. Long before computers, yeomen were clerical assistants charged with manually typing, filing, and maintaining the ship's voluminous paper records. Personnel records alone for a fifteen-hundred-man crew were daunting. By the time Thomas became a chief yeoman, his duties were those of an administrative assistant and included drafting letters for the captain and other officers, handling routine mail, responding to social invitations, and preparing requisite thank-you notes.

By 1934, the Depression had a firm grip on rural Alabama, and eighteen-year-old Luther Murdock followed his big brother's example. A little over three years later, then nineteen-year-old Melvin did, too. By all accounts, the Murdocks were a close-knit family, and it was no surprise that Luther and Melvin requested duty on the *Arizona* along with Thomas. Both younger brothers became watertenders.

In the fall of 1939, all three Murdock brothers got leave at the same time to visit their family in Alabama. They left Long Beach at 2:00 a.m. one morning planning to take turns sleeping and drive straight through. Two days into the trip, with Luther behind the wheel, their 1938 Chevrolet coupe ran into a stopped truck in a fog near Vicksburg, Mississippi.

They were lucky. Thomas, who was in the front passenger seat, received cuts on his head and knees and strained his right ankle. He ended up on crutches. Luther's knees were also bruised along with a sore chest and cut lip from hitting the steering wheel. Melvin, asleep in the back seat, awoke to ask what the fuss was about but later learned he had three broken ribs. Thomas sent their parents, C. W. and Sleatie, a telegram announcing, "Arriving Friday noon with tape, bandages and crutches."

Sleatie gathered in her brood and rejoiced to have her

older boys home safe. Friends and neighbors wore "the hinges off the Murdocks' doors," the local newspaper reported, "eager to see the boys and congratulate them on their narrow escape." Broken ribs or not, Melvin's injuries didn't stop him from looking up all the girls he knew who were still single. "The Murdock boys are true blue one hundred per cent Navy," the paper concluded. "When a Navy man gets hurt he smiles."[1]

By the fall of 1941, Luther was a Watertender, First Class, while Melvin wasn't far behind with his rating as a Watertender, Second Class. Back home in DeKalb County, their younger brother, Verlon, had just turned eighteen and was planning to follow his older brothers and enlist. Meanwhile, oldest brother Thomas had gotten married. His seniority gave him regular liberty privileges ashore, where his wife, Ruth, rented an apartment in Honolulu after the *Arizona* began basing from Pearl Harbor. Luther Murdock had liberty ashore Saturday evening and joined Thomas and Ruth for dinner. They invited him to spend the night. Luther thought it over, but decided to return to the *Arizona* and younger brother Melvin.

During its Saturday-morning rehearsal, the *Arizona*'s band had had to compete with the construction noise of the workers from the *Vestal*. After eating lunch and playing its usual 12:30 concert for the crew, the band held an abbreviated afternoon rehearsal. Bandmaster Kinney and his musicians were preoccupied and eager to go ashore on liberty. The entire crew had just been paid, and purchasing Christmas gifts for sweethearts and family back home was a high priority. There weren't many quality items in Honolulu that were affordable on an enlisted man's pay, and most purchases—such as a set of drinking glasses with decals of hula dancers on them—fell into the tourist-trinket category. But such gifts would remind recipients where their boys had been during this tumultuous year.[2]

Books were heavy and expensive to mail back to the states, but for those looking for something for special friends in the fleet or on Oahu, there were plenty of choices. Ernest Hemingway's *For Whom the Bell Tolls* was still quite popular, as were new novels from two well-established favorites: *Oliver Wiswell* by Kenneth Roberts and *Saratoga Trunk* by Edna Ferber. *Curious George,* the tale of a mischievous monkey and the man with the yellow hat, had just made its debut as a children's book. It would go on to become a perennial favorite of millions of postwar baby boomers and their offspring.

In nonfiction, 1941's top bestseller was CBS correspondent William Shirer's *Berlin Diary*. Recounting Shirer's time in the German capital as Hitler marched toward war, its publisher unabashedly called it "the most important book for Americans today" in an advertisement in the *New York Times*.[3] Douglas Miller's *You Can't Do Business with Hitler: What a Nazi Victory Would Mean to Every American* was also timely and well-read.

If one was just looking for an afternoon matinee in Honolulu to unwind in the cool of a theater, *A Yank in the R.A.F.,* starring Tyrone Power and Betty Grable, had just opened at the Waikiki Theater. According to a review in the *Honolulu Advertiser,* "Power is seen as a cocky American aviator who joins up with the RAF to be near his American girl friend, Betty Grable. The latter is an entertainer in a night club and is featured in several peppy song and dance numbers."[4]

Other movie offerings around Honolulu included *The Great Lie,* a drama of marital intrigue starring Bette Davis, at the Kaimuki; Robert Taylor in *Billy the Kid,* at the Kapahulu; and *Dive Bomber,* with Errol Flynn and Fred MacMurray, at the Waialua on the north shore. One of the top-grossing movies of 1941, *Dive Bomber* featured an improbable script that pitted Flynn and MacMurray against each other as rivals in the air and on the ground, fighting over a divorcée played by Alexis Smith. The film was saved only by its pioneering use of Technicolor, gung-ho spirit for the US Navy, and cameo appearance by the carrier *Enterprise*.

Attractions coming soon included *Badlands of Dakota,* opening at the Princess. A baby-faced Robert Stack, a poised Ann Rutherford, and a relative unknown listed in the credits as Brod Crawford starred in a frontier drama that managed to include Wild Bill Hickok, Calamity Jane, and George Armstrong Custer. Or, one could wait until the next week for the opening of Mickey Rooney and Judy Garland—"together again," as an ad proclaimed—in *Life Begins for Andy Hardy*.[5]

After their shopping excursions, the musicians of the *Arizona*'s band met up at Bloch Arena. They had reason to celebrate and feel confident. On November 22, the band had taken second place in the first round of the semifinals of the Battles of Music. Competing bands came from *Arizona*, *California*, the minelayer *Oglala,* and the Marine Corps Barracks. Scuttlebutt had it that the *Arizona* band was clearly the best but that the Marines had marched en masse to the arena and whistled and applauded the loudest while sailors split their enthusiasm among the Navy bands.

Tonight, Kinney and his musicians were only interested spectators. Contrary to many accounts, the *Arizona*'s band was not playing because it had already earned a spot in the finals through its second-place finish on November 22.

Bands from *Pennsylvania, Tennessee,* the auxiliary ship *Argonne* (AG-31), and the submarine base competed for the remaining two slots in the finals. The sub base band was a last-minute substitute for the cruiser *Detroit* (CL-8) after its bandmaster pulled out of the contest to protest the judging by applause.

Three of these bands were older and more established, but the *Tennessee*'s contingent had graduated from the Navy School of Music with the *Arizona* band. There were many friendships between the two bands because of this, and *Tennessee* was the sentimental favorite among the *Arizona* musicians — at least until the finals. That would be serious business and big stakes. Wayne Bandy, a cornet player who doubled on vocals for the *Arizona* men, wrote home that the winning band would be assigned to a one-year tour of the states. That was almost assuredly wishful thinking, but the rumor kept competitive juices flowing.

When the last notes died away and the applause stopped, the *Pennsylvania* band was judged the winner and the *Tennessee* men came in second. What a final four it would be. *Pennsylvania, Tennessee, Arizona,* and the Marine Corps Barracks — three battleships and the Marines — would toot it out for top band two weeks hence, on December 20. The *Arizona* men were excited. All they had to do was play their hearts out and figure out how to keep away as many Marines as possible.

As Clyde Williams, another cornet player in the *Arizona* band, was leaving the arena that night, someone called out his nickname, Okmulgee. Williams turned around and came face to face with Leonard Yandle, the bugler from the *Pennsylvania.* They had been rivals on competing sports teams in Okmulgee and Henryetta, Oklahoma, south of

Tulsa, during high school, and now they laughed about ending up as rivals in music half a world away.

Williams also met up with Henry Brown, a friend from Okmulgee who had just performed as a member of the *Tennessee* band. Williams and Brown visited at length, talking about their hometown, and then made plans to meet the next day and look up yet another Okmulgee lad, nineteen-year-old Asa Everett "Ace" Streight, Jr., who was stationed on the *Nevada* as a member of one of its fourteen-inch-gun crews. Ace had been a wrestler and football player in high school and joined the Navy while he was a senior. Williams and Brown parted and went back to their respective ships, expecting to see Ace Streight the next day.[6]

In Washington, the evening had not been so peaceful. By 7:00 p.m., Navy cryptographers finished decoding the first thirteen parts of the intercepted message to be tendered by the Japanese ambassador the following day. Copies were made for distribution to the highest security list, and at about 9:00 p.m., a naval intelligence officer began to make the rounds delivering them in locked briefcases.

Chief of Naval Operations Harold Stark was at the theater with guests attending a performance of *The Student Prince* and could not readily be reached. Army Chief of Staff George Marshall was home enjoying his usual quiet evening with his wife, Katherine. His aides decided that the import of the thirteen sections received so far was more diplomatic than military and elected to wait for the final fourteenth part before giving them all to Marshall in the morning.

President Roosevelt's copy of the first thirteen parts made its way through the White House usher's office to the president's study, where he was conferring with trusted aide

Harry Hopkins. Roosevelt took about ten minutes to read the assembled sheaf of fifteen typewritten pages and then handed the batch to Hopkins. When Hopkins had finished reading, he handed it back as Roosevelt intoned, "This means war." Whether Roosevelt meant war against the United States specifically or merely that the British could expect a Japanese attack at Singapore would never be entirely clear.[7]

Lieutenant Kleber Masterson's wife, Charlotte, always told him that she would follow him anywhere. When *Arizona* and the Pacific Fleet called at Pearl Harbor during the spring 1940 maneuvers, Charlotte packed up their two young boys and sailed to Honolulu for what was supposed to be a ten-day visit. When the fleet was ordered to remain in Hawaiian waters, Charlotte and the boys did, too.

Even on an officer's salary, it wasn't easy to find suitable accommodations. Masterson remembered that they "lived all over Hawaii in the year and a half before the war," but it was better than being apart. Some men faced what at the time seemed like a relatively non-consequential choice between spending Saturday night ashore or returning to the *Arizona*. For Masterson, there was no question about what he would do. He did not have duty, had regular liberty, and his wife and children were there—he would spend the night with them.[8]

Another of those spending the night ashore was Machinist's Mate, First Class, Everett Reid, still onboard the *Arizona* and happily married two and one-half years after Admiral Kidd—then still *Captain* Kidd of the *Arizona*—had graciously offered Reid the use of his gig on Reid's wedding day. Reid turned twenty-four on December 6, and while he was scheduled for weekend duty, he persuaded Machinist's Mate, Second Class, Samuel Gemienhardt of Ohio to substitute for him so that he could attend a birthday party thrown by Reid's wife, Barbara.

Like Charlotte Masterson and a few other wives, Barbara Reid had made the move to Honolulu only that September to be closer to her husband. Official Navy policy frowned on such family moves, particularly among lower enlisted rates, because of the uncertainty about future deployments. Everett asked Barbara to remain stateside, but she came anyway and set up rudimentary housekeeping. When one was young and in love, it was enough. Just the day before, they had moved into a little studio apartment on Cleghorn Street, four blocks up from Waikiki Beach.

Reid invited Elmer "Bennie" Schlund of Nebraska, another machinist's mate from the *Arizona,* to party with him and Barbara, and they went out for drinks and dinner with other shipmates at a Waikiki watering hole. No matter the establishment, jukeboxes were almost certain to reverberate with the sounds of the Andrews Sisters belting out "Boogie Woogie Bugle Boy" once, twice, or multiple times during the evening.

When the three of them returned to the Reids' tiny apartment, Reid offered to set up a place for Schlund to sleep on the floor instead of returning to the ship. Schlund was appreciative of the offer but declined. "No, I'm going back to the ship," he told the Reids. "I've got a bed on the ship. Why would I sleep on the floor?" He departed before midnight and caught the crew boat back to the *Arizona.* Reid, Gemienhardt, and Schlund: three men, three seemingly innocent choices. For them and so many others, it would prove to be the luck of the draw.[9]

*   *   *

Among those on the *Arizona* not going ashore for Saturday liberty were the members of the ship's Marine Detachment. They were expecting a new commanding officer to replace well-liked Major Alan Shapley, whose recent promotion from captain to major made him over-rank for a captain's billet as the commanding officer of a battleship detachment.

The incoming commander, Captain John H. "Jack" Earle, had faced a similar promotion issue. Serving with the MARDET on the *Tennessee* as a first lieutenant since June 1940, Earle had just been promoted to captain. This made him over-rank to remain on the *Tennessee* because another captain commanded its MARDET. It took Earle a few weeks to report to his new billet as the detachment commander on the *Arizona* because, being in different battleship divisions, *Tennessee* and *Arizona* were rarely in port at the same time. When Earle saw the *Arizona* tie up astern of the *Tennessee*, he could at last carry out his transfer orders.

Packing all his personal gear, Captain Earle reported to Major Shapley aboard the *Arizona* late Saturday afternoon. Shapley immediately presented Earle to Captain Van Valkenburgh as his relief, and the two Marine officers began the laborious but time-honored inventory of the detachment's clothing and gear that was required before an official change of command. It was a lengthy process, and much of it had to be done deep within the lower compartments of the ship where it was stiflingly hot. Well into the evening, Shapley suggested they take a break and go ashore for a beer at the Officers' Club before completing the task. Earle readily agreed.

The Officers' Club was located on the south side of the

Southeast Loch within yards of the fleet landing. Enlisted men streamed eastward from the landing to Bloch Arena or on buses into Honolulu while officers strolled westward to partake of the amenities of the club. On a Saturday night, those in attendance were mostly junior officers who were either single or what were called geographical bachelors, meaning their wives were stateside. Those few lucky enough to have their wives with them in Honolulu were likely at home or out partying with them in the establishments along Waikiki.

Jack Earle fell in the latter category of the lucky few, but because of his change of command responsibilities, he had not been home to see his wife, Barbara, since the *Tennessee* returned from its latest two weeks of sea duty. The Earles lived in what Jack recalled was a "termite-infested cheap wooden apartment building" in Waikiki a few blocks from the Royal Hawaiian. The rent was sixty dollars per month, about one-third of Jack's salary, but Barbara had gotten a clerical job with Naval Intelligence to supplement their income.

Sipping beers at the Officers' Club, Shapley and Earle joined a group of officers from the *Arizona,* one of whom was celebrating his birthday. Farewell toasts for Shapley, who was due to leave for his new assignment on the mainland, mingled with birthday toasts, and at some point Shapley turned to Earle and said, "Why don't you go home to your wife and come back in the morning to finish the inventory?"

Earle needed no encouragement. He said good night and hailed a cab to take him into Honolulu. By now, it was after 10:00 p.m. and there was little traffic going into the city. In the other direction, long lines of cabs and buses were hauling sailors and Marines back to their ships before their liberty expired at midnight—hence the term "Cinderella liberty." Jack Earle got home to his apartment and fell into Barbara's arms, glad to be able to spend the night with her. Alan Shapley raised another glass or two and then made his way back to the *Arizona* to spend the night aboard.[10]

Several hundred miles to the west, another group that had dreamed of the weekend accepted its fate. Bill Halsey and *Enterprise* were behind schedule. Halsey had planned to arrive back in Pearl Harbor late on Saturday, but high winds and battering waves cracked a seam in one of the escorting destroyers and slowed refueling operations. Halsey shrugged it off, but for his sailors an arrival on *Sunday* instead of Saturday meant that their weekend had all but evaporated. Only the pilots of the air squadrons, scheduled to fly off in pre-dawn darkness and land ahead of the task force, stood half a chance of salvaging a few hours.

For the crew of the *Enterprise,* Saturday night entertainment would be limited to gathering on the hangar deck and watching Gary Cooper in *Sergeant York*. Cooper went on to win an Academy Award for his role, and *Sergeant York* became the top-grossing film of 1941. A good-looking hero initially refusing to fight because of his convictions but who did just that with a vengeance when left with no other choice said a lot about what America was about to become.

In the *Arizona*'s makeshift theater space on the fantail, there was no pitching deck to distract during the regular Saturday night movie as Spencer Tracy fought the waves of good and evil in *Dr. Jekyll and Mr. Hyde*. It proved one of Tracy's less memorable roles, but the fact that one could see first-run movies aboard a Navy vessel within weeks of their release was a morale-booster for enlisted men, especially those not due for liberty.

Other 1941 movies likely shown aboard the *Arizona* included *High Sierra,* a jewel heist drama that turned Humphrey Bogart into a leading man. Bogey's follow-up hit, *The Maltese Falcon,* debuted October 18, but never made it to the makeshift theater on the *Arizona.*

Seaman, Second Class, Kenneth Warriner may have seen it nonetheless. Since mid-October Ken had been assigned to temporary duty at the Fleet Signal School in San Diego. Ken was twenty-six hundred miles away from his brother and the *Arizona,* where Morse code and semaphores were the order of his day. His older brother, Russell, a month shy of his twenty-sixth birthday, had his heart set on a boatswain's mate rating and may well have spent part of the weekend doggedly studying for his next promotion. The Warriners were the only set of brothers aboard the *Arizona* to be temporarily separated by such a great distance. That had not always been the case.

Following their 1911 marriage in Chicago, the boys' parents, Sherman W. Warriner and the former Alma Schmiedel, had arrived in Camp Douglas, a little lumber camp in northwest Wisconsin, and somewhat belatedly for the times—he was thirty-eight, she was four days shy of thirty—began a family that would eventually number one girl, first-born Arlene, and four boys. Russell Walter was born on January 20, 1916, followed by Rudi Arthur two years later. By the time Kenneth Thomas came along on April 11, 1923, the family had moved south to Clinton, just east of Beloit, on the Wisconsin-Illinois border and later into Beloit proper.

Sherman Warriner was variously employed as a laborer, most likely for a lumber company or farm. In September 1935, Sherman died ten days short of his sixty-first birthday. Ken was only twelve and the youngest brother, Lyle, just eight. Although still in their teens, Russell and Rudi took on the roles of family breadwinners. By the fall of 1940, approaching twenty-five and having completed a stint with the Civilian Conservation Corps, Russell enlisted in the Navy in search of a steady income. He saw the service, he later recalled, "as a way of staying alive."

An eighteen-year-old from nearby Janesville, Herbert Vincent Buehl, joined up at the same time, and the two Wisconsin men went through basic training together at Great Lakes. After a brief Thanksgiving leave at home, they reported aboard the *Arizona* as apprentice seamen on December 9, 1940, while the ship was undergoing its final overhaul at Bremerton.

Sometime prior to shipping out, Russ Warriner met a girl at Turner Hall in Monroe, thirty-some miles west of Beloit. Turner Hall was a gathering place for many German-speaking Swiss immigrants in south-central Wisconsin. There, they continued their cultural traditions, including lively polka music, dancing, and especially gymnastics. Elsa Schild, a brunette with blue-gray eyes, was a *"turner"*— German for gymnast—who had come to America from Switzerland as a little girl. By the time Russ marched up the *Arizona*'s gangplank, he and Elsa, almost five years his junior, had an understanding.

On the home front, Rudi Warriner worked to support the family and help his mother. Three months before younger brother Ken turned eighteen, Alma gave her permission for him to follow Russ into the Navy. It was indeed the one steady job to be found, and if Ken had stayed home, he would have been another mouth around a sparse table. Ken enlisted on January 7, 1941, and caught up with the *Arizona* on April 29, shortly after it arrived at Pearl Harbor.

Their Navy training aside, neither of the Warriner broth-

ers were great swimmers. It was Russ who had the closest
call. One day while the *Arizona* lay at anchor—likely in
Lahaina Roadstead off Maui—Russ was swimming with
a bunch of shipmates, as was the norm. Such dips were
good recreation as well as a better bath, albeit with saltwater, than the single bucket of freshwater they were allot-
ted aboard ship. While swimming near a coral reef some
distance from the ship, Russ cramped up and started to
flounder. A muscle-bound guy, who couldn't swim very
well either, came to his rescue. Russ didn't know him, but
Russ was convinced that he would have drowned without
his help. It would not be the last time he would have such
thoughts.

It is likely that the Shive brothers spent the hours of Saturday evening aboard the *Arizona*. Gordon Shive's Marine
Detachment was expecting the change of command between Major Shapley and Captain Earle. After his eighteenth birthday celebration, Malcolm was not one to party
ashore. Having grown up with little money, both brothers
were inclined to save every penny and think long and hard
before spending any.

A few months before, Gordon had written his mother,
Lois Westgate, about one such quandary that he resolved on
the side of thriftiness. "Dear Mom," Gordon began his letter, "This morning was pay day again which is a good way
to start a day off right." Then, after recounting details of
the ship's last cruise, Gordon told her, "I was going to get
myself a watch, but I got to thinking the idea over and I decided that I wouldn't need one any more than a dog needs
two tails." Instead, he sent twenty dollars home and asked
her to keep it for him until his next leave or use it for herself if she needed it. Once Malcolm reported aboard, both

brothers had ten dollars per month automatically taken out of their pay and sent by check to their mother.[11]

Gordon and Malcolm Shive both wrote devoted letters to their mother, and each was also sweet on a girl back home. The Shive and Balfour families had been close growing up in Laguna Beach. Weston Balfour was about Gordon's age, and the three boys palled around together. "Wess" had two younger sisters who were usually in the mix. As everyone grew older, twenty-year-old Gordon developed more than a crush on Marge Balfour, who was two years his junior, and although the relationship was much lower key, eighteen-year-old Malcolm had more than a passing interest in sixteen-year-old Jeanne.

Gordon's correspondence with Marge Balfour reveals the sort of uncertainties and subtle innuendoes that affect many a long-distance relationship by mail. Having been childhood friends and parted as such, Marge expressed some worry in a letter to Gordon during his first cruise to Pearl Harbor that she was destined to be an old maid— hardly a concern yet at eighteen. "I wouldn't worry about being an old-maid," Gordon reassured her; "I figure it is just the opposite, that someone else is hoping that you will be an old-maid for a while anyway."[12]

By the time Malcolm reported aboard *Arizona*—perhaps with fresh intelligence from the home front—there had been an uncomfortable silence from Marge. "What's the matter, am I poison?" Gordon asked her at the start of a letter written on November 2, 1941. Then, he got to the heart of the matter: "I have heard that you and Harry had ideas of getting hitched, well if you do I hope that you will be happy." Those magnanimous words aside, he crossed out a couple of words and then added, "No that isn't cursing, but just a misprint."[13]

Marge's response, which has been lost, evidently set Gordon straight. "Doggone, was I glad to hear from you," Gordon wrote back. "I thought that you were on the outs — but I see that I was badly mistaken." Calling himself a "dope for doubting" and promising not to get "any more of those silly ideas," Gordon confessed that this was the second letter that he had written to her in response to her most recent one but that he couldn't bring himself to mail the first one — he wanted to give it to Marge in person. "So will keep it," he now wrote, "till I see you again if nothing doesn't happen, but if something should happen you will get it in the mail. It will be dated Nov 20, 1941 in the heading so if you ever get it through the mail — I hope that that doesn't sound too mysterious — it shouldn't."[14]

The father-and-son team of Gussie and William Free was momentarily splitting up. According to family lore, Gussie was a patient in the *Arizona*'s sick bay, which was located just forward of Turret No. 1 and one deck below the chief petty officers' mess. No records survive from the ship to confirm Gussie's presence there or what ailed him, but in those days a man of fifty was getting on in years, and Gussie may have presented with any number of maladies. William, on the other hand, was a month shy of an energetic eighteen and had liberty ashore.

William spent the evening with his cousin, Beulah May-wald Hodge (Gussie was her mother's first cousin) and Beulah's husband, Calford Thomas Hodge. "Tom" was a Machinist's Mate, First Class, on the *Dobbin* (AD-3), a destroyer tender moored northeast of Ford Island with a bevy of five destroyers in its care. Tom wasn't quite the old salt that Gussie was, but he had lied about his age to enlist in 1929 and had been on the *Dobbin* for almost two years.

Like the repair ship *Vestal,* destroyer tenders such as the *Dobbin* spent a lot of time in port, and Tom Hodge was fortunate that Beulah and their two children, Philip and Patty, were able to live in Honolulu with him and afford him time ashore.

William Free likely enjoyed a home-cooked meal with the Hodges and then made his way back to the *Arizona.* It is not known whether he stopped by sick bay to check on his father or decided that he would do so in the morning. After all, it was already late, and Sunday mornings were usually pretty quiet aboard ship.

Somewhere below decks, a young sailor was writing a letter to his mother.

CHAPTER 8

Dawn

Sunday, December 7

At 2:38 a.m. Washington time on December 7, Tokyo finally sent its embassy the fourteenth and final part of its reply to the American proposal of November 26. It was neither a formal declaration of war nor a severance of diplomatic relations, but it was ominous nonetheless. "The Japanese Government regrets to have to notify hereby the American Government," it concluded, "that in view of the attitude of the American Government it cannot but consider that it is impossible to reach an agreement through further negotiations."

By 7:30 a.m., the fourteenth part had been intercepted and decoded in Washington, and once more naval intelligence officer Lieutenant Commander Alwyn Kramer made the rounds delivering top-secret copies. Because they were housed in the same building, Main Navy on Constitution Avenue, Admiral Stark saw his copy first. Kramer then delivered the president's copies to the White House a few blocks away. Considering his comment of the night before, Roosevelt's reaction was mild. He shook his head and muttered, "It looks as though the Japs are going to sever negotiations."

As official Washington read and digested the full four-teen parts of Japan's message, a short "execute" missive arrived. It instructed Ambassador Nomura on when he was to deliver the complete document, the fourteenth part of which was still being typed hunt-and-peck style, to make it effective. "Will the Ambassador please submit to the United States Government (if possible to the Secretary of State)," Nomura's instructions read, "our reply to the United States at 1:00 p.m. on the 7th, your time."[1]

Colonel Rufus Bratton, Chief of the Far Eastern Section of the Army's Military Intelligence Division, was greatly alarmed. Such precision, particularly on a Sunday, was hardly the diplomatic norm. Given Japan's long tradition of launching preemptive attacks without a formal declaration of war—most famously against the Russians at Port Arthur in 1905—Bratton was convinced that something major was about to happen in the Pacific. He tracked down General Marshall, who had been out for his morning horseback ride, and offered to deliver the message to him immediately. Marshall assured Bratton that he would be in his office in the Munitions Building adjacent to Main Navy shortly and told him to wait.

When Marshall read the execute message with the 1:00 p.m. time notation, he, too, became alarmed. Marshall reached for a pad of paper and scrawled a longhand message to be sent to his major Pacific commands: "Japanese are presenting at one p.m. eastern standard time today what amounts to an ultimatum; also they are under orders to destroy their code machine immediately. Just what significance the hour set may have we do not know but be on alert accordingly. Inform naval authorities of this communication. Marshall."[2] It was high noon in Washington, DC, and 6:30 a.m. at Pearl Harbor. Thirty minutes earlier, six

Japanese aircraft carriers had turned into the wind some two hundred miles north of Oahu and begun to launch their complements of planes.

Sunday, December 7, 1941, was a big day for the Miller family of Ostrander, Ohio. George Harley Miller and his wife, Mary, were hosting a family dinner to celebrate their thirty-seventh wedding anniversary. They lived on a farm near the Union–Delaware county line about twenty miles northwest of Columbus. During their marriage, Harley— no one called him George—and Mary had made a living farming and raised four children. Frank, the oldest, was married with a three-year-old daughter of his own, named for her grandmother. Rachel, the youngest and only girl of Harley and Mary's four children, would be twelve in February.

The "boys," as their mother always called them, who were in between Frank and Rachel in age and now absent around the Miller table were Jesse Zimmer Miller and George Stanley Miller. Jesse, the older of the two, was born in 1914. Stanley—like his father, for whom he was named, no one ever called him George—was six years younger and had just turned twenty-one. Despite their age difference, big, tough Jesse—he and Frank were of similar solid builds—had always tended to look after gangly Stanley, who had been rather frail and sickly as a child. Until recently, Jesse pumped gas at brother Frank's filling station, and Stanley worked as a hired hand for a neighbor. Neither had more than an eighth-grade education.

Having never taken to farm chores, Stanley repeatedly talked about joining the Navy to learn a trade. He persuaded Jesse to share his plan, and the two Miller brothers enlisted together at Cincinnati on October 7, 1940. Two months later, after training at Great Lakes, they reported aboard the *Arizona* while it was moored at Bremerton. Almost a year to the day later, they were still serving aboard it. Jesse was training as an electrician and Stanley was on a gun crew.

Harley and Mary's little granddaughter, three-year-old Mary, would always carry one lone memory of her Uncle Jesse from the final meal the family shared together before the boys reported aboard the *Arizona*. "Uncle Jesse stood up," Mary later recalled, "and drained his water glass. Then, he looked down, smiled at me and winked. That's it. Just one picture in my mind."

The boys took turns writing letters home to their family, but both of them always signed each letter. That's the way they had always done things: the two of them together. "Oh, Frank," one of them enthused to their older brother in one such missive, "you should have been with us Saturday night. We went into town and some of the guys got drunk and got into a big fight. Somebody called the MPs and some of the guys landed in the brig. What a night! I wish you could have been with us."

Now, it was Harley and Mary's turn to wish that Jesse and Stanley could be home with them for this special day. As the Miller family—minus "the boys"—sat down to share a big midday dinner in honor of Harley and Mary's thirty-seven years together, no one thought to interrupt the celebration by turning on the radio.[3]

Forty-five hundred miles and six time zones to the west of the Miller dinner table, the skies over Pearl Harbor slowly lightened. Plodding along at five knots, the destroyer *Ward* (DD-139), an aging four-stack *Wickes*-class veteran of World War I, patrolled the waters outside the entrance channel. Its captain, Lieutenant Commander William W. Outerbridge, a 1927 graduate of Annapolis, was only two days into his first command and it had already been a busy morning. Receiving a report from the coastal minesweeper *Condor* (AMc-14) of a narrow wake of a submarine periscope, Outerbridge had ordered the *Ward* to general quarters and conducted a futile pre-dawn search.

Barely two hours later, the officer of the deck summoned the captain back to the bridge. The supply ship *Antares* (AG-10) was inbound to Pearl Harbor, heading toward the submarine nets protecting the entrance channel. Between *Antares* and the barge it was towing, Captain Outerbridge made out the unmistakable silhouette of the conning tower and periscope of an unknown submarine. There was no doubt in his mind that this was an intruder intent on following *Antares* through the open submarine nets and into the harbor.

Outerbridge called for speed and ordered a turn toward the target as the *Ward* surged to twenty knots. At 6:45 a.m. the destroyer fired two shots from its four-inch guns. The first passed directly over the submarine's conning tower and missed. The second hit the submarine at the waterline between the conning tower and its hull. As the *Ward*'s action report later characterized it, "This was a square positive hit." The target heeled over to starboard and appeared to slow and sink, drifting into a tightly spaced salvo of depth charges set for 100 feet that the *Ward* dropped as it crossed the submarine's bow.

Outerbridge couldn't be certain, but a large oil slick on the surface after the depth charges exploded indicated that his quarry had likely sunk. He radioed a voice transmission saying the *Ward* had "dropped depth charges upon subs," but two minutes later, fearing that the report might be taken merely as one more in a long line of sketchy contacts, Outerbridge made clear that this had been no illusion: "We have attacked, fired upon, and dropped depth charges on a submarine operating in defensive sea area," he radioed. Seconds later, just to be certain his information had been received, Outerbridge queried, "Did you get that last message?"

The answer was yes, and the report made its way up the chain of command, reaching Admiral Kimmel about forty minutes later. Like others who'd relayed the message, Kimmel was skeptical. "I was not at all certain that this was a real attack," he later told investigators. It would take sixty years before a Japanese midget submarine was discovered in some twelve hundred feet of water with a hole in its conning tower—evidence that Outerbridge and the *Ward* had indeed inflicted the first casualties of the day.[4]

By all accounts, Captain Outerbridge and the crew of the *Ward* performed their duties vigilantly and aggressively. No doubt their actions were the sort Secretary of the Navy Frank Knox had in mind when he affirmed the superiority of the United States Navy for the *New York Times*. Readers opening their Sunday morning newspapers found Knox's comments under the headline, "Navy is Superior to Any, says Knox." Citing record expansion in new ships and planes and a war footing, Knox asserted: "I am proud to report that the American people may feel fully confident in their Navy. In my opinion, the loyalty, morale and technical ability of the personnel are without superior. On any comparable basis, the United States Navy is second to none."[5]

In its "News of the Week in Review" section, the *Times* sounded a similarly optimistic note. "Big Forces are massed for showdown in Pacific," it warned, but because of American, British, Chinese, and Dutch interests in Southeast

Asia, any aggressive moves by Japan "will have to meet superior strength of ABCD Powers." A large map accompanying the article, captioned "Possible Path of Widening War," pointed the way past China and the increasingly isolated American Philippines to Singapore and the heart of the Netherlands East Indies. The Hawaiian Islands and Pearl Harbor were located far to the east on the map and appeared to be well out of harm's way.[6]

There was, of course, more mundane news. Christmas was coming, but many in Hawaii and the Philippines would have to do without Christmas trees. On Oahu and in Manila there was a bona fide tree shortage. While mainland residents were buying more than ever, thousands of trees that would normally have been shipped overseas to US possessions had been crowded off freighters by more important cargoes—much of it of a wartime nature. Even with the stateside surplus, tree prices were up about ten percent this season because of rising labor and transportation costs.[7]

The biggest sporting news from Saturday's collegiate football games was the mincemeat the Texas Longhorns made of the Oregon Ducks before twenty-six thousand spectators in Austin. Striving to prove that they deserved a higher AP ranking than Texas A&M, the Longhorns steamrollered the Ducks in a 71-7 shellacking. Oregon managed its only score on a tricky hand-off reverse in the second quarter and finished the season 5-5. Southwest Conference Champ Texas A&M beat Washington State in Pullman, in far less spectacular fashion, 7-0. It was the last game for the Aggies until their scheduled matchup against Alabama in the Cotton Bowl on New Year's Day.[8]

National Football League games underway or about to begin on the mainland included the traditional interborough rivalry between the Brooklyn Dodgers and the

New York Giants and a crosstown scuffle between the Chicago Bears and the Chicago Cardinals. In the nation's capital, quarterback Sammy Baugh and his Washington Redskins were hosting the Philadelphia Eagles.

On the *Arizona,* it was baseball that was still on the mind of newly-minted Marine Major Alan Shapley. He was up early for breakfast with a full day ahead. He not only had to complete the equipment inventory with incoming Captain Jack Earle before a change of command, but also hoped to participate in one more game with the *Arizona*'s baseball team before his departure stateside. Shapley was both the coach and first baseman of the team that had won the battleships championship and was scheduled to play a team from the *Enterprise,* the victor among the aircraft carriers and cruisers. Shapley didn't know that *Enterprise* had been delayed by weather on its return from Wake Island and was still inbound to Pearl Harbor.[9]

Out on the deck of the *Arizona,* Boatswain's Mate, Second Class, John Delmar Anderson turned a critical eye to the rows of chairs that the work detail under his command had just finished setting up for Sunday church services on the *Arizona*'s fantail. A large awning covered the entire stern area and was usually in place whenever the ship was in port to afford some measure of shade. Similar awnings covered the forecastle at the bow and portions of the quarterdeck. Anderson gave a nod of satisfaction to himself. The rows were neat and correctly spaced, and the chaplain's lectern stood at the front of the assembled chairs. Anderson dismissed his men and went below decks to eat breakfast.

Elsewhere on the *Arizona,* its crew stirred. Francis and Norman Morse were excited over the rumors—by now confirmed by Captain Van Valkenburgh as true—that the

Arizona would be in Long Beach, or at least somewhere between there and Bremerton, over the Christmas holidays. They knew that their devoted mother would be thrilled when she learned the news. Having no one but her two boys, May Morse was indeed the 1940s version of a twenty-first-century helicopter mom. Her boys in turn had long shown that they were equally devoted to her.

The three of them had been through a lot together since the boys were born in Lamar, Colorado. At an elevation of thirty-six hundred feet and thirty miles from the Kansas border, Lamar is about as far downstream on the Arkansas River as one can get and still be in Colorado. Sugar beets were an important crop, especially after the American Beet Sugar Company built a processing plant in 1905 and proceeded to acquire land for company farms.

In 1917, their father, Royal Bernard Morse, a Spanish-American War veteran from Winona County, Minnesota, received an early discharge from service in World War I so that he could manage one of American Beet Sugar's farms. The following year, Roy, as he was called, married Clara May Dyer, a native of Tennessee sixteen years his junior, in the First Methodist Church in Lamar.

When Clara gave birth to her first son on November 22, 1919, they named him Francis Jerome Morse. On July 19, 1921, Norman Roi Morse joined him. This unusual spelling of Norman's middle name seems to have been derived from his father's. To say that these two boys, born twenty months apart, were May's pride and joy would be an understatement. In fact, they were her everything.

Roy and May Morse proved to be pillars in the Lamar community. Roy served on the school board and May was a Republican precinct committeewoman for Prowers County. Francis and Norman grew up in a solid middle-class family with plenty of time outdoors, but in 1930, Roy died in a farming accident. May moved the boys into town and tried to adjust to life without him.

Eleven-year-old Francis turned his attention to music and joined the Lamar Junior High School Band. He discovered what his mother called "an inborn talent–interest in the clarinet." Norman took up the cornet. Norman was the reader of the two, preferring books to going places, and his mother knew that she "could always find him at the library."

Two years after Roy's death, May relocated to Denver and enrolled the boys in East High School. They continued their interest in music but also participated as cadets in Junior Reserve Officers' Training Corps (JROTC). Francis got his first job running a paper route for the *Denver Post*. May called him the "dater" of her two boys and wasn't surprised when he announced his plans to take a girl to the annual military ball in 1935. May *was* surprised, however, to learn that a friend had loaned Francis his car for the occasion. "Until that time," she recalled, "I did not even know that he could drive!"[10]

Shortly afterward, Francis declared his intention to join the Navy. Despite his father's service in the Army, Roy Morse had always "talked Navy" to the boys, perhaps because life at sea seemed preferable to the malaria-ridden field camps he had experienced. A further influence may have been a set of history books about the Navy, which the boys read time and time again. Most of all, despite Francis's recent job delivering telegrams for Western Union, long-range job prospects in Denver were bleak.

May Morse gave her permission somewhat reluctantly, but at the time judged it a good thing. Her firstborn enlisted at Denver on December 11, 1936. May long remembered the cold December night at Denver's Union Station when they said their goodbyes. "Francis left for Calif. Friday at 8:30 p.m. wearing a blue suit, blue tie, white shirt and a smile," May recorded on a scrap of paper. "Also his mother was wearing a smile too. Age 17 years 20 days," she wrote.[11] After undergoing basic training at San Diego, Francis reported to the *Arizona* in the spring of 1937.

When Norman graduated from high school two years later, there wasn't much question what he wanted to do. This time, May was even more reluctant to give her permission, but she did so and Norman enlisted on August 13, 1938. Once again, there were goodbyes at the railroad station. As she had done for Francis, May made a little note as her younger son headed off for boot camp. Norman left wearing a yellow sweater and May claimed that she was smiling just as she had at Francis's departure.

Norman reported to Naval Station San Diego for basic training. Francis was close by when the *Arizona* came in and out of San Pedro. Francis soon told May that he had received a letter from Norman and that Norman didn't like training, but Francis assured her that he had "felt the same way when I was there" and he thought Norman would like it better once he was "out here in the fleet."

Always the attentive son, Francis asked May to confirm she had received three dollars he had sent and told her he was sending five more on his next payday. As for Norman, Francis promised to see him sometime soon. "I'm going to try and get my girl to take me down in her car," he told his mother, adding, "Getting high class, aren't I?"[12]

After Norman finished basic training, he reported to the *Arizona* and joined his older brother. That was the way they wanted it, and it made them both very happy. According to May, "Francis was beside himself with joy because his brother had made it aboard."

But by the following spring, May was feeling decidedly alone. "This is my wedding anniversary 21 yrs ago today [and] I find myself all alone," she wrote on one of the many scraps of paper she routinely saved. "My boys are at sea. I love them." Then, echoing the sentiments of many a mother whose sons had joined the military, she added, "Francis don't seem to be the same. Norman has not changed yet."[13]

Part of Francis's change may have been that there was now a steady girl in his life. Having been the "dater" of the two brothers, Francis met Dorothy Fletcher of Portland, Oregon, through mutual friends while the *Arizona* was undergoing an overhaul at Bremerton early in 1939. With Norman as best man, Francis and Dorothy married at Long Beach on August 17, 1939, in an evening ceremony officiated by the chaplain of the *Arizona*. Dorothy may not have understood what life would be like married to a sailor, whose whereabouts were not of his own doing, but she settled down to wait for Francis in Long Beach along with so many others. As May had just written to Francis, his young wife and her mother-in-law were not close, but kept similar vigils.

Meanwhile, Marvin and Wesley Becker were feeling content. They had opted to remain on the *Arizona* the night before and give their big brother, Harvey, some time alone with his wife, who had only recently come out from the mainland. If the *Arizona* sailed east as just announced, Marie Becker might be left alone in Honolulu for Christmas. Civilian travel between the islands and the mainland by air was almost prohibitively expensive on an enlisted man's salary, and last-minute shipboard passages were increasingly difficult to obtain. Marvin certainly didn't begrudge Harvey some privacy, particularly as he was busy packing for his scheduled annual leave at the end of the month regardless of the *Arizona*'s schedule.

By all reports, old-timer Gussie Free was still confined to sick bay, located below decks just forward of Turret No. 1. Given the quiet Sunday morning, Gussie's son, William, was in no particular rush to check on his father. William had been ashore the night before with relatives and he was taking his time with breakfast. Gussie, free-spirit that he was, may well have been passing the time daydreaming about what part of the world he hoped to visit once his final hitch was finished.

Gordon Shive was not part of the four-man Marine color guard about to assemble in their dress uniforms for the 8:00 a.m. colors ceremony, although he had done that duty many times. Gordon was preparing to eat breakfast in the Marine area and still glowing over the latest letter he had received from Marge Balfour. They appeared to have something going after all, and Gordon was thrilled. He contemplated how he might be able to deliver his unmailed letter to Marge personally when the *Arizona* moored in California in a week or two.

Navy brother Malcolm Shive, always a bit of a tinkerer, may well have been reading some radio manual or preparing for his next watch. Neither of the Shive boys had any way of knowing that their best buddy from Laguna Beach, Weston Balfour, and the 24th Pursuit Group to which Wess was assigned as a member of the Army Air Forces had had a little excitement the night before when P-40 fighters from Iba Airfield north of Manila scrambled in response to unidentified aircraft flying off the coast.

Like many of his shipmates, Russ Warriner had a habit of sleeping out on deck, savoring a cool breeze on nice nights when the *Arizona* was in port. If he did this on the night of December 6, his hammock and those of others doing the same thing would have been smartly stowed away shortly after reveille. This complete, Russ washed up, glanced at the Hamilton watch on his wrist—it was American-made and a favorite of US servicemen—and headed for breakfast in his assigned eating area. Breakfast on Sundays was a bit more leisurely, with time for a second cup of coffee.

The other Warriner brother, Ken, had been up several hours ahead of his shipmates because of the time difference with his temporary duty station at Fleet Signal School in San Diego. Ken was well into a low-key day, but elsewhere around San Diego Harbor, things were hopping. At the Naval Air Station, squadron personnel from the air group assigned to the carrier *Saratoga* scurried to ready their planes and equipment to be hoisted aboard. Having completed a refit at Bremerton, the *Sara* was making its way into the harbor after a three-day voyage down the West Coast. In addition to its air group, a squadron of Marine fighters bound for Oahu was to be put aboard before the carrier sailed west for Pearl Harbor the following morning.

As the *Arizona*'s men gathered for breakfast and the enemy submarine report from the *Ward* made its way up the naval chain of command, the Army's Opana Mobile Radar Station at Kahuku Point on the northern tip of Oahu shut down for the day. Privates Joseph Lockard and George Elliott had been on duty since 4:00 a.m., and their three-hour shift training on a relatively new warning system was over. Lockard had been instructing Elliott in reading the radarscope, but just as he reached to turn it off, a large image began to march across his screen from the north.

Lockard's first thought was that something had gone haywire with his set, but when everything checked out, he and Elliott called in a report of what appeared to be more than fifty planes approaching Oahu about 130 miles out. The Information Center at Fort Shafter, to which they reported, was charged with directing pursuit aircraft to intercept any incoming threat, but it was also shutting down for the day. The senior officer remaining at the Information Center was First Lieutenant Kermit Tyler, the executive officer of the 78th Pursuit Squadron, who was serving only his second day of duty at the center.

Tyler would always be adamant that it never crossed his mind that these incoming planes could possibly be enemy aircraft, particularly as a far more likely explanation presented itself. Two squadrons of B-17 bombers, totaling twelve aircraft, were nearing Hickam Field from the northeast that morning after an overnight flight from California. After refueling, they were supposed to continue on to the Philippines to augment General MacArthur's air force. Tyler was convinced that the Opana station had detected this flight of bombers and told Lockard and Elliott, "Well, don't worry about it."[14]

Lockard and Elliott were, of course, looking at far more than fifty planes. In fact, the first wave of Japanese attackers approaching northern Oahu numbered 183 aircraft: 43 Mitsubishi A6M "Zero" fighters; 51 Aichi D3A "Val" dive-bombers; 49 Nakajima B5N2 "Kate" bombers deployed with bombs for a high altitude attack; and 40 "Kate" bombers armed with torpedoes. Even as Lockard and Elliott watched this mass come closer, 170 more planes, part of a second attack wave, rose from their carrier decks and streaked south.[15]

Lieutenant Commander Sam Fuqua joined Marine Major Alan Shapley for breakfast on the *Arizona* in the officers' mess just forward of Turret No. 3 near the base of the main mast. Fuqua was the command duty officer for the day because the night before he had volunteered to take the twenty-four-hour shift so that the *Arizona*'s gunnery officer, Lieutenant Commander Bruce Kelley, could spend Saturday night and Sunday ashore with his family. Also at the table were the ship's senior medical officer, Commander, Medical Corps, Samuel Johnson, and its chaplain, Captain, Chaplain Corps, Thomas Kirkpatrick. Talk centered around Shapley's pending departure for the states and his replacement, Captain Jack Earle, who, thanks to Shapley's similar kindness, was home in Honolulu with his wife.[16]

As Fuqua and his breakfast companions sipped second cups of coffee, the first wave of Japanese planes crossed the northernmost point of Oahu and flew almost directly over the startled faces of Privates Lockard and Elliott at Kahuku Point. The Zero fighters surged ahead to suppress any resistance from Army Air Forces fighters from Wheeler, Kaneohe, and Hickam airfields. Val dive-bombers climbed to twelve thousand feet and cut directly across the island to approach Pearl Harbor from the northeast. Kates carrying torpedoes dropped to near sea level and split into two groups to come at the harbor from opposite directions. The Kates assigned to high-altitude bombing made a lazy circle over the western point of the island and then turned northeast, heading straight up the entrance channel toward Battleship Row.

At precisely 7:50 a.m. the Marine bugler with the duty on the *Arizona*, Field Musician Don Edgar Hamel from Chicago, put his shiny bugle to his lips and sounded the brief notes of "Band Call." In response, the twenty-one members of the *Arizona*'s band assembled in formation on the quarterdeck. The four-member Marine color guard

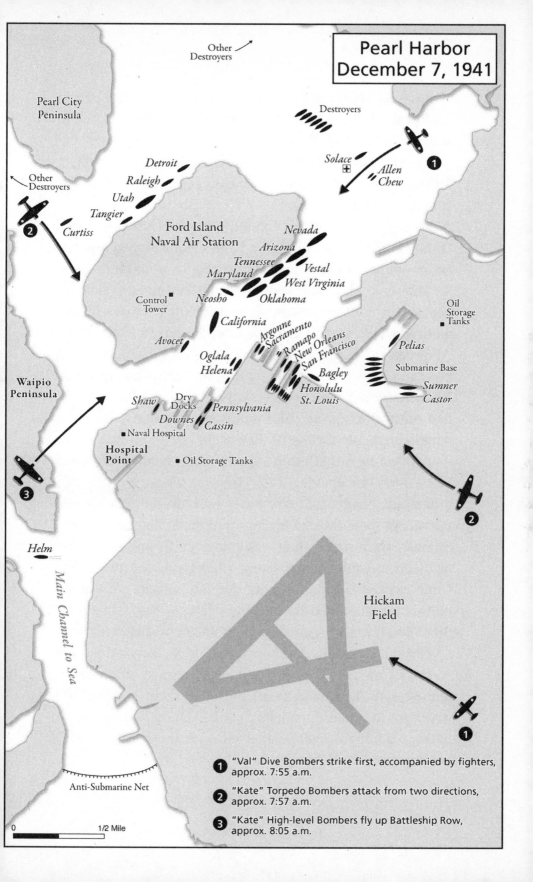

Pearl Harbor
December 7, 1941

Other
Destroyers

Destroyers

Pearl City
Peninsula

Solace ⊞

Allen
Chew

1

Other
Destroyers

Detroit

Raleigh

Utah

Tangier

2

Curtiss

Nevada

Ford Island
Naval Air Station

Arizona

Tennessee

Maryland

Vestal

West Virginia

Control
Tower

Neosho

Oklahoma

Oil
Storage
Tanks

California

Waipio
Peninsula

Avocet

Argonne
Sacramento

Ramapo
New Orleans
San Francisco

Pelias

Submarine Base

Oglala
Helena

Bagley

Sumner
Castor

Honolulu
St. Louis

Shaw

Dry
Docks

Pennsylvania

Downes

Cassin

■ Naval Hospital

3

Hospital
Point

■ Oil Storage Tanks

Helm

2

Main Channel to Sea

Hickam
Field

1

Anti-Submarine Net

0   1/2 Mile

1 "Val" Dive Bombers strike first, accompanied by fighters,
approx. 7:55 a.m.

2 "Kate" Torpedo Bombers attack from two directions,
approx. 7:57 a.m.

3 "Kate" High-level Bombers fly up Battleship Row,
approx. 8:05 a.m.

stood by ready to do the flag-raising honors on the ensign staff at the stern. Smaller ships relied on a bugler alone to sound "To the Colors" as the national ensign was raised, but on the battleships, their bands played the National Anthem for colors seven days a week unless excused by their ship's commanding officer.

Five minutes later at 7:55 a.m., bugler Hamel sounded "First Call" and the color guard and band marched into position on the fantail. The usual procedure would have been for Hamel to play "Attention" seconds before 8:00 a.m. All persons in uniform within sight or hearing, unless in formation, would stop in their tracks and render a hand salute. At precisely the hour, Bandmaster Kinney would sweep his hands upward and the strains of "The Star-Spangled Banner" would resound across the *Arizona*'s deck. At the first notes the Marine color guard would smartly hoist the American flag to the top of the ensign staff.

All along Battleship Row, the bands of each battleship—except the *West Virginia,* whose captain had granted its band a rare reprieve—took up positions on the fantails of their respective ships and made the same preparations. They timed their individual performances to the band on the ship of the senior officer present afloat. For some reason this morning, the *Nevada*'s band got a jump on this time-honored routine and began to play "The Star-Spangled Banner" several minutes ahead of schedule.

On the *Arizona,* Bandmaster Kinney frowned at the *Nevada*'s breach of protocol. His bandsmen stood at attention with their instruments poised at their lips, but they never got the chance to make a sound. The escalating drone of approaching aircraft competed with the martial strains coming from the *Nevada*'s fantail.[17]

*   *   *

The Christiansen boys—Sonny, the baker, and Buddy, the newest brother to join the *Arizona*—had risen and eaten early. Dressed in their whites, they were intent on heading into Honolulu on liberty to have a photo taken together as a Christmas present for their mother back home in Columbus, Kansas. The brothers stood on the quarterdeck waiting for the 8:00 a.m. colors ceremony and a chance to be in the first load of sailors to climb down the ladder to the crew boat and be taken ashore to the fleet landing.

Buddy Christiansen may have made a younger brother smirk as he pointed out a blemish in Sonny's attire. All was neat and proper except for a black smudge on Sonny's white sailor's hat. That would not do for their photo, and it certainly wouldn't pass the eyes of the officer of the deck as they presented their liberty cards and requested permission to go ashore. Sonny shook his head in disgust. "Wait here," he told Buddy. And with that Sonny Christiansen disappeared below decks to return to his locker to find a replacement.

Ensign Henry "Hank" Davison, an Arkansas native and member of the Annapolis class of 1940, had the duty as officer of the deck for the four-hour watch beginning at 8:00 a.m. The Christiansen brothers and all those going ashore would have to pass under his scrutiny. As was customary, Davison had relieved the previous officer of the deck a few minutes before the official start of his watch. The just-relieved officer ducked into the wardroom mess and sat down for breakfast near Lieutenant Commander Sam Fuqua and Major Alan Shapley.

Barely had he done so, when the notes of "Air Defense" blared out of Field Musician Don Hamel's bugle instead of the expected "Attention" for the colors ceremony. Fuqua furrowed his brow and quickly inquired of the just-relieved officer of the deck, "Is this a drill?" And what about the antiaircraft batteries? Were they manned and ready? "I think so," came the reply to both questions.

Fuqua was hardly satisfied, and he tried to call Ensign Davison to confirm that the ship's antiaircraft guns were manned and ready for the usual tracking exercises required during such a drill. When Fuqua was unable to raise Davison on the telephone, he exited the wardroom, went up a ladder, and stepped onto the quarterdeck on the port side of the ship adjacent to where the *Vestal* was moored.

A glance toward the stern of the *Arizona* showed the Marine color guard and the ship's band in place on the fantail preparing to raise the American flag. The escalating whine of diving aircraft grew louder. Why were so many planes in the air on a quiet Sunday morning? The Army must be out of its mind. What sounded like real explosions inland on Ford Island sent plumes of thick black smoke spiraling into the air.

Just then, a plane passed low overhead with its machine guns chattering. Fuqua looked up. The big red "meatball" on the underside of one wing left no doubt in his mind that the aircraft was Japanese. But in that instant, Fuqua could not comprehend the magnitude of the disaster that was about to descend. Surely, Fuqua thought, this is a single errant plane, probably launched from a submarine. No doubt it would quickly be shot down.

Fuqua ran around the aft end of Turret No. 4 to reach the officer of the deck station and order General Quarters. Someone, perhaps Ensign Davison, was ahead of him. Field Musician Hamel bugled "General Quarters" for all he was worth, and claxons resounded throughout the ship.[18]

Over on the *Vestal*, Ensign Fred Hall was just going off duty as that ship's officer of the deck. Hall had gotten almost no reaction in the *Vestal*'s wardroom the night before when he suggested that when it came to war in the Pacific, the Japanese would "attack right here." Hall, too, looked up at the sound of machine gun fire and immediately recognized the red circle under the wing of the attacking aircraft. "Sound General Quarters," he yelled. When the quartermaster simply stared back at him in disbelief and didn't move, Hall barked, "Goddamn it, I said sound General Quarters!" and reached past the frozen crewman to pull the signal himself.[19]

On the *Nevada*, its band was well into its early playing of the National Anthem. Bandmaster Oden McMillan apparently did not hear the General Quarters alarms sounding on the *Arizona* and *Vestal*. *Nevada* was moored aft of the *Arizona*, bow to stern, and McMillan's position on his battleship's fantail put him more than six hundred feet away. Still, there were those on the *Arizona* and the *Vestal* who would recall hearing the strains of "The Star-Spangled Banner" as they rushed to their battle stations. They assumed these were coming from the *Arizona*'s band, but in fact the *Nevada*'s musicians were the only band to play that morning.

By the time McMillan saw the attacking aircraft and realized what was happening, he sped up the tempo and, after the last notes, hurried his bandsmen, most with instruments in hand, to their battle stations. In the rush, Musician William E. Clemons threw his big bass horn over the side so that it would not clog up a hatchway.

On the *Arizona*, Bandmaster Kinney looked up at the sounds of the bugled "Air Defense" call and shouted to his men to take their battle stations as "General Quarters" rang out. They ran from the fantail and disappeared down a hatchway near the base of the main mast. Their duties now were to man the ammunition hoists in Turret No. 2.

As the musicians ran forward toward the turret, they may have dropped their instruments in the band room along the way or put them in whatever nook they judged to be secure. These shiny trumpets and ebony clarinets were personal property and likely the most important possession many had. Some bandsmen were still making payments on them. With instruments stored, their owners lined up along the hoists carrying powder bags from the magazines to the breeches of the fourteen-inch guns. They were to make sure that the silken bags did not become snagged as they rode up the hoists.[20]

Commander Fuqua's breakfast companions also headed for their battle stations. Dr. Johnson and Chaplain Kirkpatrick went forward past Turret No. 2 toward their assigned areas in sick bay. Major Alan Shapley heard a thud overhead and thought one of the ship's forty-foot boats had fallen off a crane and onto the deck. Shapley followed Fuqua topside to investigate and found himself surrounded by chaos. He moved to rally the Marines, who were still his charges pending a transfer of command, but Shapley could scarcely believe his eyes or ears. As he rushed past several sailors, Shapley heard one of them exclaim, "This is the best goddamn drill the Army Air Force has ever put on."[21]

CHAPTER 9

"Andy, Who Are Those Guys?"

Sunday, December 7

Boatswain's Mate John Anderson was just digging into his breakfast and enjoying his first cup of coffee when a loud explosion shook the Sunday morning calm. Anderson's first thought was, "What the dickens was that?" One of the mess cooks peered out a porthole to survey the growing buzz of airplanes. "Andy," he said evenly, "you served in China. Who are those guys? They look like Japs."

Anderson ducked through a hatchway and stepped onto the deck. Looking skyward, he could plainly see the big red circle underneath the wings of a diving Zero. "My god," Anderson exclaimed, "those sons of bitches are here!" In later telling, Anderson would sometimes avoid repeating that characterization or apologize for what he termed his "bad word," but at the time there was no denying how he felt.[1]

Buddy Christiansen had been waiting patiently on the quarterdeck for his brother, Sonny, to fetch a clean hat. Buddy first sensed something was amiss when a big splash of water, likely from a bomb dropping alongside the ship off the starboard quarter, flew upward and washed over the quarterdeck. A petty officer stuck his head out a porthole and

sharply ordered all hands within earshot to close all portholes
as standard operating procedure for damage control. Gee,
thought Christiansen, he's pretty bossy for a Sunday morning, but just as quickly Christiansen realized the gravity of
what was occurring. As General Quarters sounded, Buddy
sprinted toward his station near the powder magazine for
Turrets No. 3 and 4. Sonny had yet to reappear on deck.[2]

Former high school basketball rivals Private, First Class,
Russell Durio and Fireman, Third Class, Archie Arnaud
from St. Landry Parish, Louisiana, had met on deck that
morning as planned. There is no way to be certain, but
it seems likely that Russell and Archie had coordinated
their liberty and planned to spend some time together in
Honolulu. Instead, when General Quarters sounded, Russell headed for his battle station on the antiaircraft batteries
and Archie disappeared below decks to his boiler station.

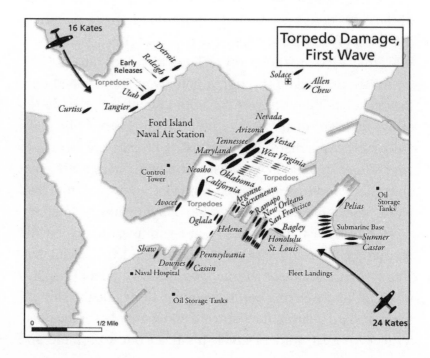

As John Anderson stared in rage at "those sons of bitches" and dive-bombers pressed their attacks against the airfield on Ford Island, the forty Kate bombers armed with torpedoes started their runs against the battleships. Sixteen Kates approached from the western side of Ford Island. Seven pilots released their torpedoes against the aging *Utah* and the light cruisers *Detroit* and *Raleigh* before they realized that bigger targets awaited them on the eastern side of the island. The twenty-four remaining Kates dove in single file from the eastern sky above Hickam Field and streaked down the Southeast Loch as if it were a giant gun sight aimed squarely at Battleship Row.

Oklahoma and *West Virginia* lay dead ahead, moored outboard to the *Maryland* and *Tennessee,* respectively. They made perfect targets for torpedoes. Three struck the *Oklahoma*. The battleship quickly began to list to port, heeling over toward the harbor and away from the *Maryland*. Two more torpedoes slammed into its side. Private Russell McCurdy, one of Admiral Kidd's orderlies on the *Arizona,* had just come off watch and remembered, "I watched the *Oklahoma* go over like a wounded whale." And the big battleship kept going, eventually turning over to expose a good portion of its hull before capsizing in the mud and entrapping more than four hundred men.

Seeing the smoke from the initial explosions on Ford Island, the officer of the deck of the *West Virginia* mistook them for internal fires on the *California,* moored by itself at the head of the battleship line. He gave the order "Away Fire and Rescue Party," and hundreds of sailors climbed above decks to obey. Had they not done so, many of them would have died as the first of seven torpedoes struck the *West Virginia* and the ship started to follow *Oklahoma*'s roll. Only aggressive counter flooding stopped the *West Vir-*

ginia's list at 25 degrees, and the ship settled onto Pearl Harbor's murky bottom on a relatively even keel.

With *Oklahoma* and *West Virginia* obviously taking a pummeling, the torpedo bombers toward the end of the twenty-four-plane string split left and right and went for fresh targets. Two Kates headed left for the *California* and released torpedoes that struck its port side and tore open a gaping forty-foot hole. Two other Kates angled right toward the *Nevada*. Machine gun fire brought one down about one hundred yards off the *Nevada*'s port quarter before it could release its torpedo. The second Kate got through the hail of gunfire, and its torpedo hit the port side of the *Nevada* between the forward turrets.

Meanwhile, five of the torpedo bombers that had approached from the west and not taken the bait of the *Utah* continued eastward over Ford Island and overflew Battleship Row, aiming for the minesweeper *Oglala* and cruiser *Helena,* moored together alongside 1010 Dock. They dropped five torpedoes, but scored only one hit. It passed under the *Oglala* and exploded against the starboard side of the *Helena,* flooding its boiler rooms. The resulting shock waves ruptured the *Oglala*'s hull. Tugs pulled it away from the *Helena* to the adjacent dockside, where it sank two hours later.[3]

So far, the *Arizona,* moored inboard from the *Vestal,* had been lucky, but more havoc was en route. High overhead, the increasing drone of high-altitude bombers filled the sky. Ten five-plane V formations of Kate bombers—one formation minus one plane—flew up the entrance channel toward Battleship Row and targeted the inboard battleships that had been largely protected from the torpedo attacks by their outboard neighbors. One wave of five planes released its 800-kilogram (1,760-pound) bombs against the *Arizona* and the adjacent *Vestal*.

These projectiles were sixteen-inch armor-piercing naval ordnance that had been converted to aerial bombs by adding four-inch-thick steel casing at the nose and directional fins at the tail. Teardrop shaped, they measured almost eight feet in length. The whole point of armor-piercing shells employed as bombs was that when dropped from an altitude that generated enough accelerating speed, the hardened casings penetrated armor and the impact triggered delayed fuses of several tenths of a second that then detonated the explosive component for maximum damage. When dropped from ten thousand feet from the Kates, these projectiles were capable of penetrating at least five inches of deck armor.

John Anderson and many others on the decks of the *Arizona* looked skyward and struggled to process why so many black objects were dropping toward them from the V-shaped formations of planes flying ten thousand feet above. Anderson started back through the hatch door, but he never reached it.

One bomb of the first salvo of five glanced off Turret No. 4 on the starboard side, likely striking the nine-inch-thick steel on the side of the turret, but it still managed to bury itself below decks and explode. Two more bombs penetrated the deck and exploded fore and aft of the base of the main mast. One, possibly two bombs, hit the *Vestal*. One of these detonated with a concussion that blew John Anderson inside the hatchway and, in his words, "knocked me silly." With bullets from Japanese fighters spraying the deck around him, Anderson came to, shook himself off, and raced to his battle station in Turret No. 4. Years of training took over. He slid into his gunner's seat and confidently announced "Manned and ready."

That was all by the book, but the big fourteen-inch guns

were meant for ship-to-ship combat and weren't going to do any good against a swarm of planes. Anderson told his turret captain, Chief Petty Officer George Campbell, "Look, what I saw out there was a number of Japanese planes. I didn't see any ships or anything and no shellfire. There's all bombs and machine gun fire. We can't do any good in here. We need some gunners on the antiaircraft batteries." Campbell asked Anderson what he wanted to do, and Anderson replied, "I'd like to get out there and get on a gun with my brother. He's an antiaircraft gun captain and he needs help." Campbell thought a second and then said, "Go for it."

But as Anderson left the turret and started up a ladder toward the antiaircraft guns on the upper decks, the entire front end of the ship erupted in a horrendous explosion. "People were blown all over the place, all kinds of body parts," Anderson recalled. "Everybody was trying to salvage somebody and get them off where they were free and clear, but nobody was free and clear."[4]

As the tightly packed formation of bombers made its way up Battleship Row, Lieutenant Commander Sam Fuqua thought the black dots dropping toward him looked like bowling balls. The blast from the initial bomb that glanced off Turret No. 4 and buried itself below decks rendered Fuqua momentarily unconscious as he ran forward on the starboard side of the quarterdeck. When he came to his senses, there was death, fire, and chaos all around.

Ensign Douglas Hein, a 1941 graduate of Annapolis and one of the *Arizona*'s most junior officers, also struggled forward, intent on making his way to the navigation bridge. As Hein neared the aft legs of the foremast and climbed to the navigation bridge, he saw Admiral Kidd on the flag bridge.

On the navigation bridge, Hein found only two others,

Captain Van Valkenburgh and a quartermaster. The quartermaster asked the captain if he wanted to go into the conning tower, a heavily armored cylinder multiple decks in height that protected key command centers during battle, but Van Valkenburgh shook his head no. Instead, he stood on the exposed bridge urgently making phone calls throughout the ship. The quartermaster started to report a hit near Turret No. 2, but he never finished his sentence.

Five more bombs from one of the other V-shaped formations of Kates had fallen toward the *Arizona.* Seeing the explosions near Turret No. 4 and near the main mast, their pilots aimed for the forward half of the ship. Two bombs straddled the *Arizona* and the *Vestal,* one falling to the shore side of the *Arizona* and the other to the harbor side of the *Vestal.* A third fell near the battleship's port bow between the two ships.

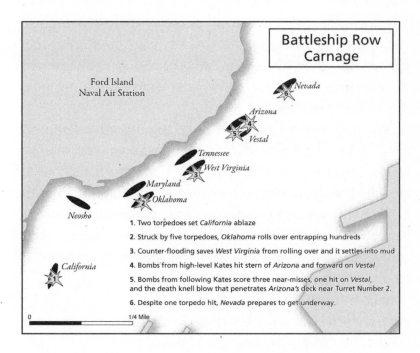

Battleship Row Carnage

Ford Island Naval Air Station

Nevada

Arizona

Vestal

Tennessee

West Virginia

Maryland

Oklahoma

Neosho

California

1. Two torpedoes set *California* ablaze
2. Struck by five torpedoes, *Oklahoma* rolls over entrapping hundreds
3. Counter-flooding saves *West Virginia* from rolling over and it settles into mud
4. Bombs from high-level Kates hit stern of *Arizona* and forward on *Vestal*
5. Bombs from following Kates score three near-misses, one hit on *Vestal,* and the death knell blow that penetrates *Arizona's* deck near Turret Number 2.
6. Despite one torpedo hit, *Nevada* prepares to get underway.

0   1/4 Mile

But there were two more projectiles in this barrage. One struck the *Vestal* on the port quarter adjacent to the *Arizona*. It passed through the carpenters' shop, shipfitters' shop, shipfitters' locker room, and four fuel oil tanks and left an irregular hole in the hull about five feet in diameter. The spaces quickly flooded with fuel and water.

The remaining bomb hit the *Arizona* on the starboard side of Turret No. 2. It passed through the five-inch armor of the first deck, continued through the second deck, and exploded on the third deck. Here, the third deck was also covered with five-inch steel to protect the powder magazines for the fourteen-inch guns that were immediately below. The explosive force from the bomb ruptured one or more of the forward oil tanks and lines and caused an intense fire on the third deck.

Five hatches led from the third deck down to the powder magazines. One hatch was over the small magazine of black powder—roughly a thousand pounds—that was used for signal guns and the catapults that launched the ship's scouting aircraft. The black powder was highly explosive, but compared to the smokeless powder used for the big guns, there wasn't much of it.

While a debate continues as to exactly what happened next, a 1944 Bureau of Ships report concluded that fire reached the black powder magazine through a hatch that the crew had been unable to close, perhaps because of an initial explosion. The black powder magazine detonated somewhere between five and ten seconds after the armor-piercing bomb exploded. This was enough of an explosion to set off the much larger magazines of smokeless powder—usually far less volatile by itself—used for the fourteen-inch guns as well as the five-inch secondary batteries. In all, these magazines totaled about one hundred tons of explosives.

Then came the volcanic explosion. According to Ensign Hein, who was on the navigation bridge with Captain Van Valkenburgh, "Suddenly the whole bridge shook like it was in an earthquake [and] flame came through the bridge windows which had been broken by gunfire." Hein and the captain staggered toward the port door of the bridge, but the shaking was too intense for them to exit. They fell to the deck just forward of the wheel and crawled back to the starboard side. Its door was jammed. As the shaking eased, they made another attempt at the port door, but only Hein made it out. He tumbled down a series of ladders. As he passed the flag bridge, he saw no sign of Admiral Kidd—alive or dead.[5]

Throughout the *Arizona,* every man, whatever his rank or battle station, felt what had happened. The explosion was horrendous, the shaking of the ship unmistakable. Coxswain Ken Edmondson was particularly graphic in remembering how it felt. He had been exhorting everyone to "get your asses" to their battle stations. "That's when," Edmondson recalled, "she come up in the air and shook like a dog."[6]

Marine Corporal Earl C. Nightingale had been at his battle station in the secondary aft director on the main mast only a short time when, in his words, "a terrible explosion caused the ship to shake violently." He looked at the deck and "everything seemed aflame forward of the main mast." Nightingale dutifully reported to Major Shapley, "the ship was aflame," which, he later admitted, "was rather needless."[7]

The initial bomb blasts left Officer of the Deck Hank Davison trapped in the OD enclosure at the break of the deck, where the quarterdeck stepped up to the forecastle deck. Then came the forward explosion with a lot of smoke and flame. "We were rapidly being roasted in that oven," Davison recalled, "so obviously we had to get out of there." Davison went over the side and into the water with the idea of swimming to the gangway and coming back on board beyond the flames. "But as soon as I was in the water," Davison continued, "and turned around to tread water and looked at the ship, why, it was obvious...she had just been virtually destroyed right then. The entire forward part of the ship had collapsed."

It was the paralyzing effect of surprise that stuck with Davison. "About half of your mentality rejects what you're seeing," he recalled decades later, "but the other half goes ahead and acts anyhow, because that's what you're trained to do. So that was that feeling, that this can't really be happening. Here's this beautiful ship, all of a sudden, that's reduced to something that will never float again."[8]

George Dewey Phraner was a Seaman, Second Class, from Pennsylvania. He had enlisted upon turning eighteen and reported to the *Arizona* a few months later in December 1940. Having been ashore on liberty the night before, Phraner was all too glad to sleep in a little Sunday morning. He and his buddies had just finished breakfast and stepped out onto the deck for some fresh air. Only as the sound of aircraft became louder did Phraner realize that it was the real thing. "At first there was a rush of fear," he recalled, then "the blood started to flow real fast." After General Quarters sounded, "everything became automatic."

Phraner's battle station was on a forward five-inch gun. It was standard practice to keep only a limited supply of ammunition at the guns—it was technically still peacetime no matter how blatant the evidence that something was about to change—and there was only one ready gun crew on each side of the ship. Phraner's wasn't one of them, and his gun captain immediately told him to go aft and bring up ammunition from the magazines. "There we were," Phraner remembered, "the Japanese dropping bombs over us and we had no ammo. All the training and practicing for a year and when the real thing came we had no ammunition where we needed it."

As it turned out, Phraner's trip below decks to fetch more ammunition saved his life. He had begun lifting shells weighing about ninety pounds onto the hoist running up from the aft magazines when there was a deafening roar and the entire ship shuddered, disintegrating the forward part of the ship. Phraner's gun crew, where he had been only minutes before, was killed outright.

The lights went out and a thick, acrid smoke filled the innards of the ship. Phraner and others groped for a hatch, found it locked, but somehow forced it open and started up a ladder to the deck. "I was nauseated by the smell of burning flesh," Phraner later admitted, "which turned out to be my own as I climbed up the hot ladder."

He almost didn't make it. As George Phraner clung to the ladder and struggled higher, all around him in the darkness he could hear the sounds of falling bodies—his shipmates who had lost the battle to survive. When at last he crawled onto the deck and collapsed, he looked toward the forward end of the ship and could see "nothing but a giant wall of flame and smoke."[9]

Over on the *West Virginia,* moored ahead of the *Arizona* off its port bow, Richard Fiske, a nineteen-year-old Marine bugler from Massachusetts, saw what happened. Three bombs rained toward the *West Virginia*'s fantail, but all missed.

163

Then, the bomb hit near Turret No. 2 on the *Arizona.* "The next thing we heard," Fiske remembered, "was this hellacious noise and we saw a big fireball. The bow of the *Arizona* came completely out of the water. She settled down and was one tremendous ball of fire. I never saw so much fire in my life."[10]

The *West Virginia*'s executive officer, Commander Roscoe H. Hillenkoetter, saw it, too. As torpedoes slammed into his ship, Hillenkoetter kept trying to make his way to the bridge. Every few steps, another explosion threw him to the deck. As the *West Virginia* listed to port, Hillenkoetter had once again gotten to his feet when he saw a flash of flame about fifteen feet high near the forward turrets on the *Arizona.* Seconds later, "there was a terrific flash of flame from the *Arizona,*" Hillenkoetter recalled, "this second flash higher than the foretop. Burning debris of sizes from a fraction of an inch up to five inches in diameter rained on the quarterdeck of the *West Virginia.*"[11]

Frank Curre was a mess cook from Waco, Texas, serving on the *Tennessee,* which was moored inboard of the *West Virginia* about seventy-five feet ahead of the *Arizona.* When he couldn't find a job after graduating from high school, Curre, still two months shy of eighteen, asked his mother to sign the papers for him to enlist or, he told her, he was going to go "downtown and get a hobo to sign 'em." She signed, and after basic training, Curre reported aboard the *Tennessee* in August 1941.

From the deck of the *Tennessee,* Curre heard a big blast, followed instantaneously by another. Turning toward the *Arizona,* Curre saw what he recalled was "the first god-awful sight I witnessed that day." The *Arizona* jumped twelve to fifteen feet out of the water and broke in two. Burning powder, oil, and debris rained down on the quarterdeck of the *Tennessee,* too, but there was more. "If you'd had a bag of popcorn," Curre remembered grimly, "and you'd a went out there in the breeze and threw it up in the air—that was bodies that went out all over that harbor."[12]

High above the *Tennessee* in the antiaircraft director atop the foremast, Seaman, Second Class, Jack Evans from California could see everything only too well. Smoke was rising from nearby Ford Island and Hickam Field to the east. A Val dive-bomber flew directly over the bow of the *Tennessee,* and the gunner in the rear seat looked directly at Evans. "If I'd had a potato, I could have hit him," Evans recalled.

Evans was still looking forward when the *Arizona* blew up. The explosion whipped his perch atop the 120-foot-tall mast back and forth in an angry, hot blast. For a moment, Evans thought it would snap like a tree in a hurricane. When Evans looked back toward the *Arizona,* the ship was out of the water and collapsing upon itself beneath a wall of flames.[13]

Along Battleship Row, the *Oklahoma* was well into its own death throes. Sensing that his ship would turn turtle, Boatswain's Mate, First Class, Howard C. French hurried the men of his division topside and then literally scrambled along the outside of the hull as the *Oklahoma* continued its roll. As French did so, he looked directly at the *Arizona.* "There was an awful blast and a terrific concussion," French recalled. "The foremast tilted forward, took a crazy angle and the ship went down immediately. I could see parts of bodies in the foremast rigging."[14]

Across the harbor from Ford Island at Hospital Point, Pharmacist's Mate, Third Class, Robert H. Meyer from Kansas had just come off the hospital's night watch and was changing into his dress whites to go into Honolulu on liberty with fellow mates. "We were gonna have a steak at a hotel, maybe go to a movie," Meyer recalled. At the sound of the first explosion, he looked out from a second-story balcony toward Ford Island. A cloud of smoke and debris rose about a quarter of a mile away, and Meyer saw another bomb fall and hit in about the same place.

Meyer sprinted to the main hospital office. The executive officer on duty ordered him to put on a shore patrol armband, grab a nightstick and helmet, and chase anyone on the grounds inside the building before attacking aircraft were tempted to strafe them. Meyer couldn't find a helmet, but ran outside bareheaded and made repeated rounds, circling the big three-story building and herding people inside.

Every time he came back to the harbor side of the hospital, Meyer looked across to Battleship Row where more and more smoke rose into the air. When one horrendous explosion wracked the harbor, Meyer didn't know at the time which battleship it was, but, as he recalled, "the sound of numerous bombs and torpedoes and the guns of our ships trying to defend themselves was deafening and almost continuous."[15]

Barely ten minutes had passed since the Marine color guard stood ready to hoist the national ensign on the stern of the *Arizona,* but the five minutes before and after 8:00 a.m. on December 7, 1941, would seem like an eternity to all who lived through it. Indeed, action reports written within days, as well as personal reminiscences decades later, tended to extend the time frame of events beyond the narrow window of minutes in which they occurred.

Russell Warriner had been eating breakfast with shipmates of his division when the General Quarters alarm sounded. His battle station was in the conning tower.

The USS *Arizona* (BB-39), once the cutting-edge weapon of its day, charges through heavy seas sometime during the 1930s. *US Navy Photo, National Archives 80-G-463589*

Esther Ross of Prescott, Arizona, and her party arrive at the Brooklyn Navy Yard beneath the unfinished hull of the *Arizona*, June 19, 1915. *National Archives, 6003992*

Miss Ross, right, prepares to christen the *Arizona* with champagne and water as one of her attendants, her mother, Secretary of the Navy Josephus Daniels, and Arizona Governor George W. P. Hunt look on. *USS Arizona Collection (AZ517). Special Collections, University of Arizona Libraries*

Arizona at anchor off San Pedro, 1935. *NH 94438 courtesy Naval History & Heritage Command*

Arizona underway in the 1930s. *NH 57660 courtesy Naval History & Heritage Command*

Isaac Campbell Kidd, USNA 1906, was a captain when he commanded *Arizona* during the late 1930s. Kidd returned to the ship as a rear admiral to command Battleship Division One early in 1941 and died on the flag bridge. *NH 97385 courtesy Naval History & Heritage Command*

Captain Franklin Van Valkenburgh, USNA 1909, took command of *Arizona* on February 5, 1941, as the capstone of his career. He rushed to the navigation bridge and was never seen again after the forward magazines exploded. *NH 75840 courtesy Naval History & Heritage Command*

Momentarily stunned by one of the bomb blasts near the quarterdeck, Lieutenant Commander Samuel G. Fuqua, USNA 1923, was the model of cool and calm as he saw to the wounded and directed the abandonment of the ship. *NH 92306 courtesy Naval History & Heritage Command*

Becker family in mid-1930s: (standing, left to right) Wesley, Harvey, Walter, and Marvin and (seated, left to right) Theresa, father Bill, Mary Ann, mother Freda, and Bob. *Becker Family*

Harvey Becker's wife, Marie, took this photo of Harvey with brothers Marvin (right) and Wesley (left) in uniform in Honolulu just before Thanksgiving 1941. *Becker Family*

When he turned eighteen, Bob Becker followed his brothers and enlisted. His mother was very upset, but Bob believed strongly that it was something he had to do.
Becker Family

Photographed from a Japanese plane near the onset of the torpedo attack, a geyser erupts from an explosion near *West Virginia* and *Oklahoma*. Moored to the north (left) are *Arizona* and *Vestal* and the solitary *Nevada*. The hospital ship *Solace* is anchored farther north. On west side, *Raleigh* and *Utah* have been hit. *NH 50930 courtesy Naval History & Heritage Command*

With more torpedoes in the water, an oil slick spreads from *California*, at right; oiler *Neosho* is next in line followed by *Oklahoma* (outboard) and *Maryland* and *West Virginia* (outboard) and *Tennessee*. Both *Oklahoma* and *West Virginia* list to port. *Vestal* is outboard of *Arizona* followed by *Nevada*, not yet hit. Across the channel at 1010 Dock, smoke engulfs *Oglala* and *Helena* and rises from Hickam Field, background. *NH 50931 courtesy Naval History & Heritage Command*

The Murdock family of Alabama: Charles Wesley "C. W." and Mary "Sleatie" and their first five children about 1920; clockwise from upper left, Thomas, Vada, Melvin, Lythonia, and Charles Luther. *Murdock Family*

The four older Murdock brothers, clockwise from top left, Thomas Daniel, Charles Luther, Verlon Aaron, and Melvin Elijah. *Murdock Family*

After Pearl Harbor, Kenneth Dewayne Murdock lied about his age and enlisted at fourteen. When he was found out in boot camp, he was discharged and sent home. *Murdock Family*

Melvin Murdock, one of three Murdock brothers on the *Arizona*, poses by his 1940 Chevrolet coupe convertible during the ship's last visit to California in the summer of 1941. He had just purchased the car and the family story is that he stored it in a warehouse in Los Angeles and it was never found. *Murdock Family*

Moments before the fatal bomb hit *Arizona*, *West Virginia* (left) and *Oklahoma* gush oil from torpedo damage. *Vestal* is moored outboard of *Arizona* and the first bombs have just struck along *Arizona*'s stern and bow of *Vestal*. *Nevada* has also taken a torpedo hit. *NH 50472 courtesy Naval History & Heritage Command*

As its forward magazines exploded, *Arizona* disappeared in a cloud of smoke. *Vestal* is still moored alongside and *Nevada* not yet underway. The stern awnings on *West Virginia* and *Tennessee* stand out as smoke pours from bombs on both ships. At far right, *Oklahoma* continues its roll. *NH 50932 courtesy Naval History & Heritage Command*

Clara May Morse photographed her sons, Francis (left) and Norman, in Long Beach in June 1941. It was the last time she saw them. *Clara May Dyer Morse collection, Mss.00453 (10039723), History Colorado*

Clara May Morse graduated from the Red Cross Nurses' Aide Program on August 10, 1942. *Clara May Dyer Morse collection, Mss.00453 (10025423), History Colorado*

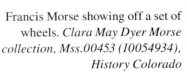

Francis Morse showing off a set of wheels. *Clara May Dyer Morse collection, Mss.00453 (10054934), History Colorado*

William Thomas Free followed in his father's footsteps. *Free Family*

Gussie and William Free while Gussie was home on leave in late 1920s. *Free Family*

Fifty years old and after almost twenty years in the Navy, Thomas Augusta "Gussie" Free, here photographed at home on what may have been his last leave, was wearing out. *Free Family*

Looking from Ford Island, this shows the absolute horror of the explosion on *Arizona*. Only the stern and mainmast remain intact. Beyond is the foremast of *Vestal*. Through the smoke at right are masts of *West Virginia*, listing to port, and the upright mainmast of *Tennessee*. *US Navy Photo, National Archives 80-G-32920*

Arizona's foremast and super-structure leaned forward as Tur No. 2 collapsed through the sha tered decks following explosion of the forward magazines. The entire forward half of the ship largely disintegrated. Marvin a Wesley Becker were stationed i Turret No. 2. *Time Life Pictures US Naval Institute/The LIFE Picture Collection/Getty Image*

Destruction of the forward half of *Arizona* included the superstruc-ture and secondary gun positions amidships. Marine PFC Gordon Shive manned one of the second-ary guns. At right are the ship's boat cranes and mainmast, includ-ing "bathtub" and director enclo-sures that became fiery ovens. *NH 97380 courtesy Naval History & Heritage Command*

Carl Christiansen at home in Kansas. *Christiansen Family*

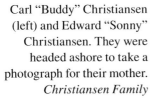

Carl "Buddy" Christiansen (left) and Edward "Sonny" Christiansen. They were headed ashore to take a photograph for their mother. *Christiansen Family*

Joseph Giovenazzo (left) and Michael Giovenazzo. *Giovenazzo Family*

Joe (left) and Mike Giovenazzo share a drink with a friend. They were seeing the world beyond Silvis, Illinois. *Giovenazzo Family*

As *Arizona* burned furiously, men on the stern of *Tennessee* directed fire hoses to keep burning oil away from their ship. *US Navy Photo, National Archives 80-G-19942*

Looking north up Battleship Row from Ford Island seaplane landing. *California* lists to port after torpedo hits. *Maryland* is upright next to overturned *Oklahoma*. Beyond, *West Virginia* lists to port and smoke obscures *Arizona*. Oiler *Neosho*, background right, has gotten underway. *US Navy Photo, National Archives 80-G-32640*

The lads of Laguna, clockwise from upper left, Malcolm Shive, friend Ed Braham, Gordon Shive, Weston Balfour. *Shive Family*

PFC Gordon E. Shive, USMC, *Shive Family*

Radioman, Third Class, Malcolm Shive, *Shive Family*

Lois Shive Westgate was among many who received returned letters marked "Unclaimed." *Shive Family Papers*

The American flag flies from stern of *West Virginia*, sunk but on an even keel after counter-flooding. Smoke pours from *Arizona* as small craft look for survivors. *USS Arizona Collection (AZ517). Special Collections, University of Arizona Libraries*

As *Arizona* settled and blazed from the maintop forward, the American flag continued to fly from the stern of the ship. Later that evening, it was carefully hauled down. *US Navy Photo, National Archives 80-G-32591*

Russell and Elsa Warriner married in 1942. *Warriner Family*

Ken Warriner (left) and Russell Warriner were the only set of brothers to both survive. Ken was on temporary duty in San Diego; Russell was badly injured. *Warriner Family*

George Stanley Miller (left) and his big brother, Jesse Zimmer Miller, enlisted and underwent basic training together at Great Lakes. December 7, 1941, was their parents' thirty-seventh wedding anniversary. *Miller Family*

Twenty-four-year-old Edward "Bud" Heidt and nineteen-year-old Donna Streur in front of her Birch Avenue home, Hawthorne, California, October 6, 1940. A year later, if Bud didn't have a ring for Donna, her family thought "he was going to get one." *Streur Family*

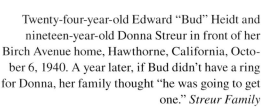

The battleship *Missouri* stands guard over the *Arizona* memorial and the sunken remains of the ship and its crew. *Marlene M. Borneman*

Lady Columbia stands above the National Memorial Cemetery of the Pacific in the Punchbowl Crater above Honolulu. Abraham Lincoln's words are carved at her feet: "The solemn pride that must be yours to have laid so costly a sacrifice upon the altar of Freedom." *Marlene M. Borneman*

Among hundreds of other pairs of running feet, Warriner attempted to claw his way to his post. Partway there, an explosion blew him off a ladder and onto the deck. He landed facefirst. Though he cringed at reliving it, Russ would always remember that the heat of the deck was like landing in a frying pan.

Months before, as Warriner had left Wisconsin for the Navy, his girlfriend, Elsa Schild, had had a terrible vision. Russ was on fire and picking pieces of steel out of his body. Now, this was as close to that dream as Russ could possibly get and it was reality. When the massive explosion below Turret No. 2 rocked the ship, the next thing Russ Warriner knew, he was in the water surrounded by burning oil. The water itself was on fire.[16]

Fireman, Third Class, Herbert Buehl, Russ Warriner's friend from Wisconsin with whom Russ had gone to boot camp, had been standing by his locker in his Electrical "E" Division, talking with a buddy about what they were going to do later that day when they each had liberty. A chief petty officer came running by, shouting, "The Japs are attacking! Close all battle ports and man your battle stations!" For a moment there was stunned silence. Then, an Electrician's Mate, First Class, said quietly, "If it's so, let's do it." Everyone broke as from a huddle and started running.

Buehl headed toward the stern to his battle station in the aft repair party. It was located three decks down and next to the doorway leading down the passageway between the No. 3 and No. 4 turrets. Only weeks before, Buehl had requested a duty change from the Power Distribution section of the E Division to the Lighting section to broaden his training. His old battle station was the Forward Power Distribution Room, which was located five decks down in the center of the ship between the twin masts.

As Buehl reached his battle station, an explosion, likely the detonation of the first bomb dropped near Turret No. 4, rocked the ship and all the lights went out. It was the job of Buehl's repair party to get them back on. Unable to contact his control station, Buehl peered down a ladder into the darkness of the passageway between the No. 3 and No. 4 turrets. As he straddled the doorway, hoping that the lights would come back on, the bomb struck near Turret No. 2. Seconds later, there was no doubt that this was the big one. Buehl remembered that it resounded and "knocked me down the ladder in one big 'swish.'" He landed on his feet and in the darkness groped for his body parts to make certain he was whole.[17]

Admiral Kimmel had been in his quarters dressing and awaiting further confirmation of the *Ward*'s submarine report. His telephone rang, and the duty officer passed on a new report that the busy *Ward* had just stopped a suspicious sampan near the entrance channel. Kimmel was still hearing about the *Ward*'s latest activity when an enlisted man interrupted the duty officer and shouted, "There's a message from the signal tower saying the Japanese are attacking Pearl Harbor and this is no drill." Kimmel slammed down the receiver and rushed onto the lawn to look down at the harbor.[18]

Two hundred miles to the west, Vice Admiral Bill Halsey and *Enterprise* neared Oahu a day late, after the delivery of fighter planes to Wake Island. Operating under radio silence, *Enterprise* had not informed Pearl Harbor that it had routinely launched eighteen of its own planes to fly off and land at the naval air station on Ford Island in advance of the carrier's arrival. Given the quiet Sunday morning, no one was likely to notice, let alone care. The phone from the bridge rang and interrupted Halsey's breakfast. His aide answered it. "Admiral," he stammered in disbelief, "the staff duty officer says he has a message that there's an air raid on Pearl!"

Thinking the aircraft from the *Enterprise* were being targeted, Halsey leaped from his chair. "My God, they're shooting at my own boys! Tell Kimmel!" Just then, Halsey's communications officer burst in with a dispatch from Kimmel to all ships: "Air raid on Pearl Harbor X This is no drill." *Enterprise* went to General Quarters.[19]

In Washington, Secretary of the Navy Knox, whose pronouncements of the Navy's prowess were still making their way around the country in the *New York Times,* had returned to his office after meeting with Secretary of State Cordell Hull and Secretary of War Henry Stimson. Chief of Naval Operations Stark joined him. An aide interrupted their conference and handed Knox a message. "My God," the secretary blurted out, "this can't be true, this must mean the Philippines." Knox handed the note to Stark, who saw its origin as Kimmel's office and knew there could be no mistake. "No, sir," Stark replied, "this is Pearl."[20]

After dispatching his "just what significance the hour set may have" message of warning to Army commands throughout the Pacific, Chief of Staff George Marshall went home to lunch at his quarters at Fort Myer. He was due at the White House for an afternoon meeting, and it was likely to be a lengthy affair. An aide in the War Department telephoned with news that had been handed to him on a scrap of paper by a breathless Navy enlisted man: "Pearl Harbor attacked. This is no drill." Replacing his napkin on the table, Marshall hurried to his waiting car.[21]

After his Saturday morning appointment with Admiral Kimmel, Joe Harsch of the *Christian Science Monitor* had taken a leisurely drive around Oahu with his wife, Anne. They headed up the west coast from Pearl Harbor to the north shore and then looped back around the eastern side to Honolulu. They stopped here and there along the way wherever they found, as Harsch remembered it, "a particularly inviting beach." After a pleasant dinner at the Halekulani Hotel amid tables of naval officers resplendent in their white uniforms, Joe and Anne retired to their little cottage in the palm grove behind the hotel and had a blissful evening, so blissful in fact that a son would be born nine months later.

Sleeping in the next morning, Harsch awoke to the booms of what sounded like distant thunder. Having read of Joe's experiences covering the war in Europe, Anne had often wondered what an air raid sounded like. "'Listen to this," Joe nudged her. "You have asked me what an air raid sounds like. This is a good imitation."

"Oh, is that what it's like?" Anne answered groggily, before rolling over and going back to sleep. According to Harsch, only after a morning swim and a genteel breakfast at a table near the wives of two admirals did he realize what was happening and head for a high spot of ground from which he could see the harbor.[22]

For the men on the *Arizona,* it was only too real. Barely had Seaman Buddy Christiansen descended below decks to his General Quarters station in the powder handling room for Turret No. 4, when the electricity failed throughout the ship and its insides were plunged into darkness. That was bad enough, but odors filling the darkened spaces brought an extra degree of terror. It may have been from chlorine gas released by spillage from the storage batteries located in each turret as a backup should the ship's electrical power fail, as it now had.

One member of Christiansen's group took charge. Christiansen never learned his identity, but he was likely an older hand who seemed to know the blackened innards of the ship by touch. The men followed this leader through the darkness, keeping a hand on the shoulder of the man in front. But there was no way out and the group returned to the handling room in Turret No. 4. Buddy remembered his shipmates as "frightened but not panicky." Where, he wondered, was Sonny? One of the group suggested lighting a match to help them see their way out. In a powder handling room yards from the aft powder magazines, this thought was quickly overruled.

Instead, they would follow their leader and try again. Once more with one hand on the shoulder of the man ahead, the group snaked its way into a passageway connecting the handling rooms of the two turrets and moved forward into the depths of Turret No. 3. Slowly, they crawled up ladders into the turret itself and found small rays of light streaming from above. Gingerly, they reached the hatch at the rear of the turret, popped it open, and amid heavy smoke climbed down the ladder onto the quarterdeck.

Buddy gulped in mouthfuls of air. Smoke laden though it was with the stench of fuel oil, it was still better than the stifling gases he had been breathing below decks. And, at least he could see again. Buddy took refuge with others under the overhang of Turret No. 3 from a flurry of machine gun fire from attacking Japanese fighters. Staying where they were was hardly an option, so they lined up their shoes and jumped over the starboard side of the rapidly settling ship. The plan was that they would swim ashore to Ford Island.

For Buddy, it was a bad mistake. Heavy fuel oil in the water made swimming feel like one was trying to stroke through heavy glue. A couple of strokes left one exhausted.

Buddy returned to the ship and climbed the starboard ladder back up to the quarterdeck. Normally, there would have been about seventeen feet of freeboard between the water and the deck, but Buddy only had to climb a few feet above the level of the water to topple over onto the deck. The *Arizona* was sinking fast.[23]

CHAPTER 10

"My Brother's Up There!"

Sunday, December 7

THE FORWARD TWO thirds of the *Arizona* was a crumpled mass of steel engulfed in flames. Having been thrown skyward by the massive explosion of the forward powder magazines, the decks collapsed one atop the other. Turrets No. 1 and No. 2 dropped to the keel of the ship like giant stones, crushing everything in their paths. The forward mast lurched toward the bow at a 45 degree angle, taking with it much of the superstructure below the pilothouse.

As Turret No. 1 collapsed, it obliterated the chief petty officers' mess and sick bay one deck below. Thomas Augusta "Gussie" Free may well have struggled to rise from his sick bay bed at the sound of General Quarters. One did not spend almost twenty years in the Navy without such a reaction being automatic, and Gussie was too much of a sailor not to have been alarmed at the sounds of the first explosions. But it was over in a heartbeat. Gussie Free never knew what hit him. His last fleeting thought, if he indeed had time to make it, was no doubt of his son. William Free met his own end somewhere in the depths of the ship.

Just as quickly, the twenty-one members of the *Arizona*'s band were gone. They had rushed to their battle stations along the hoists that carried powder bags up from the forward magazines to the breeches of the fourteen-inch guns in Turrets No. 1 and No. 2. Hundreds of sailors in the forward part of the ship shared their fate.

Theresa Becker had long considered her older brothers Marvin and Wesley to be her special heroes. One day years before while the three of them were making the two-mile walk home from the one-room Point Pleasant School—Theresa was about six or seven—Marvin and Wesley ran ahead to get their chores done while Theresa took her time playing along the road. Looking up, she was surprised to see Marvin and Wesley running back toward her and yelling at her to hurry. The brothers swooped in, one on each side, and picked her up. "Look behind you," they told her as they spirited her toward home.

Theresa did and saw a huge dust storm barreling down on them. Marvin and Wesley carried her all the way to the underground storm shelter at the farm and barely had time to put wet cloths over their faces before the towering wall of dust hit. It was a close call, and thereafter Theresa always thought of Marvin and Wesley as her guardian angels. Now, it was Marvin and Wesley who needed a guardian angel.

In Honolulu, Harvey Becker, the oldest of the Becker trio, was jolted awake by the sound of explosions coming from the harbor. He rushed toward the naval base and tried to return to his ship. What little he could see showed the *Arizona* enveloped in flames and sinking. There was no sign of Turret No. 2. Harvey was well aware of where his younger brothers would have been.[1]

Others also awoke in Honolulu and knew immediately that their duty—and in many cases their brothers—lay aboard the *Arizona*. Thomas Murdock's brothers, Luther and Melvin, were watertenders, and Thomas was certain they would have been far below decks amid the mass of boilers and piping. If only he and his wife, Ruth, had tried harder to have Luther spend the prior night at their apartment. Like so many, Thomas Murdock hurried toward the harbor with the sickening feeling that there was little he could do.

Ray Chandler did the same. He was at home in Honolulu on weekend liberty with his wife, Mary Louise. After two married years mostly apart, they had been enjoying the weekends when the *Arizona* was in port ever since Mary Louise's arrival in the islands in August. Somewhere in the harbor, Ray's brother, Marine Private Don Chandler, was fighting for his life.

Anthony Francis "Tony" Czarnecki was every bit as lucky and as sad as Ray Chandler. Tony, too, was married and at home with his wife, Dorothy, in Honolulu in a little apartment on Lusitana Street near the slopes of an old volcanic crater called the Punchbowl. They were having breakfast and looking forward to having Tony's kid brother, Stanley, over for dinner that night. Stanley had rushed to his battle station far below decks to fire up the boilers and produce steam in preparation for getting underway. But the *Arizona* was not going anywhere.

Tony and Dorothy's neighbor heard the first bulletin about the attack on the radio, and Tony immediately hopped a ride to the harbor upon hearing the news. "We had to get out of the car once on the way back," Czarnecki later recalled. "We thought we were going to be strafed." By the time he got to the *Arizona*, "there wasn't a sign of life aboard." Stanley never showed up for dinner.[2]

At Joe and Helen Giovenazzo's little apartment on Kapahulu Avenue, Joe was still feeling a bit under the weather when KGMB, Honolulu's major radio station, interrupted its program of easy listening at 8:08 a.m. for a special announcement. Without giving any reason, the radio directed all Army, Navy, and Marine personnel to report to their duty stations immediately. KGMB went back to music but broke in again seven minutes later with the same announcement.

Joe Giovenazzo caught a ride with a neighbor and headed for the harbor. His ship, the *Vestal,* was shrouded in smoke, but the *Arizona* was almost invisible. Joe had the same thought as many others: *Where is my brother?* But another thought also tortured him: Joe Giovenazzo knew all too well who had encouraged his younger brother Mike to enlist.

Marine Captain Jack Earle, about to assume command of the *Arizona*'s Marine Detachment, awoke in Honolulu with his wife, Barbara. Major Alan Shapley's generosity the evening before had sent his replacement home to Barbara instead of returning him to the *Arizona* and the drudgery of completing the detachment inventory before their change of command. Earle's next-door neighbor, a Navy commander on Admiral Kimmel's staff, banged on the door of his apartment and shouted, "Pearl Harbor is under attack!"

Earle looked out from his porch in the direction of the harbor and could see black antiaircraft bursts popping above it. Barbara Earle later remembered that Jack was "out the door in five minutes," flagging down a taxi and racing for the harbor with a friend from the *Tennessee,* his latest post.

Earle was still emotionally tied to the Marines on the *Tennessee,* but there was so much smoke and fire drifting over the ship from the *Arizona* that it was difficult to ascertain its condition. A firestorm of burning powder, oil, and debris continued to rain on the quarterdeck of the *Tennessee.* Two bombs from the high-level Kates also struck the ship, one atop Turret No. 3 and another on the center gun of Turret No. 2, but compared with the *Arizona*'s cataclysmic explosion, the damage to the *Tennessee* was relatively moderate.

On the *Arizona,* Captain Earle's Marines were giving a good account of themselves, but their casualties were mounting. Veteran First Sergeant John Duveene, six months shy of twenty years of service, stood by the ventilator shaft on the starboard side of the quarterdeck. He was burned almost beyond recognition, but his booming voice was unmistakable. Duveene had always called his charges champions, and now he yelled out to them: "Swim for it, champions. Don't try to go back inside; everything in there is all burned up. I'm not going to make it. Get the hell out of here!"

One of Duveene's men was unsure what to do. Eighteen-year-old Private Leo Amundson from Wisconsin had enlisted just five months before and only reported aboard the *Arizona* on Saturday. He had yet to be assigned duties or a battle station. Amundson was last seen sitting on a bench inside the Marines' area looking very frightened and very confused. Told to "sit down right there, and stay until this is over," Amundson did so and was never seen again.[3]

*   *   *

Private, First Class, Gordon Shive was manning one of the five-inch guns amidships. His brother, Malcolm, likely would have been in one of the radio rooms or attempting to get there. Gordon's good buddy, Private, First Class, Edward Braham, was also manning guns above decks. Braham's battle station was on the .50-caliber antiaircraft guns in the birdbath atop the main mast. Shive and Braham, who hailed from Iowa, had met when both were assigned to the *Arizona*'s MARDET.

When Gordon and Malcolm's boyhood chum, Weston "Wess" Balfour, showed up in Hawaii as an Army private en route to—well, no one was supposed to know where—the three Laguna Beach lads had gladly included likeable Ed Braham and made it a foursome for their liberty outing. The quartet took a photo together in Honolulu, and Gordon sent his mother a photo postcard of the occasion.

Writing Lois Westgate and others about Wess's passage through the islands, Gordon was careful not to divulge his destination per censor instructions, but in Gordon's last letter to Marge Balfour, he inadvertently let it slip that Wess was on his way to "the P.I." It had "worked out swell," Gordon wrote Marge, "that Wess, Mac and I were all together again as this will probably be our last for a long time." As Ed Braham and the Shive brothers fought off the attacking Japanese above Pearl Harbor, Wess was about to do the same five thousand miles away in the Philippine Islands, loading ordnance for MacArthur's air force.[4]

Despite the exposed position of the aft secondary near the top of the main mast, most of the Marines assigned there, including Ed Braham, would be lucky. Along with his enlisted men, Major Alan Shapley climbed to this aerie and took charge as attacking planes riddled it with heavy machine gun fire. The aft secondary had directional control over the five-inch guns. With the redundant directional station on the foremast blasted out of commission, it was up to this unit to direct any return fire from the secondary guns. But that was not going to happen, and Shapley was frustrated. These were not antiaircraft guns, and elevating them high enough to do any damage to the attackers was out of the question.

When the sailors and Marines manning the antiaircraft machine guns higher up in the birdbath ran out of ammunition—there were only two hundred rounds of ready ammunition at the guns—they descended to the aft secondary platform and joined its occupants in gawking at the mayhem on the decks below.

As the forward magazines exploded, one of the Marines huddled there described the sound as more of a rushing *whoosh* than a sharp bang or a boom. The resulting fireball swept toward the stern, but the superstructure and foremast partially shielded the director stations atop the main mast. Marines Gordon Shive and Don Chandler weren't so lucky. Shive was out in the open manning one of the five-inch guns, and the force of the blast blew him off the ship and into the oily water. No one could be certain where Chandler had been. No one ever saw him again.[5]

At times, it seemed that the only person not running for cover was Lieutenant Commander Sam Fuqua. The ship's damage control officer stood on the quarterdeck and was a model of calm for anyone who looked his way. Fuqua remembered that when the forward magazines blew "the whole ship erupted like a volcano."[6] Captain Van Valkenburgh was last seen on the navigation bridge, but now the bridge was a crumpled mass of red-hot steel. Admi-

179

ral Kidd, gripping the railing on the flag bridge a level below, met a similar fate. Sam Fuqua was suddenly the senior officer onboard, and he looked in the direction of John Anderson.

The forward magazine explosion had knocked Anderson momentarily unconscious as he exited Turret No. 4 and ran toward a ladder leading to the antiaircraft batteries on the upper decks. He was determined to find his twin brother, Jake, who was stationed there, and help him defend the ship. Just before the massive blast, Anderson had reached out to grab a sailor by the hand whose clothes were on fire from prior explosions. When Anderson came to, he still had Gunner's Mate, Third Class, James William Green by the hand. Miraculously, Green survived.

But John Anderson had to find his brother. Encountering Lieutenant Commander Fuqua, the officer told him to get Green and others who were badly wounded into one of the small boats that were tied alongside or beginning to circle close through the oil-covered waters. Anderson shook his head. "My brother's up there," he told Fuqua. "I've got to find him."

"He couldn't have made it," Fuqua shouted back. "Get to the boats; we've got to save as many men as we can." Fuqua literally gave Anderson a shove toward the starboard ladder, and Anderson did as he was ordered. He ended up the coxswain in a small boat that ferried a load of wounded men from the *Arizona* to Ford Island. Anderson was momentarily safe, but his thoughts were still focused on Jake, who Anderson was certain was still somewhere on the burning *Arizona*.

Anderson looked around for a way to get back to the ship even as those near him warned him not to try. "Don't be crazy," someone said. "If you go on that ship, I'm gonna kill ya," yelled another. Anderson shook them all off. "I've got to go," he replied. "My brother's up there. I've got to find my brother."

There was a small boat floating nearby with no one in it—perhaps the one they had just unloaded. Anderson turned to Boatswain's Mate, First Class, Chester Clay Rose, a big guy—190 pounds and six feet tall—who played on the *Arizona*'s football team. "Rose," Anderson said evenly, "are you ready to drive out there and go at it again?" By Anderson's telling, Rose thought a second and then replied, "If you are, I am."[7]

Besides John Anderson, there was another brother feeling a stab of pain for his twin. Warren Joseph Sherrill and John Benjamin Sherrill were born in Republic, Kansas, on September 29, 1920. They enlisted together right after they turned eighteen in the fall of 1938. After basic training at San Diego, the Sherrills reported directly to the *Arizona* while it was at Bremerton for its 1939 overhaul. Warren worked up to a Yeoman, Second Class, and also became a chaplain's assistant. His twin brother, John, was a Fireman, Second Class, who later transferred to the destroyer *John B. Ford* (DD-228).

On this morning, the *Ford* was operating out of Cavite Naval Base in the Philippines as part of Admiral Hart's Asiatic Fleet. Those sailors would soon have their hands full in the Philippines, but when John Sherrill heard word of the attack on Pearl Harbor, he knew instantly that something was wrong. "My twin brother is on the *Arizona*," John said worriedly, "and I just know he's dead or seriously wounded—I feel it."[8]

John's gut was all too correct. Warren Sherrill, who

likely had been helping to prepare for morning church services on the fantail, hurried toward his battle station in the conning tower and was killed while delivering a message to the officer of the deck. In the coming months, John Sherrill and the *Ford* would go on to serve in the thick of the naval battles around Java.

The massive magazine explosion doomed the *Arizona,* but the *Vestal* moored alongside it still had a fighting chance. Having taken two direct bomb hits and sustained two more near misses, the repair ship was on fire fore and aft when the forward half of the *Arizona* erupted skyward. The concussion consumed the air above the *Vestal* and had the effect of momentarily tamping down the worst of its fires. Tons of debris from the explosion, however, rained down on the *Vestal*—parts of the ship as well as parts of men. It was a sickening scene to all who witnessed it, to see charred and blackened limbs and torsos, as well as complete but lifeless bodies. The *Vestal*'s crew rushed to help those horribly burned who showed any signs of life, whether on its decks or in the adjacent waters.

The explosion also blew about one hundred crewmen who had been above decks on the *Vestal* overboard. Among them was Chief Boilermaker John Crawford, who recalled that the *Arizona* "blew up like a million Fourth of Julys." Crawford flew off the starboard side of the *Vestal* and landed in the main channel. He didn't know how high the explosion flung him, "but, by God," he said, "it was high enough, because I was stunned when I hit the water, and my right hand and the left side of my face were burned."[9]

Among others on the *Vestal* who were tossed into the water by the *Arizona*'s explosion were gunners on several

182

antiaircraft guns and the *Vestal*'s captain, Commander Cassin B. Young. With the captain in the water and his fate unknown, the *Vestal*'s officer of the deck gave the order to abandon ship.

Just as the first of the crew started to obey, a wobbly figure dripping in oil clawed his way up a rope ladder from the blackened harbor waters and demanded, "Where the hell do you think you're going?" Told that men were abandoning ship, the grimy face of Commander Young quickly set them straight. "Get back aboard ship!" Young roared. "You don't abandon ship on me!"[10]

The *Vestal*'s officers and crew turned about and worked feverishly to save their ship. With burning fuel oil on the waters between it and the *Arizona*, the only way to do so was to get away from the *Arizona*. Young gave the order to prepare to get underway. Crewmen cut the forward lines that held the port bow of the *Vestal* to the port quarter of the *Arizona*. As they prepared to do the same to the stern lines, frantic calls drifted across the fiery waters from the crumpled foremast on the *Arizona*.

Minutes earlier, Seaman, First Class, Don Stratton and Firecontrolman, Third Class, Lauren Bruner had scrambled to their battle station in the port antiaircraft director five ladders up the foremast. As they did so, Bruner took a bullet in the lower leg from a strafing Zero and trailed a stream of blood behind him as he crawled the last few feet into the enclosure. Among others that Stratton remembered being assigned to the port director were Boatswain's Mate, Second Class, Alvin Dvorak; Seaman, First Class, Harold Kuhn; Seaman, First Class, Russell Lott; and Gunner's Mate, Third Class, Earl Riner.

Ensign Frank Lomax, a 1940 graduate of Annapolis, was the officer in charge of the port director station, but he faced a quandary similar to that of Alan Shapley on the secondary battery director. Those antiaircraft batteries still operational couldn't target the low-flying attackers without risking a hit to a friendly vessel, so they pointed ninety degrees straight up and tried to hit the high-level bombers. Antiaircraft shells had fuses timed to explode so many seconds after firing, but even after increasing that length of time, the shells were exploding well below the level of the Kates. Ensign Lomax went below in search of more ammunition for the batteries under his direction and was not seen again.

When the forward magazine explosion toppled the foremast forward, the port antiaircraft director hung out over the flaming waters between the *Arizona* and the *Vestal* like a pig roasting on a spit. Indeed, the men inside were roasting. The steel enclosure all around them and the deck was red hot. As Stratton remembered, "The metal floor was so hot we could feel the heat through the soles of our shoes." They hopped from one foot to the other and looked to the crumpled decks below for help.

Russell Lott wrapped a nearby blanket around him and attempted to climb down the ladder, but flames blocked any notion of escape. The metal enclosure became so heated and claustrophobic that two men jumped out. They, too, were never seen again. The six men who remained looked across the fiery waters to the port quarter of the *Vestal* where Boatswain's Mate, Second Class, Joseph Leon George was swinging a fire ax, cutting his ship's aft lines. George looked up when he heard their cries for help.

Joe George immediately saw the dilemma and grabbed a monkey's fist, a lightweight heaving line coiled around a metal ball that could be thrown and used to pull over a thicker line. Twice George heaved the monkey's fist toward the *Arizona* only to have it fall short of the cauldron of the port director and its six occupants. His third try hit the mark, and Don Stratton and his companions soon had a heavy line rigged between their airy perch and the *Vestal*.

Harold Kuhn went first, hauling himself hand over hand across the fiery waters that lay between the two ships. As Kuhn was about halfway across, another Zero strafed the ships and sent a flurry of bullets ricocheting around the remaining men in the director. Kuhn made it across to shouts of encouragement from both sides and then it was Don Stratton's turn. Lauren Bruner, his leg still dripping blood, followed, as did Russell Lott, Earl Riner, and Alvin Dvorak. As Lott later recalled, they went "hand over hand, like a band of monkeys." In all, Joe George was responsible for saving the lives of six men, though most were by now badly burned.

As George finished cutting the aft lines that tied the *Vestal* to the *Arizona*, a small boat darted along its starboard side and evacuated the six battleship survivors to a hospital ashore. As it did so, a tug pulled the *Vestal*'s bow away from the *Arizona* and the repair ship got underway. By now, the Arizona's quarterdeck was almost awash. The *Vestal* itself was taking water aft and beginning to ride low in the stern and list to starboard. Commander Young initially anchored the *Vestal* about half a mile to the northeast off McGrew Point, but the ship continued to sink, so he ordered it beached just to the east in Aiea Bay.[11]

The other ship moored near the *Arizona* and trying to get away from it was the *Nevada*. The battleship sat by itself astern of the *Arizona*'s flaming wreckage. Earlier that morning, the *Nevada*'s officer of the deck had ordered a second boiler lit in addition to the one boiler providing routine power throughout the ship. The plan was to switch the power load from one boiler to the other shortly after the forenoon watch began at 8:00 a.m. Before that could happen, however, all hell broke loose. But with two boilers lit, the *Nevada* had the advantage of being able to get up steam far more quickly than its sisters.

Gilbert Patten, one of the six Patten brothers aboard the *Nevada,* had been standing in line waiting for the ship's store to open at 8:00 a.m. Less than patient, Gil counted thirty-four sailors ahead of him and decided to come back later. Brother Allen had just finished a hot dog sandwich and beans for breakfast. He was sipping coffee with his messmates and discussing the upcoming Rose Bowl game between Duke and Oregon State.

At the sound of General Quarters, all six Patten brothers rushed to their battle stations in the boiler rooms and went to work lighting the remaining four boilers. According to Allen, "we had all six boilers off in ten minutes—record time."[12]

The one torpedo hit to the *Nevada*'s port side caused a list to port of about five degrees, but aggressive counter flooding by the damage control crew returned the ship to an even keel. Determined to get underway, junior officers on the bridge—the captain was ashore—and a veteran quartermaster took charge. The deck force cut the mooring lines with axes and the ship backed away from the quay.

Then came the signal for all ahead. The helmsman put the wheel hard over to port, and the *Nevada,* with the six Patten brothers sweating in its boiler rooms, turned outbound from Ford Island and made its way toward the head of Battleship Row and the open ocean. A weary cheer rose from parched throats all along the line. *Nevada* would be the only one of eight battleships to get underway that day.

Ahead and outboard of the *Arizona,* the *West Virginia,* too, was hoping to escape the billowing black smoke and raft of oily flames reaching around its stern. But the damage from seven torpedo hits was too great for the ship to get underway. From its decks, Marine bugler Richard Fiske wasn't the only one staring at the carnage coming from the *Arizona.* Harold Flanders, the step-uncle of the two Heidt brothers, Bud and Wesley, knew that the Heidts' battle stations were well below decks in the *Arizona*'s engine rooms. Like Joe Giovenazzo, Harold Flanders also knew who had encouraged the Heidt boys to enlist.

The Heidt brothers' fellow firemen, brothers Masten and Bill Ball, had battle stations somewhere other than below decks, where the Heidts were tending to the boilers. According to family lore, Masten was on deck when he was blown off the ship and into the water. His younger brother, Bill, evidently went below decks after the attack started to check on a buddy or fetch more ammunition. Bill was never seen again.

Being above decks in the forward part of the ship when the forward magazines exploded was almost as automatic of a death sentence as being below decks in that area. Men were burned to an unrecognizable crisp, incinerated in an instant, or buried under tons of molten steel.

Being blown off the after decks into flaming waters clogged with debris was hardly a guarantee of survival, but it gave some a fighting chance. From his battle station on one of the five-inch guns, Marine Gordon Shive went airborne and into the greasy waters. He had no idea where his brother Malcolm might be.

Having skidded across the sizzling frying pan of a deck, Russ Warriner landed in the same waters and made an effort to swim toward shore. But it was no use. Try as Russ might, he could make no progress. It was just like that simpler time when he had cramped up swimming near the coral reef and been rescued by a buddy. This time, Russ was on his own. Or was he?

An oily hand reached out from the blazing waters and grabbed at his tattered clothes. Russ wasn't certain whether he was a shipmate from the *Arizona* or someone off another ship. Given the blinding oil and heat, he may not have recognized his rescuer in any event. The apparition kept a desperate hold on him and dog-paddled until they were both near shore. Russ Warriner never knew who his rescuer was or whether he made it all the way, too.

Through these deathly waters, John Anderson and Chester Rose made their way in their commandeered boat back to the pyre that was the *Arizona*. As they got closer, the oily water was so choked with bodies that it was difficult for Anderson to tell who was dead and who needed help. He and Rose hauled three sailors into their boat and then turned back toward shore. As he did so, Anderson swallowed hard. There was no sign of his brother, Jake.

They almost made it. Near the beach, machine gun fire from a strafing plane ripped through the boat, blasting it apart. Only Anderson survived. "I lost them all," John recalled, "including Rose." Later, John learned that Jake had likely met a similar fate when he was hit by machine gun fire while manning his antiaircraft gun.[13]

On the sinking quarterdeck, Sam Fuqua was still the model of calm. The situation, however, was clearly well beyond anyone's control. Gunner's Mate, Third Class, L. Howard Burk of Missouri had been assigned to Turret

No. 3. After the forward magazines exploded, he was ordered out of the turret to fight the resulting fires. Burk did his best. Others around him did the same. Finally, Burk turned to Sam Fuqua and shouted the obvious. "Commander, there's no use in fighting it anymore."[14]

CHAPTER 11

"*Abandon Ship!*"

Sunday, December 7

Fᴏʀ ʟᴏɴɢ ᴍɪɴᴜᴛᴇꜱ, the skies above Pearl Harbor were clear of enemy planes, but the respite did not last very long. Just as the *Nevada* appeared to be making progress at getting underway, the sounds of more planes filled the sky. The second wave of Japanese attackers was less than an hour behind the first. This time, knowing the defenders would be on the alert, slow-flying, low-altitude torpedo planes were judged too vulnerable to antiaircraft fire and were not included in the attack.

Only Val dive-bombers and high-altitude Kates delivered the punches, but they reversed the targets of their comrades an hour earlier. Instead of the battleships, the Kates dropped their bombs on planes and installations on Ford Island and at Hickam Field. Eighteen struck Ford Island, although the billowing smoke from the *Arizona* and other fires was so intense that it obscured much of the target. Twenty-seven bombers hit Hickam, while the remaining nine Kates pummeled Kaneohe Naval Air Station on the eastern shores of Oahu.

The eighty Val dive-bombers largely sought targets of opportunity among the undamaged ships throughout the harbor. Judging that resistance from American fighters had been suppressed by the first strike, the thirty-six Zeroes accompanying the second wave broke into two groups and went after their own targets. Eighteen hit Kaneohe and Bellows Field, while the remaining Zeroes strafed service buildings and parked aircraft at Hickam Field. Even if few American planes were flying, a barrage of antiaircraft fire from ships in the harbor shot down six Zeroes and fourteen Vals in this second wave.

As this second wave of the Japanese attack swarmed in, the *Nevada* was the only capital ship underway and it made an inviting target. Dive-bombers attacked the battleship with a fury. As the *Nevada* passed the *California* at the head of Battleship Row and drew abreast of 1010 Dock on the opposite side of the harbor, a dozen bombs splashed into the water around it.

Then, Japanese pilots found the range, and five bombs struck the ship. Three hit forward of Turret No. 1 and left the bow a mangled mess. One of these ignited a gasoline storage tank and started a blaze that might have proven as catastrophic as that on the *Arizona* but for the fact that as part of a regular ammunition rotation, the *Nevada*'s crew had yet to reload twenty-eight hundred bags of powder into its main magazines.

The other two bombs exploded at the base of the main mast and smokestack, damaging the director stations on the foremast. Rather than risk the ship sinking and blocking the entrance channel, the senior officer afloat ordered the *Nevada* to beach near floating Dry Dock No. 2, adjacent to Hospital Point. When the *Nevada* nosed ashore, Pharmacist's Mate Robert Meyer was still making his patrol rounds

191

outside the hospital. "I stood looking almost straight up at the bow," he recalled.

As the Val dive-bombers sought other targets in addition to the *Nevada,* they found the battleship *Pennsylvania* as it sat in Dry Dock No. 1 along with two destroyers, *Cassin* and *Downes.* The lone occupant of Dry Dock No. 2 nearby was the destroyer *Shaw.* Several attacking planes dropped 550-pound bombs on the *Shaw.* Two penetrated the main deck near the five-inch guns forward of the bridge. A third went clean through the bridge superstructure and ruptured fuel tanks, setting the front half of the *Shaw* ablaze.

This fire caused the forward magazines to detonate just as they had on the *Arizona.* A huge explosion, second only to that on the *Arizona,* sent a mass of flames and mangled metal into the air. A great deal of it landed on the decks of the nearby *Nevada,* making it twice in less than an hour that the battleship had come under such an assault. Meanwhile, the *Shaw* broke in two.

Finding Hospital Point not so hospitable, a tug pushed the *Nevada* off the beach and across the channel to a new resting spot aground on Waipio Peninsula across from Ford Island. As Robert Meyer observed, the battleship "kept its deck above water but not by much." Meanwhile, the *Arizona* and the rest of the battleships strewn along Battleship Row were not going anywhere.[1]

About 9:00 a.m., in the midst of the second wave of attackers, KGMB Radio in Honolulu once again interrupted its morning broadcast. This time, Webley Edwards, host of the popular *Hawaii Calls* program of island music, provided plenty of detail and stressed the seriousness of the situation. "All right now, listen carefully," Edwards began. "The island of Oahu is being attacked by enemy planes. The center of this attack is Pearl Harbor, but the planes are attacking airfields as well. We are under attack. There seems to be no doubt about it. Do not go out on the streets. Keep under cover and keep calm. Some of you may think that this is just another military maneuver. This is not a maneuver. This is the real McCoy! I repeat, we have been attacked by enemy planes."

Edwards left no doubt who the enemy was. "The mark of the rising sun has been seen on the wings of these planes, and they are attacking Pearl Harbor at this moment," he continued. "Now keep your radio on and tell your neighbor to do the same. Keep off the streets and highways unless you have a duty to perform. Please don't use your telephone unless you absolutely have to do so. All of these phone facilities are needed for emergency calls. Now standby all military personnel and all police—police regulars and reserves. Report for duty at once. I repeat, we are under attack by enemy planes."[2]

The few men remaining alive aboard the *Arizona* were under no illusion about that. Death was everywhere. Any chance of survival for those walking or crawling its decks was tenuous. Having gone over the side only to find the thick oil covering the water too difficult to swim through, Seaman, Second Class, Carl "Buddy" Christiansen, a long way from Columbus, Kansas, and several of his shipmates climbed back onto the *Arizona*'s main deck. The ship had settled into the mud on the bottom of the harbor so quickly that they could do so without using the usual lines and boarding ladders. These were underwater, and the deck itself was almost awash.

"Time goes real fast," Buddy later recalled. "When the ship blew up, we didn't know it had been damaged that bad." At first, he had not been able to find a way out of his battle station in the depths of Turret No. 4. Now, he had to find a way off the ship.

Several sailors commandeered the captain's gig that had been tied up alongside the *Arizona*'s starboard quarter. Dead on the bridge, Captain Van Valkenburgh no longer had any need of it. The gig made repeated trips between the *Arizona* and Ford Island, ferrying all the men it could carry. The distance was only about one hundred yards, but mangled wreckage and flaming water made for hazardous and circuitous routes.

When it was Buddy Christiansen's turn, he and a handful of shipmates tumbled into the gig and it made yet another run to shore. The day before, Ford Island had been just a pile of rocks and dirt. Now, it was a desperately sought haven from an inferno of unspeakable horrors. Buddy had no idea what had happened to his brother, Sonny, but it did not look good. Save for those men in the two aft turrets, like Buddy himself, very few survivors emerged from below decks. Buddy was right: "Time goes real fast." Never had firm ground felt so good.[3]

Seaman, First Class, Clyde Jefferson Combs of Indiana was also one of the lucky ones. He had been in the chief petty officers' quarters near the bow folding laundry when he heard one of the chiefs shout, "Hey, the *California* is on fire." Combs looked out to see a Japanese plane strafing Ford Island. "I didn't have to think," he remembered. "I knew we were being attacked so I did a hundred-yard dash aft to my battle station." Rushing aft to Turret No. 3 saved Combs's life. In the turret, he was protected from the main blast; the chiefs' quarters where he had been were obliterated.

When Combs finally struggled out of the turret and onto

the main deck after the second attack, he found it "riddled with bullet holes, and body parts were scattered everywhere." The body of one of his friends hung from a ladder on the main mast. Like Buddy Christiansen, Combs jumped into the water and tried to swim the hundred yards to Ford Island. Finding that impossible, he, too, climbed back onto the sinking quarterdeck.

A ghost of a sailor walked out of a burning hatchway and pleaded, "Help me, Combs." The man was burned beyond recognition, but Combs and others did their best. The captain's gig came alongside and they lowered the burned sailor into the boat. He died on the way to the beach, and only later did Combs learn that the blackened shape was one of his best friends, Seaman, First Class, Wilfred John Criswell, also from Indiana.[4]

Seaman, First Class, Clinton Howard Westbrook, born in Brooklyn within sight of the *Arizona*'s own birthplace, was the bow hook on one of the fifty-foot whaleboats running errands throughout the harbor that morning. "Looks like the flyboys are out early," he had remarked to his coxswain as the first attackers flew over. The insignia of red balls under the wings shouted otherwise, and as bombs began to fall, Westbrook's whaleboat pushed off from the *Nevada*, where it had been about to load passengers for church services, and hurried back toward the *Arizona*.

Westbrook's whaleboat joined other small craft in picking up men who had been blown off or jumped overboard. "The adrenaline came out of no place and you just instinctively reacted," he recalled. All around, the battle raged and for hours afterward Westbrook didn't realize that at some point he had been wounded by a piece of shrapnel. "We'd been carrying casualties and we had the burnt flesh from picking them up, blood from the wounds, oil from the water from people we'd pulled out. If somebody had knifed me, I probably wouldn't have known it. It was that bad."[5] And it only got worse.

Having been rescued himself, Yeoman, Second Class, Martin Benjamin Bruns, a poor farm boy from Fredericksburg, Texas, who had joined the Navy for thirty-six dollars a month because he "was sick and tired of making two fifty a week as an itinerant farmhand," gladly became a rescuer and returned to the *Arizona* time and again. Unlike most others, Bruns claimed to have barely felt the death-knell explosion, but its result was obvious. He saw the foremast crumple and pitch forward, and watched as men "with their shoes blown off and blood pouring out of their ears and noses straggled from the doomed ship's hatches to stand dazed in the morning light."

"The flames and smoke were vicious," Bruns recalled. "By the time we began to evacuate the ship, there were dying men everywhere." Picked up by a motor launch, Bruns stayed aboard and made trips between the *Arizona* and Ford Island, hauling wounded men off the ship or out of the burning water and taking them to shore. Bruns also remembered swimming "with soot-blackened, nearly exhausted men...begging them to keep kicking to make it to shore." For Martin Bruns, the decision to risk his life over and over again was easy. "Those were guys I'd gone to sea with," he remembered, "guys I sat down at mess with. They were my friends."[6]

Among those Martin Bruns may have helped rescue was Chief Gunner's Mate John Andrew Doherty. His battle station was one of the antiaircraft batteries. As the ship exploded, Doherty "saw the forecastle waving up and down and fire and smoke coming up through seams of the deck." Doherty ran from one side of the ship to the other to make certain that the ammunition hoists were rigged and operating. Just as he noticed that one AA-gun wasn't firing due to a mechanical malfunction, a shock wave hit Doherty and he was "suddenly surrounded by smoke and flames." He tried to back away from the billowing smoke, but it engulfed him. Doherty didn't remember anything else until he found himself floundering in the water. Friendly hands reached out and dragged him into a boat.

It was John Andrew Doherty's subsequent after-action report that provided John Anderson with the only clue about his brother Jake's fate. Jake Anderson had been manning one of the antiaircraft guns. Doherty wasn't certain, but he thought he saw Jake hit by machine gun bullets. John Anderson never found his twin, nor did anyone else.[7]

At some point in the midst of the second wave of the attack, Lieutenant Commander Sam Fuqua, the senior surviving officer aboard the *Arizona,* reluctantly, but with the decision all too necessary, gave the formal order to abandon ship. Most who could were already doing so. Fighting the fires had long since become a lost cause, but Fuqua remained solidly on the quarterdeck, shepherding wounded and burned sailors into the circling launches. His "amazingly calm and cool manner and . . . excellent judgment," the citation for his subsequent Medal of Honor read, "inspired everyone who saw him and undoubtedly resulted in the saving of many lives."[8]

Sam Fuqua was always modest in his own accounts, but the rank and file sang his praises long after that dreadful day. When Gunner's Mate, Second Class, Earl Pecotte of Michigan climbed out of Turret No. 4, the first thing he saw was Fuqua exposed to machine gun fire but calmly directing the removal of the wounded. "Scared?" Pecotte recalled. "Hell yes, we were scared! Once you have men die in your arms and carry them around in pieces...you don't get used to that."

Two motor launches from the hospital ship *Solace,* which was anchored nearby, were among the small craft picking up the wounded, and Fuqua personally saw to it that some thirty or forty badly burned souls made it into the boats. When it was Pecotte's turn to board one of the launches, he stumbled and became entangled in lines until someone pushed him free and into the water. He couldn't see, but Pecotte never had any doubt that it was Fuqua who helped him over the side.[9]

The Marines, too, thought that Fuqua was the model of cool *under* fire. Major Alan Shapley and his men in the aft director station on the mainmast had been literally *over* fire. Shapley looked down from their perch and thought, "We were all going to get cooked to death because I couldn't see anything but fire down below." Shapley nonetheless led his men back down the mast to the quarterdeck. The ladders and handrails were red hot, and they burned many a palm. Corporal Earl Nightingale, who had rather blandly reported to Shapley that the *Arizona* was ablaze, was the last to leave his post. Shapley exchanged a few words with Fuqua. Nightingale thought Fuqua was "exceptionally calm" as Fuqua ordered Shapley and his Marines over the side. "Charred bodies," Nightingale remembered, "were everywhere."

Nightingale was fumbling to remove his shoes and Shapley was looking around to account for as many of his men as possible when a secondary explosion blew both of them into the water. Private Russell McCurdy, Admiral Kidd's orderly, had been at his battle station in the director with the others and was also blown over the side. Although Marine Gordon Shive had been manning antiaircraft guns and was not among the escapees from the director, he, too, had been blown over the side and was in the water somewhere nearby.

McCurdy had also been trying to take off his shoes—they were Marine high-tops, not conducive to swimming—but he ended up in the water kicking like crazy with them still on his feet. Blazing oil blocked the direct route to Ford Island, so these Marines first swam away from the ship and out toward the harbor to detour back through oily waters to which the fire had not yet spread.

With Major Shapley giving orders and shouting encouragement "to hang in there," the swimmers took a few strokes underwater and then popped up through the thick goo to catch pungent breaths. Bombs were still falling and explosions going off, which sent concussions through the water and added to the difficulty. "That vibration," McCurdy recalled, "moved your flesh like your flesh was going to leave your legs."

Earl Nightingale lost sight of Shapley but decided to swim to a pipeline extending out from shore about fifty yards away. He was about halfway there when his strength failed him in the thick waters. Nightingale was about to go under when a hand reached out and grabbed his shirt. It was Shapley, who told Nightingale to hang onto his shoulders while he swam the remaining distance.

Nightingale did so, but less than twenty-five feet from the pipeline, Shapley's strength failed him as well. Nightingale let go and told Shapley to leave him and make it on his own. Shapley shook his head, grabbed Nightingale with a vise grip, and refused to let go. Nightingale was adamant about the outcome: "I would have drowned," he said, "but for the Major." Alan Shapley received the Silver Star for his bravery and went on to become a lieutenant general. Nightingale became a widely known broadcaster.[10]

Whether Gordon Shive could have used such a guardian angel or whether he was dead as he hit the water, no one could say. Of the eighty-eight members of the *Arizona*'s Marine Detachment, only fifteen survived the attack. Among the seventy-three Marines who perished, only sixteen bodies were ever recovered, including that of Gordon Shive. The remaining Marines lie entombed in the depths of the *Arizona* with their Navy comrades.

The ranks of other contingents on the *Arizona* were also dwindling. Radioman, Third Class, Glenn Harvey Lane was assigned to the *Arizona*'s Aviation Unit. He grew up in tiny Williams in the heart of Iowa, a bit east of where the Patten brothers on the *Nevada* called home and west of the Ball and Sullivan brothers' homesteads around Waterloo. Lane took his uncle's advice and enlisted in the Navy rather than wait to be drafted into the Army. After the bomb went through the deck near Turret No. 4, Lane manned the nozzle of a fire hose and yelled for two sailors to turn on the water. They did, but no water filled the hose. Lane turned around to check the hose for kinks just as the forward magazines exploded. The next thing he knew, Lane was in the water, covered with oil.

In the thick goo, Lane had one of two choices. He could strike out for Ford Island, which, he remembered, "looked a mile away," or he could try to reach the *Nevada,* which at that point had not yet begun its run through the harbor. Lane chose the *Nevada,* and though suffering from burns and shrapnel injuries, he and several shipmates managed to climb up one of its ladders and collapse on the deck. "We were so black, filthy with black oil," Lane recalled, "that we were dirtying up their whole ship."

Crewmen on the *Nevada* called sick bay and reported that they had found an injured "mess steward." Such mess attendants were almost always African Americans or Filipinos. "I am no mess attendant!" Lane asserted indignantly, but he was led to a mirror to show him the proof. "I was black as coal and my hair was singed about that short, and I looked like a mess attendant, a black guy, 'cause I was coal black from oil," Lane recalled. "So they gave me a bucket and some saltwater soap...and I began to wash up [but] when I washed, the skin started coming off my arms." Hours later, Lane was on the *Solace* being treated for severe burns.[11]

Back on the *Arizona,* there were only two African American messmen who would survive the day, along with two Filipinos and one Guamanian, out of a Steward's Branch contingent of approximately forty men. One of those survivors was Mess Attendant, First Class, Joseph Henry Washington of Charleston, South Carolina. Washington's father died when he was young, and his mother took in washing to put food on the table. Washington later said that he was determined to see the world, but he likely needed a job, too, when he enlisted in the Navy on August 9, 1937. He underwent basic training at Norfolk and soon found himself assigned to the wardroom on the *Arizona.*

There wasn't much upward mobility for a black man in the pre-war Navy, but Washington attended Cook and Stewards School and was assigned to steward's duty. He was serving breakfast in the wardroom when the first explosions resounded from Ford Island. Washington closed the portholes per procedure and then attempted to return to his quarters. He found hatches dogged, and at the sound of General Quarters, he made his way on deck. The move likely saved Washington's life.

As the captain's gig and other motor launches collected the wounded and dying from the burning ship, Washington went overboard and helped rescue others. He finally escaped by swimming ashore. "It was a miracle that I came through the bombing," Washington recalled. "I was one of the lucky ones." Indeed, he came through without a scratch.[12]

As its decks emptied of the pitifully small number of survivors, the *Arizona* was not the only ship being abandoned. The *West Virginia* had sustained multiple torpedo hits as well as bomb blasts. With its captain dead on the bridge, the executive officer, Roscoe Hillenkoetter, gave the order to abandon ship without being in direct communication with damage control parties working to counter-flood the vessel and keep it from rolling over. The confusion was soon sorted out and the order countermanded, but in the interim, men went over the side.

Marine bugler Richard Fiske jumped overboard and swam to Ford Island along with some sailors. They reached shore and, in a hail of bullets from strafing planes, ran across the runway to get as far away from Battleship Row as possible. An ensign ordered them back across the runway to help with the wounded arriving in motor launches or struggling ashore by themselves.

Fiske remembered seeing sailors swimming in circles near the sunken *Arizona*. Their eyes were so full of oil that they couldn't see where they were going. Fiske and about twenty-five other men jumped into the water and helped guide some of them to shore. Later that morning, their task became grimmer as they pulled more and more dead bodies ashore. As Fiske remembered it, "My life changed from a nineteen-year-old kid to a nineteen-year-old man in a matter of hours."[13]

Moored alongside the *West Virginia* inboard to Ford Island, the *Tennessee* had taken two bomb hits from the high-altitude bombers of the first wave. Far more seriously, the *Tennessee* had been inundated by a wall of blazing oil and debris blowing onto its stern from the burning *Arizona*. The heat was intense, and fires started on the stern and port quarter of the ship.

There were no thoughts about abandoning ship, but with his crew engaged in major firefighting efforts, the *Tennessee*'s captain tried to move his ship forward to escape the inferno astern. He signaled for all engines ahead five knots, but the *Tennessee* didn't budge. The battleship was wedged too tightly against the quays by the stricken *West Virginia*. Nonetheless, its engines were kept turning throughout the day and long into the night so that the propeller wash would keep the burning oil from the *Arizona* away from its stern as well as the *West Virginia*. As it was, one of the *Tennessee*'s motor launches caught fire from the burning oil and sank as it tried to rescue survivors.

The grim reality was that there were far too few survivors from the *Arizona*. From Admiral Kidd and Captain Van Valkenburgh down to the greenest seamen recently arrived aboard — Malcolm Shive and William Thomas Free among them — death was indiscriminate. Among hundreds dead in an instant were Chief Watertender Clem "Maw" House, who had first reported aboard the *Arizona* in 1921 and who was never too busy to show new sailors the ropes, and Carpenter's Mate Al Konnick, who had hit his share of home runs for the *Arizona*'s baseball team.

Admiral Kidd died on the flag bridge, his hands gripping the railing in front of him. Among the young enlisted men whom Kidd had encouraged and taken an interest in over the years, two met very different fates. Seaman, Second Class, James Randolf Van Horn, who had heard the admiral speak at his Tucson high school and rushed to enlist, was dead somewhere below decks. His body was never found. Machinist's Mate, First Class, Everett Reid, who years before had arrived for his wedding day in the captain's gig, was far luckier. Reid was safe at home in Honolulu with his wife on the morning of December 7. His friend and shipmate, Elmer "Benny" Schlund, who had declined the Reids' offer to sleep on their floor, was never seen again.

Safe in one of the rescue boats headed toward the Ford Island shore, Gunner's Mate Earl Pecotte looked back at the *Arizona*. "The last thing I saw," Pecotte remembered, "was Mr. Fuqua alone on the quarterdeck and the ship ablaze from Turret Three forward." Fuqua remained there until everyone who could be saved was off the ship. Only then did he climb into the last boatload to leave.[14]

Once ashore at the fleet landing, Fuqua made an effort to rally the few survivors from the ship and to account for those sent to hospitals. Thomas Murdock and Larry Elliott were among the crew members who had spent the night in Honolulu, and they eventually joined up with Fuqua. Elliott was a Machinist's Mate, First Class, whose job it was to maintain the pumps and external fittings on the boilers in the center pump room. Elliott was well acquainted with Murdock's brothers, watertenders Luther and Melvin.

When a car full of uniforms screeched to a stop at the corner where Murdock and Elliott were looking for a lift out to the harbor from Honolulu, a lieutenant behind the wheel shouted, "I've got room for one more." Both Murdock and Elliott piled in.

As they roared along the two-lane road that led to the harbor, the last of the second wave of attackers was still bombing and strafing. A Zero targeted the highway dead center with an aim so accurate that its bullets chewed the asphalt out of the white line in the middle of the road. "I was glad he was accurate," Elliott recalled, "because if he had been over to the right, he'd have got us."

As Murdock and Elliott reached the landing and joined Fuqua, the view across the harbor to the towering column of smoke where the *Arizona* lay did not bode well for Thomas Murdock's brothers. Just then, another Zero made a strafing run along the dockside. Those who had been on the ship ducked for cover, but Murdock and Elliott seemed transfixed by the scene before them.

As the plane climbed away, Thomas Murdock reached down and picked up a spent bullet. It was still hot, and he bounced it in his hands. "You know, Silas," Murdock said, calling Elliott by his nickname, "when these things were addressed, Silas Elliott, or Thomas Murdock, it doesn't bother me. But when they're addressed to whom it may concern, that's the ones that bother me."[15]

IN GRATEFUL MEMORY OF

𝔐𝔢𝔩𝔳𝔦𝔫 𝔈𝔩𝔦𝔧𝔞𝔥 𝔐𝔲𝔯𝔡𝔬𝔠𝔨

WHO DIED IN THE SERVICE OF HIS COUNTRY AT

𝔓𝔢𝔞𝔯𝔩 𝔥𝔞𝔯𝔟𝔬𝔯, 𝔗.𝔥., attached 𝔘.𝔖.𝔖. Arizona, 7 December 1941

HE STANDS IN THE UNBROKEN LINE OF PATRIOTS WHO HAVE DARED TO DIE

THAT FREEDOM MIGHT LIVE. AND GROW. AND INCREASE ITS BLESSINGS.

FREEDOM LIVES. AND THROUGH IT. HE LIVES—

IN A WAY THAT HUMBLES THE UNDERTAKINGS OF MOST MEN

Franklin D Roosevelt

PRESIDENT OF THE UNITED STATES OF AMERICA

However noble the words, however famous the signature, commendations such as this for Watertender, Second Class, Melvin Elijah Murdock did little to ease the grief of a family's loss.
Murdock Family Papers.

PART III

"There's Never a Day Goes By..."

CHAPTER 12

The Waiting

Sunday, December 7

A<small>T</small> P<small>EARL</small> H<small>ARBOR</small>, the waiting began almost as soon as the last attacking plane of the second wave disappeared over the horizon. Everyone was apprehensive that yet another attack was coming. Long into the afternoon of December 7, as survivors worked to save the remaining ships and care for the wounded, their eyes turned upward at the slightest sound and scanned the skies for signs of a third attack. It never came.

The rumors did. They came in "fast and furious," Storekeeper, Third Class, Jack Rogo remembered. Assigned to clerical duties at the supply depot on Ford Island, Rogo had been eating breakfast in the mess hall when the attack began and volunteered to go to the small boat landing and help pull wounded ashore.

"We couldn't tell truth from fiction," Rogo recalled of the many reports circulating along the crowded shore: "'The Japs were landing at Hickam Field,' 'They are landing on Oahu,' 'They are landing north of us.'" Rogo planned to be ready in any event and swapped out his pistol for a Springfield .30-caliber rifle. "The waiting game starts," he later wrote. "The USS *Arizona* is close by, and we watch it burn and burn and burn."[1]

But as stunning as the losses were that morning, the failure of the Japanese to launch a third attack was fortuitous. The American battleship fleet was crippled, but oil storage tanks, dry dock facilities, and the submarine fleet were largely intact. Most critically, the American aircraft carriers were at sea and safe.[2]

That perspective would only come, of course, with future victories. For the present, news of the attack on Pearl Harbor was met with a profound shock, anxiety, and rage second only to that just experienced firsthand by those on the decks of the *Arizona*.

At the White House, Eleanor Roosevelt was finishing a luncheon in the Blue Room for thirty-some assorted guests. The First Lady had hoped that the president might drop in to say hello, but she was accustomed to his absences and made her usual apologies on his behalf. Franklin was very busy, Eleanor told her guests, because "the news from Japan was very bad." For another few minutes, she had no idea how bad.

Franklin Roosevelt was momentarily finishing his own lunch. It had been delivered to his study on a tray along with one for confidant Harry Hopkins. The telephone rang and the president answered it. A long seventeen minutes after being assured by Admiral Stark that the scene of the attack was indeed Pearl Harbor, Secretary of the Navy Knox, who insisted on being put through directly to the president, broke the news. "Mr. President," Knox began very quietly, "it looks as if the Japanese have attacked Pearl Harbor."

Roosevelt reacted with some measure of disbelief and

it was a short conversation. It went without saying that Knox would gather what details he could—they would be in short supply for days—and come to the White House immediately. Roosevelt returned the receiver to its cradle and turned to Hopkins. "If the report is true," said the president, "it would take matters entirely out of my hands."[3]

Roosevelt turned back to the telephone and called Secretary of War Henry Stimson, who had gone home for lunch after a lengthy morning meeting with Knox and Hull. "Have you heard the news?" the president asked in what Stimson recalled was "a rather excited voice." Stimson assumed Roosevelt meant the most recent reports of Japanese advances against Malaysia. "Oh, no. I don't mean that!" Roosevelt exclaimed. "They have attacked Hawaii."

Having spent most of his morning meeting with Knox and Hull discussing what the United States should do if Japan attacked the British in Malaysia, Stimson realized, "now the Japs have solved the whole thing by attacking us directly in Hawaii." It was "staggering," Stimson wrote in his diary, that "our people there...should have been so caught by surprise." But he admitted, "My first feeling was of relief that the indecision was over and that a crisis had come in a way which would unite all our people...this country united has practically nothing to fear."[4]

Roosevelt next reached Cordell Hull at the State Department, where Hull was about to receive Japanese Ambassador Nomura and Special Envoy Kurusu. The two diplomats were almost an hour late in delivering the completed typescript of Japan's long-awaited fourteen-part response. Say nothing, Roosevelt instructed his secretary of state. "Receive their reply formally and coolly and bow them out."

Briefly scanning the proffered answer—Hull had read

the decoded version hours earlier—and knowing what had just transpired at Pearl Harbor, Hull could barely restrain himself. "In all my fifty years of public service," he told the Japanese, "I have never seen a document that was more crowded with infamous falsehoods and distortions." Until today, Hull had not judged "any Government on the planet was capable of uttering them."

Nomura started to protest, but Hull held up his hand and pointed to the door. The audience was over. Supposedly, Nomura and Kurusu did not know what had happened at Pearl Harbor until they returned to their embassy. It would have made no difference to Hull. By some accounts, he reverted to his country-boy roots in northeastern Tennessee and had only two words for them as they took their leave. They were "scoundrels," Hull reportedly said, and "piss-ants!"[5]

One thousand miles to the northwest of Pearl Harbor and still some four hundred miles shy of Midway, the carrier *Lexington* and its escorts prepared to launch the delivery of eighteen Marine Vought SB2U-3 Vindicators toward their final destination. With the skies above Pearl Harbor barely clear of the second wave of attackers, Admiral Kimmel ordered *Lexington* to abort its delivery and rendezvous with Halsey and his *Enterprise* task force west of Oahu. Kimmel also ordered Wilson Brown and his ships back north from their foray to Johnston Island. Contrary to long-held opinion, the Japanese attack had not come from that direction.

These three task forces turned toward the rendezvous site, anticipating that their combined forces, with Halsey in command, would seek out and extract some measure of vengeance on the Japanese fleet. But the Japanese were already retiring westward. One of the great what-ifs of the early Pacific war—aside from the failure of the Japanese to launch a third strike against Pearl Harbor—is what might have resulted had the Japanese fleet paused to capture Midway en route back to Japan. The decisive battle off that atoll just six months later might have occurred differently.

Meanwhile, Honolulu, too, had been under attack—or so it seemed. Japanese aircraft had not dropped bombs on the city, but American antiaircraft shells, most improperly fused for detonation at altitude, had fallen on it. This unintended bombardment caused about forty explosions and added sixty-eight civilian deaths to the rising toll in the harbor. By about 10:30 a.m. Pearl Harbor time, the *Honolulu Star-Bulletin* rushed out the first of three extras that day, and Japan, with most of its attacking planes safely back on its carriers, had formally declared war on the United States and Great Britain.

Not knowing the extent of the losses that had befallen the *Arizona*'s Marine Detachment, Captain Jack Earle was doing his best to return to his new command and his new ship. After a wild taxi ride from his apartment to the main gate, Earle made his way to the fleet landing at Merry Point and looked out across the harbor. "It was a mess," Earle recalled. "Flames and smoke hung over Battleship Row...*Arizona* was burning like crazy; a huge cloud of black smoke billowed skyward. *West Virginia,* next to my old ship the *Tennessee,* was burning furiously."

But Earle's most poignant memory was of the many small boats that came into the landing from the harbor. Coxswains aboard them called out the names of their ships to pick up shipmates who had been ashore and ferry them out to their stations. "I noticed immediately," Jack Earle remembered, "that no boat came in from the *Arizona*."[6]

*   *   *

As President Roosevelt summoned his senior political and military advisors to the White House—Hull, Stimson, Knox, Stark, and Marshall would all be there along with Harry Hopkins—the president's press secretary, Stephen Early, gave assembled reporters what little he had. It wasn't much, and consequently, the first reports received by the public were maddeningly brief.

About 2:30 p.m. Eastern time, NBC Radio broke into its afternoon programming with a terse bulletin: "From the NBC News Room in New York," the announcer intoned. "President Roosevelt said in a statement today that the Japanese have attacked the Pearl Harbor, Hawaii, from the air. I'll repeat that. President Roosevelt says that the Japanese have attacked Pearl Harbor in Hawaii from the air. This bulletin came to you from the NBC News Room in New York."

Indeed, the news needed repeating. Some thought it a hoax or bad joke. There were memories of Orson Welles and the *Mercury Theatre on the Air*'s "War of the Worlds" broadcast of Sunday, October 30, 1938, reporting that Martians had landed in New Jersey. But this was neither a hoax nor a bad joke.

Music lovers who tuned into their CBS radio affiliates a few minutes early for a 3:00 p.m. Eastern time performance by the New York Philharmonic, heard twenty-seven-year-old John Charles Daly, not yet the broadcast legend he would become, say: "The Japanese have attacked Pearl Harbor, Hawaii, by air, President Roosevelt has just announced. The attack was also made on naval and military activities on the principal island of Oahu." In his excitement, Daly pronounced the last word as "O-ha-u."

Without the benefit of a radio, concertgoers gathering in Carnegie Hall for the symphony's live performance listened without distraction as Artur Rodziński conducted Dmitri Shostakovich's Symphony No. 1. The New York Philharmonic was celebrating its centennial season, and this performance was its 3,799th of that century.

At intermission, a wave of unease swept through the crowded lobby as incomplete news trickled in from passersby on the street. Nonetheless, the audience settled back into its seats as Arthur Rubinstein took the bench at the Steinway for Brahms's Concerto for Piano and Orchestra in B-flat Major. Only after the last notes did announcer Warren Sweeney confirm the rampant rumors. Rodziński and Rubinstein looked at each other and began to play "The Star-Spangled Banner." Afterward, according to the *New York Times,* "there was no applause and the audience streamed silently from the hall."[7]

Around the country, crowds at National Football League games learned the news by word of mouth and in bits and pieces as loudspeakers blared requests for certain military personnel and newspaper staff to report for duty. In Washington's Griffith Stadium, it had looked bad for the Redskins after the Philadelphia Eagles scored first, but tough defense and three second-half touchdown passes from Sammy Baugh saved the day. The Redskins prevailed 20–14. No general public announcement of the attack was made because stadium management didn't want to create hysteria.

At the Polo Grounds in New York, fifty-five thousand fans were also kept in the dark even as a buzz built among the crowd after public address announcements summoned senior military types to telephones. The Brooklyn

Dodgers were up 21–0 when the New York Giants scored a last-minute, face-saving touchdown. Only after the game was it announced that *all* Army and Navy personnel should report to their stations. With the loss, the Giants still finished the season one game up on the Dodgers to win the Eastern Division. They would go on to lose to the Chicago Bears in Chicago in the championship game two weeks later.[8]

At Soldiers & Sailors Memorial Hall & Museum in Pittsburgh, a crowd of almost three thousand gathered on a dreary December afternoon for what promised to be the America First Committee's signature event of the week. While two out of three Americans opposed intervening in the war against Germany, it was no secret that this group was made up of hard-core isolationists. They gathered in anticipation of hearing Republican senator Gerald Nye of North Dakota rip into Franklin Roosevelt.

Just before the program began, a journalist informed Senator Nye and event organizers of the attack on Pearl Harbor. Nye was skeptical. Was this sabotage, a ruse, or a merely an attempt to distract or quiet him? They decided to proceed as planned, without seeking confirmation or making any announcement to the audience.

The Bellevue Methodist Church choir sang several selections, and warm-up speakers fired up the crowd. When former state senator C. Hale Sipe took the podium, he embarked on a lengthy denunciation of Roosevelt as "the chief warmonger in the United States." That was enough for Enrique Urrutia, Jr., an Army reserve colonel, who had heard the Pearl Harbor news on the radio and entered the event late to see how the crowd would react. Incensed by the attack on the president with the nation now at war, Urrutia tried to interrupt Sipe. "I wonder if the audience knows,"

Urrutia shouted, "that Japan has attacked us and that Manila and Pearl Harbor have been bombed by the Japanese."

The audience heard little of the substance of Urrutia's interruption, but booed and jeered in response. To cries of "throw him out," organizers hustled the white-haired colonel and his wife out the door even as he denounced the gathering as "a meeting of traitors." At the podium, Sipe continued his rant. Calling Urrutia an interventionist plant, Sipe quipped, "Don't be too hard on this bombastic man. He is only a mouthpiece for Franklin Delano Roosevelt—only another sounding board for the warmongers."

Then, it was Senator Nye's turn. With a speech entitled "Christianity and Intervention," Nye argued that the two concepts were "as completely opposite as anything under God." Handed a note confirming that Japan had declared a state of war against the United States and Great Britain, Nye still did not pause. "Whose war is this?" he asked, speaking about the conflict in Europe. "Roosevelt's!" the crowd thundered in response.

Only after being handed more messages did Nye finally halt his prepared remarks. Calling it "the worst news that I have encountered in the last twenty years," Nye, in somewhat of a daze, read a journalist's report of the Japanese declaration of war. The audience, too, sat stunned. Nye tried to pivot back to the war in Europe, lambasting Roosevelt's Lend-Lease program and questioning the facts in the sinking of the *Reuben James,* but the fire had gone out of the crowd as rapidly as a deflating balloon.

The meeting came to a close. A few stalwart supporters pushed to the stage to congratulate Nye on his remarks, but the majority melted away quickly and quietly. In an editorial the next day, with reports of the Pearl Harbor disaster spread across its front page, the *Pittsburgh Press* labeled the Sunday gathering the most "disgraceful meeting in all Pittsburgh's history" and concluded, "those who partici- pated in it should forever hang their heads in shame."[9]

In the basement of a classic New York townhouse in the heart of Greenwich Village, Woody Guthrie and his fellow musicians in the Almanac Singers were playing one of their Sunday "hootenannies." Having been transi- tioning from peace songs to more patriotic verses, they sang sets that included "The Sinking of the *Reuben James*"—not yet recorded—and "Mister Charlie Lind- bergh," a mocking tale of Lindbergh and the America First movement. At one point in the performance, there was a commotion in the back of the room. Someone hur- ried to the stage and whispered to the performers. One of them took the microphone and announced, "The Japanese have just attacked the American fleet at Pearl Harbor." There would be no more peace songs for Woody Guthrie and the Almanac Singers.[10]

For many, the news and subsequent waiting would be far more personal. At the Community Presbyterian Church in Laguna Beach, its longtime pastor, the Rev. Raymond Brahams, had preached his morning sermon as usual. Over the years, Gordon and Malcolm Shive had both taken their turns ringing the bells in the church's lofty Spanish-style tower. After this morning's service, eleven-year-old Robert Shive went with his mother, Lois, and stepfather, Frank Westgate, to San Pedro to check on rental property that Westgate owned. Most of Westgate's tenants had connec- tions to the Navy.

As Westgate finished his business—likely collecting December rent that was late—the car radio blared out a report of the attack in Hawaii. Confronted with alarming news and uncertain what might happen next, Frank, Lois, and young Robert headed straight home. Passing through Long Beach, they picked up a sailor frantically hitchhiking his way south to join his ship in San Diego. They drove him along Highway 1, the Pacific Coast Highway, as far as Laguna Beach and wished him Godspeed. Then, like so many others, they went home and sat down to wait.[11]

In Long Beach, Clara May Morse was beside herself. She did the only thing she could think of that might give her some solace. She wrote letters to Francis and Norman. "My dear son," each began. "I have sat here by my radio and I know what has happened," May wrote to Norman. "God bless you and our whole US Fleet. We shall win, keep up your chin dear son. And I am fine and of course feel too sadly to write a letter, but will wait to hear from you my boy.

"Try to see Francis if you can," May added. "And my heart is too heavy to write more always my own dear sweet devoted son, who has been the dearest pal in the world." May signed off, "Lovingly your own Mother," promising to "write again soon."[12]

To Francis, May wrote much of the same, assuring him that she was all right and only worried "about my dear boys." Of Francis, she asked a similar question: "Have you seen Norman?" She acknowledged a letter written on Francis's twenty-second birthday, November 22, and promised that she was going to try to get in touch with Francis's wife, Dorothy. Then, she concluded, "Now dear son, I repeat that you have always been the best son a Mother ever had. God bless you and Norman and all men and officers of our Big Fleet, so I will say goodbye now, and, may God bless you and keep you. Lovingly, your Mother."[13]

In Silvis, Illinois, twenty-two-year-old Teresa Faye

Giovenazzo Ickes, married with two children and one of the two sisters between Joe and Mike Giovenazzo in age, was frying chicken when she heard the news bulletin on the radio. Teresa turned off the stove and ran to a neighbor's house to use their phone to call her parents. Had they heard, she asked? George and Concetta Giovenazzo had never understood why Joe had chosen to leave Silvis and join the Navy. The town was safe, secure. Then, Mike had followed his big brother. George and Concetta's bewilderment—as well as their fear of the unknown—was doubled. Yes, they had just heard, Concetta told her daughter. But what was the fate of her sons?[14]

Later, memories of that day and recollections of exactly when someone had learned of the attack would blur. Is that what you remembered, or what you were told? The Heidt brothers, Bud and Wesley, were both on the *Arizona* that morning. Bud's girlfriend, Donna, was home in Los Angeles with her family. Bud had once brought Donna's little sister, Fran, a stuffed panda bear when he was home on leave.

"The next thing I remember," Fran later recalled, "or at least I was told and now believe I remember, is that my mom, sisters, and I were baking cookies that Sunday morning when the announcement came over the radio that Pearl Harbor had been severely attacked. I don't recall the unceasing keening of my sister, but I'm told it went on for hours."[15]

The Heidt brothers' father, George, a typesetter at the *Los Angeles Times*, had the unenviable task of setting in print the news for the morning edition. "Japs Open War on U.S. with Bombing of Hawaii" the front-page headline screamed. George's heart screamed to know the fate of his sons. The boys' stepmother, Hazel Flanders Heidt, also had

220

worries of her own. Her brother, Harold, was on the *West Virginia*.[16]

The woman who was still living on the farm that Bill and Freda Becker had just purchased near Savonburg, Kansas, heard the news on the radio and ran out to the sheep barn where Bill and his youngest son, Bob, were in the midst of another long day of construction work. Pearl Harbor bombed by the Japanese? Their first reaction was disbelief. As Bob later recalled, "The first impression on something tragic like that is one that you just can't believe that this is happening."

With no way to call home and not knowing the fate of the trio of Becker brothers, father and son immediately packed up the truck and began the drive of almost three hundred miles back to Freda and the family in Nekoma. It was a grim and heart-wrenching journey that went by hour after long hour at a speed of about forty miles an hour. Near Great Bend, well past the early sunset of the December evening, the headlights on the truck burned out. Father and son slowed, but kept going the last forty miles in the dark. They had to be together with the rest of the family.

Word of the attack had already reached the Beckers' Nekoma farm. Freda, too, was in shock and disbelief. Walter Becker, the oldest of the Becker brothers, remembered, "We heard on the radio the *Arizona* was hit. We didn't know how bad it was damaged. They didn't say it went down." And so, the Becker family, like so many others in America that evening, gathered and waited.[17]

In St. Landry Parish, Sunset, Louisiana, Marine Private, First Class, Russell Durio's fifteen-year-old brother, A. D., was in his Boy Scout uniform helping to direct traffic at a church function a few miles from their home. A. D. heard the news of the attack from people in the crowd and rushed home to tell his folks. They all gathered around the radio for more news, but it was agonizingly slow in coming. A. D.'s eight-year-old sister Charlsey's memories of that day are that she spent most of the afternoon on the porch swing. People kept coming over all day long to the Durio house, she said, but "they didn't even notice I was there." That evening, at a special meeting of the town board, Sunset's trustees, not knowing how widespread the attacks might be, voted to hire a man to guard the town water supply.[18]

Across the Atlantic Ocean at Chequers, the British prime minister's official country residence northwest of London, it was 9:00 p.m. Winston Churchill was finishing a typically late dinner with guests that included the American ambassador, John Gilbert Winant, and Roosevelt's Lend-Lease czar and special envoy, W. Averell Harriman. Churchill asked for his portable radio, a recent gift from Harry Hopkins. It turned on when one lifted the lid. Churchill did so, and those around the table heard snatches of words that at first did not make sense: "Japanese, aircraft, Pearl Harbor, attacked, American base, Hawaiian Islands."

According to Churchill, amid a flurry of "what did he say?" around the table, Churchill's butler entered the room saying, "It's quite true. We heard it ourselves outside. The Japanese have attacked the Americans." Ambassador Winant immediately put in a call to the White House for confirmation. Within two or three minutes, Roosevelt himself was on the line. "Mr. President, what's this about Japan?" Churchill asked him. "It's quite true," Roosevelt replied. "They have attacked us at Pearl Harbor. We are all in the same boat now."[19]

As Roosevelt's senior advisors saw to their various

tasks, the president began to formulate the message he would deliver to a joint session of Congress the following day asking for a declaration of war against Japan. Roosevelt dictated much like he spoke before audiences, slowly and deliberately. As his faithful secretary Grace Tully took down his words, he seemed even more so: "Yesterday comma December 7, 1941 comma a date which will live in world history dash."

Cordell Hull had urged him to refute the inaccuracies of Japan's fourteen-part response line by line, but Roosevelt knew the American people. This was not the time for a lengthy recital but rather a pithy punctuation mark. Five hundred words would do it. Miss Tully typed it up, and Roosevelt prepared to show it to his cabinet that evening. Already he had marked changes on what would be the first of five drafts. Among the changes, he crossed out *world history* and replaced it with *infamy.*

After dining quietly with Harry Hopkins, Grace Tully, and his son, James, the president received his cabinet at 8:30 p.m. Save for Hull, Stimson, and Knox, most knew little more than the radio bulletins they had heard. Several had just hurriedly arrived back in the capital by plane.

Calling it "the most serious meeting of the Cabinet that had taken place since 1861"—the opening of the Civil War—Roosevelt reported what he knew and then slowly read his proposed message to Congress. There were questions from cabinet members about collusion among the Axis Powers; Stimson wanted to ask for a declaration of war against Germany, too. Roosevelt brushed that thought aside. This had been a blatant, surprise attack—a dastardly deed—and he wanted Congress, as well as the country, unified against Japan. He would deal with Germany in due time.

Thirty minutes later, the leaders of the House and Senate joined the cabinet, including Speaker of the House Sam Rayburn and Chairman of the Senate Foreign Relations Committee Tom Connally. Connally was particularly incredulous. "Why were all the ships crowded together?" he wanted to know. "Protection against submarines," Knox replied. "Then you weren't thinking of an air attack?" Connally asked. "No," Knox admitted.

The meeting with congressional leaders lasted a full two hours. As it broke up, there was no question but that the country was united. Never before in American history had a single event galvanized a national consensus so quickly. The America First movement was dead. Isolationism was dead. Japan had done more to accomplish that in two hours in the skies above Pearl Harbor than Franklin Roosevelt had been able to do in two full terms.

Young men from one shore of America to the other and the heartland in between had paid for it with their blood—many more would do so—but within hours, perhaps mere minutes, of learning of the surprise attack on Pearl Harbor, the United States stood united and defiant. As he left the White House, Republican minority leader Joseph W. Martin told the *Washington Post*, "Where the integrity and honor of the Nation is involved there is only one party."[20]

In Hawaii, it was still midafternoon. A few hours earlier, with rumors of Japanese troops landing throughout Oahu, the territorial governor had agreed with General Short to declare martial law. The governor assumed it would be in effect a few days; instead, it lasted three years. Short seemed leaden at times, but he exploded in rage when an aide handed him Marshall's much-delayed "just what significance the hour set may have" message at about 3:00 p.m. Still in his headquarters overlooking the harbor, Admiral Kimmel had a similar reaction when his copy arrived a few minutes later. Kimmel balled it up and threw it into the wastebasket.[21]

In the harbor beyond Kimmel's window, a flotilla of motor launches and small boats spread out across the water like frenzied water spiders. They carried the wounded first to the hospital ship *Solace* and then, after its hastily enlarged trauma space overflowed, to the main medical facilities on Hospital Point and a triage area set up on 1010 Dock adjacent to the *Argonne*. Some of the wounded were carried aboard the *Argonne,* where the warrant officers' mess was converted into an emergency operating room. By midmorning, personnel from the *Argonne* and other ships had also set up a field hospital at the nearby Officers' Club.

On Hospital Point, Naval Hospital Pearl Harbor was a state-of-the-art facility with about 250 beds, but the carnage quickly taxed it well beyond anything its staff had ever imagined. The first casualties arrived even as the second wave of attackers still pounded the harbor. As more poured in, ambulatory patients on the wards with far less critical conditions were discharged or evacuated to vacant outbuildings and hastily erected tents behind the hospital. Within three hours, the hospital received 546 casualties and 313 dead.

They arrived mostly from the small boats combing the harbor. Those who could do so walked into the hospital from the shore, some assisted by buddies, others staggering in on their own two feet. Oozing second- and third-degree burns covered many bodies. Blackened faces showed only two hollow eyes. "Some were so badly burned," Pharmacist's Mate Robert Meyer recalled, "that skin hung in large sheets from their arms." Nonetheless, he said, "they made little or no complaint, and their silence was eerie." Shock, no doubt, played a major role.

After the second wave was over, Meyer left his outside patrol and entered the hospital to do what he could for the burned and wounded. Everyone on the staff was pressed into service far beyond his or her level of training. Meyer sutured a twelve-inch wound on a sailor's leg that was open clear to the bone and sewed a young lieutenant's ear back in place. "We did things," Meyer remembered, "we never thought we would have to do."[22]

"The attack brought the very best out of them," Navy nurse Lieutenant Ruth Erickson remembered of the hospital's personnel. They "worked as though it was their last day on earth." For all too many, it was. For Erickson, who would go on to command the Navy Nurse Corps, "it was like watching a movie reel speeded up to the point where the frames ran together in a featureless blur." But there was one inescapable memory that pervaded everything—the stench of burned flesh. "I can still smell it after thirty years," Erickson recalled, "and I think I always will."

By the end of the day, the hospital had taken in 960 casualties. When there were no more survivors, the water spiders turned to the gruesome task of hauling bodies out of the oily water. Many were burned beyond recognition; some were so charred that they fell apart at one's touch.[23]

Marine Captain Jack Earle finally caught a boat out to Ford Island. He worked his way to the shore adjacent to what was left of the *Arizona*. There, in a makeshift bomb shelter, he found Major Alan Shapley and the few surviving members of his Marine Detachment. "They were a dazed, bedraggled-looking bunch," Earle recalled, "soaking wet, no shoes, missing parts of uniforms—and mentally exhausted." Earle shepherded them to the *Tennessee* for a good scrubbing and fresh clothes. His former comrades there embraced them all. They had been certain that Earle had perished on the *Arizona*.[24]

Just because the day was drawing to a close without a third attack didn't mean that tensions were easing. Pearl Harbor, Honolulu, and all of Oahu remained on edge. Having conducted a fruitless search for the Japanese fleet west of Oahu, torpedo planes and scouting aircraft from the *Enterprise* returned to their carrier while six Grumman F4F Wildcat fighters low on fuel flew on to Ford Island.

During the chaos of the morning attacks, planes inbound from *Enterprise,* as well as a squadron of B-17 bombers coming from the mainland, had come under assault—from the attacking Japanese as well as the defenders. That was somewhat coincidental and to some extent unavoidable. *Enterprise* lost six planes in the melee. Halsey had been right to be worried. They were indeed shooting at his boys. By evening, however, defenders should have been alert to distinguish between friend and foe.

"Don't shoot, don't shoot, incoming friendlies," the control tower on Ford Island advised all ships and shore installations as this second group of aircraft from the *Enterprise,* the six Wildcats, entered the pattern with landing lights ablaze. But over the dry docks, nervous gunners on the *Pennsylvania* opened fire. That was all it took. The entire harbor erupted in gunfire. Four of the six Wildcats were shot down and three American pilots killed.

Darkness finally fell shortly before 6:00 p.m. local time. It had been a long day. For too many, it would be an even longer night. Having been full on December 3, the moon was waning and would not rise for three more hours. All of Oahu was darkened because of lingering fears of another attack. Nonetheless, fires continued to burn and light the sky, especially above what was left of the *Arizona*. December 7 would turn out to be the hottest day of the month in Oahu—a high of 86 degrees Fahrenheit. While the mercury dipped below seventy during the night, it would not give much relief to men who had walked scorching decks or grasped hot railings and who now lay badly burned.

In the flickering light of the fires burning along its decks, the *Arizona* appeared deserted, an eerie ghost ship. But in the fading twilight, two men climbed from a motor launch onto its quarterdeck, which had remained barely above water. One of them, Lieutenant Kleber Masterson, was the *Arizona*'s gunnery officer. Masterson had been ashore with his wife the night before. "The only reason I'm alive today," he later grimly observed, "is that my wife was out in Hawaii. If she hadn't been there, I would have been on board ship."

Masterson was one of the few men from the *Arizona* who refused to entertain any measure of survivor's guilt. "I hated to lose so many shipmates," he lamented long afterward, "but I have never wished that I was on board during the bombing, because I couldn't have done a thing about it." He would have been trapped in the plotting room, Masterson said, and couldn't have helped with the antiaircraft batteries. "That's the only consolation I have."

Masterson had reported to the *Arizona*—really the shore of Ford Island nearest the burning ship—as soon as he could make his way to Pearl Harbor and get across the harbor. He spent the afternoon helping Sam Fuqua detail the few men who had escaped uninjured to duty aboard other ships. Masterson and Ensigns Leon Grabowsky and James Ashton Dare ended up on the *Maryland*.

As night fell, Masterson along with Grabowsky—

accounts differ, it may have been Dare—took a launch from the *Maryland* and headed back to the *Arizona*. There was one more job that needed to be done. The large American flag that had been hoisted up the ensign staff on the stern was still flying. Proper etiquette required it be hauled down at sunset. Because it was a Sunday, the "Sunday ensign," a larger-sized flag than usual, likely about nine feet by seventeen feet in size, was being flown as part of the ship being what was called "dressed."

Masterson and Grabowsky tied up alongside the *Arizona*'s sunken quarterdeck and climbed aboard. "We heard no noises," Masterson recalled, "because there were, of course, no survivors under that little bit of deck we could walk on." The Sunday ensign hung limp at the stern. It was oil-stained, riddled by shrapnel, and dragging in the water, but it was still there. The men hauled the flag down and folded it neatly. Then, they returned with it to the *Maryland*.

Exactly what happened to the flag after that, no one knows. Masterson remembered that he handed it to the *Maryland*'s officer of the deck with the wish that "it be preserved as a reminder of their ship." But he never saw it again. Apparently, no one else ever saw it after that night. It may have been burned out of respect. As Grabowsky remembered it, "Nobody knows where that flag is. It is a relic that got lost in the process." Whatever their exact association with the *Arizona*'s flag, Masterson, Dare, and Grabowsky went on to long and distinguished careers in the Navy. Masterson retired a vice admiral, Dare a rear admiral, and Grabowsky a captain.[25]

Anyone who may have seen the American flag come down from the stern of the *Arizona* that night no doubt watched with a lump in his throat. But there was a much more poignant scene if one looked downward into the waters of Pearl Harbor. In the darkness, the objects were barely visible, but as the moon rose and cast long beams over the blackened waters, splotches of white appeared. Floating on the oily surface—dirty and soiled—were dozens and dozens and dozens of white sailor hats.

CHAPTER 13

"*Yesterday, December 7...*"

Monday, December 8

O N MONDAY MORNING, December 8, dawn lit the eastern sky above Pearl Harbor as usual, but the fiery glow in the harbor had been present all through the night. The *Arizona* continued to burn and would do so for three more days. Launches from the *Solace* and other vessels returned to the gruesome task of combing the oily waters along Battleship Row looking for bodies or, as the case might be, parts of bodies. It was an ugly business and would become even grimmer when *Arizona* survivors were ordered back aboard their ship to collect the remains of their fallen shipmates.

The *Honolulu Advertiser* put out a newspaper on December 8, but it wasn't easy—or without misinformation. Its rival, the *Honolulu Star-Bulletin,* had cranked out three extra editions on Sunday, but a broken gear on the *Advertiser*'s presses curtailed its normal run. The *Star-Bulletin* graciously allowed the *Advertiser* to print an eight-page Monday issue on its presses.

In the rush to get back on the street, the *Advertiser* missed a few beats. "Saboteurs Land Here! Britain, Australia Declare War!" its bold headline claimed. The war declarations were true, but the report of saboteurs could be chalked up to the Army's erroneous claim that invaders had landed on northern Oahu early Sunday afternoon and been recognized by the "red disks on their shoulders."

"Raiders Return in Dawn Attack," the *Advertiser* went on to assert. "Renewed Japanese bombing attacks on Oahu were reported as Honolulu woke to the sound of antiaircraft fire in a cold, drizzling dawn today." There may well have been a few scattered antiaircraft bursts fired into the clouds above Hickam Field by nervous gunners and "brief machine gun firing" at several points along the waterfront, but reports of parachutists dropping into the Kalihi neighborhood of Honolulu nearest Pearl Harbor were without foundation.

Overall, Honolulu and all of Oahu conducted itself without panic. "Under the first baptism of fire," the *Advertiser* editorialized, "Honolulu acquitted itself with calmness. In the days ahead, that shall be Hawaii's motto: 'Be calm.'" But for the present, there would be no more editorials about treating nisei as Americans first.[1]

In Washington, it was a few minutes past noon. A caravan of black limousines, bristling with machine gun–toting federal agents, left the White House and drove up Pennsylvania Avenue to the Capitol. The air temperature was 46 degrees, but a stiff southwest wind made it feel much colder. Shrouded in the dark blue naval cape that he adored, Franklin Roosevelt stared out the window of his heavily armored vehicle at the December sky. Even the president did not yet know the extent of the losses at Pearl Harbor, in the Philippines, and across America's Pacific outposts.

Entering the chamber of the House of Representatives,

Roosevelt made what for him was a painful personal effort—he walked. Leaning heavily on the arm of his son, James, Roosevelt swung the leaden steel braces gripping his legs forward one awkward step after the other. This was no time for America's commander in chief to be seen sitting down. Cheers and applause greeted him as he moved to the rostrum. Sam Rayburn, the speaker of the house, introduced him, and after more warm applause, the president got right to the point:

"Yesterday, December 7, 1941—a date which will live in infamy," Roosevelt began, "the United States of America was suddenly and deliberately attacked by naval and air forces of the Empire of Japan." Emphasizing that this was a long-planned surprise attack and pledging to remember "the character of the onslaught against us," Roosevelt cataloged the extent of Japanese assaults throughout the Pacific. Then, before the subdued chamber, he asked that, "the Congress declare that since the unprovoked and dastardly attack by Japan...a state of war has existed between the United States and the Japanese Empire."[2]

Congress responded with a prolonged standing ovation and quickly agreed to the president's request. Within the hour, the Senate voted 82-0 in support of a joint resolution for war. Senator Gerald Nye, his recent America First harangues notwithstanding, voted in the affirmative. While some members from both chambers were unable to return to Washington in time for the president's address and the subsequent votes, it is doubtful that even hard-core isolationists would have voted no. The vote in the House of Representatives was 388-1. Shortly after 4:00 p.m. that same afternoon, Roosevelt signed the declaration of war against Japan.

Montana Republican Congresswoman Jeannette Rankin,

late of the America First Committee but voting more as a lifelong pacifist than an isolationist, cast the only vote in opposition despite boos and jeers from the gallery. Colleagues implored Rankin to switch her vote and make the declaration of war unanimous, but she refused. "As a woman, I can't go to war," Rankin explained, "and I refuse to send anyone else." The deluge of angry telegrams and telephone calls started at once, including one from her own brother, a former Montana state attorney general, who cabled, "Montana is 100 percent against you."

While widely criticized for her vote, Rankin nonetheless found a champion for her conscience in Kansas newspaper icon William Allen White. "Probably a hundred men in Congress would have liked to do what she did," the sage of Emporia wrote, but "not one of them had the courage to do it. The *Gazette* entirely disagrees with the wisdom of her position. But Lord, it was a brave thing! And its bravery someway discounted its folly." Miss Rankin did not seek re-election in 1942.[3]

President Roosevelt's address to the joint session of Congress was broadcast to the nation via radio. From DeKalb County, Alabama, to Nekoma, Kansas, to Laguna Beach, California, and ten thousand points in between, America reacted with a steely resolve. In Fonda, Iowa, Martha Patten's husband, Ernest Sporleder, visited the Western Union office at the Illinois Central Railroad Station, hoping for some word about Martha's six brothers serving on the *Nevada*. There was no telegram for Martha, and Sporleder returned again the following day—still nothing.

Ted Patten, the only Patten brother who had left the Navy after his enlistment was up, made similar visits to the naval station in Long Beach. When Ted finally learned that all six of his brothers were alive and safe, he wired Martha a terse message: "All okay." That was enough, and Martha broke down with tears of relief. For his part, Ted Patten immediately reenlisted in the Navy.[4]

Other men rushed to do the same barely before the president's words had faded from the airwaves. Among them were younger brothers of men who had already answered the call. There were also some well-known names.

Twenty-three-year-old Bob Feller was an ace starting pitcher for the Cleveland Indians. "Rapid Robert," as the Cleveland press fondly called him, was coming off a stellar 1941 season: twenty-five wins, six shutouts, and 343 innings pitched. Feller heard the news of the attack on his car radio just after he crossed the Mississippi River at Davenport, Iowa, after visiting his terminally ill father in Des Moines. He was on his way to Chicago to meet the general manager of the Indians and sign his 1942 contract. Instead, the day after the president's speech, Feller enlisted in the Navy, becoming the first big-name athlete to do so.

"I had planned on joining the Navy as soon as the war broke out," Feller recalled. "Everybody knew that we were going to get in it sooner or later and that was the day."

No less than Joe DiMaggio, who would later enlist in the Army Air Forces, said of Feller, "I don't think anyone is ever going to throw a ball faster than he does. And his curveball isn't human." As for Feller's broad American appeal, *Life* magazine had written only months before that Feller was "unquestionably the idol of several generations of Americans, ranging in age from 7 to 70."[5]

Bob Feller ended up on the battleship *Alabama* (BB-60) and saw front-line service in both the Atlantic and Pacific theaters. His hiatus of almost four full seasons at the height of his baseball career almost surely cost him a lifetime record of more than 300 wins. He finished with 266 but never expressed any regrets. Bob Feller was proud that he had had a chance to serve his country.

Ensign Joseph Langdell was also gladly serving his country, but he was soon assigned to a task both heartbreaking and life changing. A former Eagle Scout from New Hampshire, Langdell joined the naval reserve officers' program at twenty-six after graduating from Boston University with a business degree. He spent the night of December 6 in the Bachelor Officer Quarters on Ford Island. When the building started rattling early the next morning, Langdell said, "We didn't think too much about it, but when we heard a big boom, we thought we better get up and see."

Joe Langdell and fellow officers rushed about one hundred yards to the water's edge opposite the *Arizona* and watched in disbelief as their ship settled into the fiery waters of the harbor. "We were just spellbound," Langdell recalled, "you couldn't think what to do." But as sailors struggled ashore at the northern end of Ford Island—away from the fiery waters engulfing Battleship Row—Langdell helped them out of the water and toward an impromptu triage station. One turned out to be a fellow ensign, although Langdell didn't recognize his oily face at the time.

Three days later, still in shock from what he had witnessed, Langdell was eating breakfast when a superior came into the room and asked, "Are there any officers from the *Arizona* here?" Langdell hesitantly raised his hand. He was ordered to report to the pier to supervise a party of enlisted men armed with sheets and pillowcases. They took a whaleboat out to what was left of the *Arizona* and collected all the human remains they could find above the waterline.

Gunner's Mate Howard Burk, who had been on the *Arizona* for exactly one year, was among those on the detail. As the boat pulled alongside the wreck, a bloated corpse floated out of the wreckage. On deck, there was a sickening odor of death as they went about their grim task. "You're not normal," Burk remembered. "You're just more or less numb, you know. You're just existing; that's about it."

No one could have been prepared for that duty. No one could have been unchanged by the time spent on the blackened decks. Langdell could hardly bring himself to talk about it even decades later. "It took two days to take all the bodies," Langdell said. "We carefully wrapped them in sheets. The body parts we put in pillowcases. We swept the decks and took the small bones. Everything was taken ashore and properly taken care of." Many of the remains would eventually rest in the National Memorial Cemetery of the Pacific in the Punchbowl. Joe Langdell choked up thirty years later when he went back to walk among the graves. Had he been on the ship that morning, his battle station would have been in Turret No. 2. Instead, he lived to be one hundred.[6]

Chief Yeoman Thomas Murdock's service to his country collided with his personal grief. Having been home with his wife, Ruth, on Sunday morning, Murdock scarcely held out any hope for his younger brothers, Luther and Melvin, but he delayed notifying his parents, C. W. and Sleatie, until he was absolutely certain they were gone.

Personal pain aside, it became Murdock's task to assist in the effort to complete a final muster roll of the *Arizona*'s crew: those confirmed deceased, those missing and presumed dead, and the eerily small number of survivors. First and foremost came the task of making certain that the badly burned and wounded in hospitals or on the *Solace* were accounted for. Those few *Arizona* sailors without injuries were assigned to other ships. In the days ahead, the muster roll would also become important to paying the survivors and making certain that the wives and dependents of the deceased were not left destitute.

Chief Murdock also passed out postcards to the handful of survivors. This was an attempt to notify family and friends quickly that their loved ones were safe without divulging pertinent war information or requiring time-consuming censorship of lengthier letters. The postcards were distributed en masse throughout Oahu to survivors of the attack and were restricted to a few simple fill-in-the-blanks.

On one side, the only permitted information was the addressee's name and address—no return address. On the business side, one crossed out the nonapplicable sentences. One first chose among "I am well," "I have been admitted to hospital as sick or wounded, serious or not serious," or "Am getting on well. Hope to return to duty soon."

There was room to acknowledge receipt of the addressee's latest letter, telegram, or parcel (again, one crossed out all but the applicable information) and to assure the addressee that a "letter follows at first opportunity." A signature and date completed the card. Twenty cents sent it via airmail, but in the deluge of mail heading east from Hawaii even this message sometimes took three to six weeks to reach parts of the United States.[7]

Lieutenant Commander Sam Fuqua, still in charge of what was left of the *Arizona*'s crew, grew uncharacteristically frustrated when Chief Murdock seemed distracted by yet another task. Fuqua put Murdock on report, only to learn that upon orders from superiors, Murdock had also been detailed to gather affidavits to support Fuqua's nomination for the Medal of Honor.[8]

More than anyone on the *Arizona*, Fuqua deserved the award, but he would always wear it humbly, as its citation concluded, the "outstanding leader of men" he was. The Medal of Honor was also awarded to Admiral Kidd and Captain Van Valkenburgh—posthumously. Both had rushed to their battle stations at the first sign of the attack. The only remnants ever found of either man were their Annapolis class rings. Isaac Kidd's class of 1906 ring was found fused to the railing of the flag bridge. Van Valkenburgh's ring, class of 1909, was recovered from a pile of ashes on the navigation bridge.

Carl "Buddy" Christiansen awoke on Monday in Naval Hospital Pearl Harbor across the channel from the carnage of Battleship Row. He immediately tried to get information about his brother, Edward "Sonny," the baker who had gone below decks to change his soiled cap moments before the first bombs fell. Buddy roamed the hospital wards but couldn't find anything with Sonny's name on it. No one had seen the likeable baker who had once provided brother Buddy's mess table with an extra cherry pie.

Among the horribly burned and maimed, Buddy Christiansen proved one of the lucky ones. He was hospitalized for about ten days from the effects of the noxious gases he inhaled while confined to Turret No. 4 and the double dose of oil swallowed during his misadventures trying to swim. His lungs improved quickly, but he still didn't know what had become of Sonny.

Fearing the worst but without definite word of his brother's fate, Buddy Christiansen was discharged from the hospital and assigned to the *Chester* (CA-27), a heavy cruiser just returned from escorting Bill Halsey and the *Enterprise* to Wake Island. With Buddy aboard, *Chester* was soon off again with Halsey and the *Enterprise* on a raid against the Marshall Islands. Taking a hit from a five-hundred-pound bomb, *Chester* limped back to Pearl Harbor on February 3, 1942, for repairs, and Buddy finally heard for certain that Sonny was dead.

Their parents, Carl and Winona Christiansen, had received the official word on January 17, while Buddy was at sea. It came to them long before they knew that Buddy was alive. When they learned that the *Chester*, with Buddy aboard, was proceeding from Pearl Harbor to San Francisco, there was only one place they intended to be. Carl and Winona were waiting on the dock in San Francisco when Buddy walked off the gangway.

Winona hugged Buddy long and hard, and his normally reserved father, Buddy remembered, did too. No doubt some of those hugs were also for Sonny. The only tangible item Carl and Winona ever got back of Sonny's was a mangled leather bag retrieved from his locker. Sonny had been in the Boy Scouts, and among the few personal items remaining intact was Sonny's Boy Scout membership card. Carl and Winona's visit with Buddy lasted only about an hour and a half, but for Buddy's parents, it was a lifetime of relief and well worth their trip halfway across the country.

Later that year, Buddy Christiansen received an honorable discharge. Having come aboard the *Arizona* only weeks after he had turned nineteen, Christiansen was the ship's youngest survivor of the attack. He returned to Columbus, Kansas, married Lenora Belle Pallett, and served thirty-six years as the town's chief of police. Carl, as he was then known, retired in 1985 and passed away in 2002.

He continued to give interviews and speak to civic organizations and schools about Pearl Harbor right up until the end. "A lot of the schools haven't gotten into this," Christiansen explained, "and the young people need to know about it. I'm keeping the history alive." The thing that Carl Christiansen kept alive most was the memory of his brother. "There's never a day goes by," he later recalled, "that I don't think of my brother, after all these years."[9]

As dusk fell on December 8, Bill Halsey and the *Enterprise* finally made their way up the entrance channel and into Pearl Harbor. There would be no baseball games played. Appalled at the destruction around him, Halsey determined not to be caught in port should there be another attack. *Enterprise* refueled and replenished throughout the night, and by 4:00 a.m. the next morning, the carrier and its escorts headed back to sea.

That afternoon in Washington, President Roosevelt held a regular press conference. It was heavily attended, but most of the questions were of a domestic nature. The depth of the loss and the sacrifices that would be demanded on the road ahead were still sinking into the American psyche. "Mr. President, are there any further details you can tell us about the attack on Hawaii?" one reporter asked. "Not yet, not yet," Roosevelt replied before launching into a discourse about what the war would mean to government censorship.

A few hours later, the president went on radio to deliver one of his patented fireside chats—the nineteenth of his presidency—and set the course for the American public: "We are now in this war. We are all in it—all the way. Every single man, woman, and child is a partner in the most tremendous undertaking of our American history. We must share together the bad news and the good news, the defeats and the victories—the changing fortunes of war."[10] For many, the news would be very bad and very personal.

Over on the *Vestal*, still beached under a waning moon in Aiea Bay, the crew, including Joe Giovenazzo, went about repairing the ship and cleaning up the wreckage littered across its decks. The drawer of a sailor's locker, blown aboard by the explosion on the *Arizona*, lay amid the debris. Only a few personal items remained in it—none very intact. But a sheet of charred paper seemed to be part of a letter written somewhere on the *Arizona* the evening of December 6. "I am going to turn in now, Mother," it concluded. "I'll finish this tomorrow."[11]

CHAPTER 14

"The Secretary of the Navy Regrets..."

T HE DAY AFTER President Roosevelt's address to Congress, Secretary of the Navy Frank Knox left Washington for Hawaii to undertake a hurried inspection trip. Knox, who had boasted of the prowess of the United States Navy, had to answer the burning question, "How could this happen?" but even more important, "What do we do now?" Arriving at Pearl Harbor, Knox declined to stay with Admiral Kimmel, saying that it might appear to prejudice his findings.

After a whirlwind six-day trip, Knox was back in Washington reporting to the president. Admiral Kimmel and his Army counterpart, General Short, were finished. There was simply no way the two officers could command the confidence of either superiors or subordinates going forward. One man, Knox argued, had to take overall command of America's Atlantic, Pacific, and Asiatic fleets and wage a two-ocean war. Knox was certain that Admiral Ernest J. King, currently commander of the Atlantic Fleet, was the obvious choice. King had a reputation as a blunt, outspoken autocrat, but also as a man who got things done. Roosevelt agreed.

Their choice of Kimmel's replacement also became obvious. They needed someone well versed in men and materiel, someone who had seen duty in the Pacific, someone who led by example and could give the men of the shattered Pacific Fleet a much-needed dose of confidence. "Tell Nimitz," Roosevelt commanded Knox, "to get the hell out to Pearl and stay there till the war is won."[1]

With agonizing slowness, word of the personal loss in the nation's tragedy made its way to families throughout the United States. "The Secretary of the Navy regrets..." are words no sailor's family wants to read. But in Silvis, Illinois; Columbus, Kansas; Ostrander, Ohio; and other towns across America, these words arrived and were read with more sadness than one family should be asked to bear. And when it came to brothers, the sadness and sense of loss doubled.

Harvey Becker spent the first days after the attack frantically searching for Marvin and Wesley in hospitals and temporary quarters throughout Oahu, but in his heart, he despaired from the start. Harvey knew that his brothers would have done their duty. He knew their General Quarters stations were in Turret No. 2. He knew that Turret No. 2 was decimated. Finally, Harvey made a pained call to his folks, Bill and Freda, in Nekoma, Kansas, and told them there was no hope that Marvin and Wesley had been spared. They would have been together, and their deaths would have been very quick.

About two weeks later, a telegram arrived in Nekoma advising that the two Becker brothers were missing in action. Several more weeks passed before Marvin and Wesley were officially declared "killed in action." It was a very hard time for Bill and Freda, but they clung to their faith and to each other. It was the first time young Bob Becker saw his dad cry. "I remember my father bawled all night," Bob recalled. "He didn't just cry. He wailed."[2]

In the midst of this grief, the Becker family held a large farm auction at the Nekoma property and moved what remained to their new farm in Savonburg. There, in the main window of the farmhouse, Freda hung a red, white, and blue banner with two Gold Stars—the symbol of having lost a son to the war—for Marvin and Wesley, and one Blue Star—signifying a child in the service—for Harvey. Still, she refused to believe that Marvin and Wesley were dead. "Mom really wouldn't concede that they were gone for a long time because they were never recovered," Bob told an interviewer more than seventy years after the attack.[3]

The jar of canned pickles with Marvin's name on it—so anticipated by Marvin for his Christmastime leave—was carefully packed and moved to the cellar of the new family home in Savonburg. It remained there unopened, still labeled for Marvin, for many years. Freda hung Marvin's and Wesley's dress suits in the front closet. They, too, remained untouched for years.

Sometimes, there were cruel delays. Sometimes, there were cruel mistakes. A few days before Christmas, Western Union delivered two telegrams to the Giovenazzo home in Silvis, Illinois. The first reported what George and Concetta had long feared: while their oldest son, Joe, was safe aboard the *Vestal*, twenty-year-old Mike was missing from the *Arizona*. Two days later, their bleak Christmas Eve turned to joy when a second telegram arrived announcing that Mike was alive. Tears of relief flooded the home.

But then, a third telegram arrived. There had been a

dreadful mistake. The Giovenazzo reported safe on Christmas Eve was in fact Joe. Mike was still unaccounted for. A subsequent letter from Secretary of the Navy Frank Knox laid bare the incontrovertible facts: "Owing to the length of time which has elapsed since your son was first reported missing and due to the fact that no further word has been received about him, the Navy Department has abandoned all hope of his surviving an engagement in the Pacific." Among the list of known dead and survivors, the name of Giovenazzo appeared as a survivor and the Navy had erroneously thought it to be Mike. "However," Knox continued, "subsequent findings have revealed that the man listed as surviving is a brother, Joseph. The Navy Department and I extend to you our sincere sympathy and deep sorrow at the loss of your son."[4]

Each of the Giovenazzo family members reacted in his or her personal way. Concetta placed a Gold Star banner in the window. Her grief went on for years. Mike's sister, Dorothy, not yet six, "grew up with the grief." His father was "really troubled." George Giovenazzo said, "What's the use of raising a boy to twenty—to adulthood—only to lose him to war?" As Dorothy remembered, "He just carried the hurt."

Seventeen-year-old Samuel Giovenazzo carried the rage and was determined to do something about it. Within hours of learning the truth that Mike was missing and presumed dead, Sam enlisted in the Navy. "Sam was going to conquer the Japanese for what they'd done," Dorothy recalled. Having already lost one brother and with another still serving, Sam was assigned to the commissary as a storekeeper, but he eventually found his way to the escort carrier *Shamrock Bay* (CVE-84) in 1944 and saw action supporting the landings in Lingayen Gulf in the Philippines, Iwo Jima, and Okinawa. Sam died in Rock Island, Illinois, in 2009.

Big brother Joe suffered a dose of survivor's guilt, compounded by his role in encouraging Mike to enlist and be on the *Arizona*. Joe remained on the *Vestal* and continued in the thick of things. The repair ship was itself repaired and soon sent to the South Pacific. There, the *Vestal* and its crew performed herculean feats, including repairing the carrier *Enterprise* and battleship *South Dakota* (BB-57) after the Battle of the Santa Cruz Islands in October 1942.

Joe Giovenazzo stayed aboard *Vestal* until November 18, 1943, when he reported to the escort carrier *Kandashan Bay* (CVE-76) and later the escort carrier *Sitkoh Bay* (CVE-86). On the latter, Joe, like his younger brother Sam, saw action off the Philippines, Iwo Jima, and Okinawa. Joe retired from the Navy as a chief petty officer after twenty years of service, including a tour in Korea. Mike Giovenazzo's best friend from Silvis, Marine Zeke Weltzer, served throughout the war with amphibious forces in the Pacific.

Joe's wife and daughter, Helen Giovenazzo and little Janean, sailed from Honolulu to the United States early in mid-February 1942, on the *President Hayes,* as dependents were evacuated from Hawaii. A second daughter, Joellen, was born in Helen's family home in Kern County, California, on May 12, 1942. It would be years before Joe met her. During Joe's absence overseas, Helen obtained a divorce, married someone else, and inexplicably told her daughters as they grew older that their father had been killed during the war. Joe's efforts to locate them were unsuccessful until the 1960s.

Even in death, Mike Giovenazzo continued to do his part. His mother, Concetta, provided a photo of him in his sailor's uniform with cap perched on the back of his head for a war bond campaign. The January 21, 1944, issue of the *Daily Dispatch* of Moline featured a full page bearing Mike's smiling face. "Most of us knew Mike Giovenazzo," it began, before recounting Mike's sacrifice and that of all the Giovenazzo family. "So when you're asked about bonds in this Fourth War Loan Drive," it pleaded, "just remember Mike, the kid who grew up out in Silvis right next door to you, and buy till it really hurts!"

But it remained the Giovenazzo family who knew best what they had lost. Mike's sister Angie, a year younger than Mike and herself married only three weeks when Pearl Harbor was attacked, asked the question so many families asked: "Of all the ships in the Navy, why the *Arizona*?" Years later, there was still no answer to that question, but Angie tearfully recalled, "Mike was loved by everybody. I especially loved him, because he was my buddy....My heart was broken for a long, long time and I'll never get over it."[5]

Clara May Morse knew what that meant. She lived with "it" the rest of her life. "Oh, God, how can I ever go on without my dear ones," she asked in her diary on Christmas Day 1941. "Every one of them has been killed, only me left."[6]

Three days after writing to her sons on the evening of December 7, May penned a letter that found its way to the desk of Sam Fuqua. The *Arizona*'s senior surviving officer aboard that day answered May on December 28, three long weeks after her last letters to her boys. Fuqua was "Commanding"—not the *Arizona*, but only what his letterhead noted was the "USS *Arizona* Administrative Office."

"It is with deep regret," Fuqua wrote May, "that I report that these two boys, Francis Jerome Morse and Norman Roi

Morse, are missing. These boys have not been seen since the attack on the U.S.S. ARIZONA, by enemy forces on December 7, 1941. No doubt you have been officially notified by the Navy Department by this time, or if not, you will receive official notification in the near future."[7]

In point of fact, it took agonizingly longer. Ominously, the letters that May had written to Francis and Norman on December 2 were returned to her with the notation "unclaimed." Then, on January 30, 1942, a Western Union telegram arrived at the address where May was staying in Newport News, Virginia. "After exhaustive search it has been found impossible to locate your sons," it began, "and they have been officially declared to have lost their lives in the service of their country as of December Seventh Nineteen forty-one. The department expresses to you its sincerest sympathy."[8]

Three days later, Secretary of the Navy Frank Knox offered "my personal condolence in the tragic deaths of your sons.... It is hoped that you may find comfort in the thought that they made the supreme sacrifice upholding the highest traditions of the Navy, in the defense of their country."[9] May Morse buried her face in her hands and sobbed all over again. If May had any contact with Dorothy, Francis's wife, after December 7, 1941, there is no record of it.

Wiley and Rebecca Ball of Fredericksburg, Iowa, received similar telegrams and letters about their son Bill. He was missing, he was presumed dead, and there was no hope. His older brother, Masten, who literally had been blown off the *Arizona*'s deck, escaped the fiery waters almost unscathed. He was soon transferred to Bishops Point on the entrance channel for duty with the Fourteenth Naval District and later served aboard the cargo ship *Sirius* (AK-15) and the carrier *Saratoga*. But Masten struggled with his grief. He was alive; his little brother wasn't.

In nearby Waterloo, Iowa, the five Sullivan brothers decided to put their grief over Bill Ball's death into action. En masse they drove to the recruiting station in Des Moines and enlisted. George and Frank Sullivan had already each done four years of service, but they signed up for more. Joe, Matt, and Al did likewise.

Twenty-year-old Albert Leo Sullivan was married with a wife, Katherine, and a baby boy, James. He could have been deferred from combat duty. Katherine, however, knew what was in her young husband's heart. "They really wanted to go, those boys," Katherine recalled decades later. "They wanted to be together. He wouldn't have been happy at all with his brothers gone in the service. You don't think anything is going to happen to them."[10]

As the Sullivan brothers had stipulated upon enlisting en masse, they were assigned to the same ship after basic training. The *Juneau* (CL-52) was an *Atlanta*-class light cruiser, freshly launched and commissioned on February 14, 1942. The five Sullivans reported aboard and were instantly poster boys for naval recruitment. How fine they looked in their uniforms peering out from photos. After a shakedown cruise and patrols in the North Atlantic and Caribbean, *Juneau* passed through the Panama Canal and steamed into the South Pacific.

Also aboard the *Juneau* was Harold Flanders, who had been on the *West Virginia* and was the brother of Hazel Heidt, Bud and Wesley Heidt's stepmother. George and Hazel Heidt were still reeling from the loss of George's two sons aboard the *Arizona,* but their bad news was not yet over, and it was about to arrive five-fold for the Sullivan family.

By Christmas 1942, Hazel Heidt had once again not heard from her brother, Harold, in some weeks—just like after December 7 the year before. On January 13, 1943, another dreadful telegram arrived at the Heidt home. The *Juneau* had taken a torpedo in the port side during heavy fighting near Guadalcanal the previous November. Steaming south for repairs the next morning in the company of two other damaged cruisers, *Juneau* caught another torpedo from the Japanese submarine *I-26*. A massive explosion lifted the ship out of the water. *Juneau* broke in two and disappeared below the waves in less than a minute.

Out of a crew of almost seven hundred officers and men, perhaps about one hundred survived the sinking, but the two accompanying ships, fearing more torpedoes and assuming the chance of survivors to be low, continued on their course without stopping to search. Whatever the number of initial survivors, only ten men lived through eight days of shark attacks on the open ocean before being belatedly rescued.

The five Sullivan brothers perished and lie in the waters off Guadalcanal. Somehow, their mother, Alleta Sullivan, was able to compose unimaginable grief and fulfill a prior commitment to christen the fleet tug *Tawasa* (AT-92) later that summer in their honor. With five Gold Stars in her window, Alleta worked tirelessly to support USO efforts throughout the war, and the Sullivan brothers became national heroes for their sacrifice.

None of that was much comfort to George and Hazel Heidt. Their boys were gone, as was Harold Flanders. His loss on the *Juneau*, like that of young husband and father Al Sullivan, cascaded upon the next generation. Harold Flanders left a wife, Elsie, and four young sons, ages eleven, nine, six, and sixteen months.

* * *

Marie Free, Gussie's daughter and the sister of William, had just turned sixteen on December 2, 1941. She was left with two Purple Hearts, one for her father and one for her brother. Marie had the extended Free family, but she was essentially alone, having been estranged from her mother since she was a young child. Marie left the Texas home of her uncle and aunt, Frank and Lillie Meads, in the spring of 1942 and enrolled in San Marcos Baptist Academy. Later, she married and had two children. An informal wedding portrait shows her to be, in the words of a family member, "the most unhappy-looking bride I've ever seen!" Marie died in California in 1990.

Gussie's sister, Lillie, who had raised his children, had something else. Years before, possibly about the time of his divorce from Myrtle, Gussie had sent Lillie a clipping from a newspaper entitled "A Sailor's Heart." On the back, Gussie wrote, "Keep this, I like it." Its beginning and ending stanzas seem to fit his life.

> *"I guess you think a sailor forgets,*
> *After he's loved and gone;*
> *And that he never thinks of the girl he left,*
> *Miles away back home.*

> *"Yes, I guess a sailor forgets,*
> *As he sails away alone;*
> *But the one that most often forgets,*
> *Is the girl he left back home."*[11]

* * *

In Laguna Beach, California, Lois Shive Westgate sat quietly and prayed. Neighbors came and went, providing what comfort they could. The Rev. Raymond Brahams of the Community Presbyterian Church called at the house. His congregation prayed, too. Lois's last letter to Malcolm, postmarked Laguna Beach, November 29, was returned to her marked "unclaimed."

Like so many anxious parents, she wrote the Navy seeking any news of her boys. Lois could not give up hope. She sent Gordon a birthday card for what would have been his twenty-first birthday on January 10, 1942: "Today is a great day, your 21st birthday and wherever you are spending it, I hope you are well and happy. Mother." The card was eventually returned to her with the same "unclaimed" marking.[12]

Not until the end of January did Lois Westgate receive the dreaded confirmation—not just one son, but both. Lois broke the news to youngest son Robert, and he "cried for two or three hours." The Navy reported that Gordon's body had been found floating face down in the harbor. It was agonizing news, but at least there was closure. Eventually, a small envelope bearing Gordon's Ronson lighter, its case badly charred, and a single brass key, its purpose unknown, made its way to his mother. Whatever Marge Balfour's feelings for Gordon in the fall of 1941, with him gone, Marge did indeed marry Harry in June of 1942.

But where was Malcolm? The same letter that confirmed Gordon's death said only, "No survivor of the *Arizona* has reported seeing your son Malcolm H. Shive since action against enemy forces on December 7, 1941 and no ship or station has reported his presence under their command. Unless something new develops or until bodies are recovered, he will be carried as 'missing in action.'"[13]

The next telegram arrived mid-February: "After exhaustive search, it has been found impossible to locate your son...and he has therefore been officially declared to have lost his life in the service of his country." Malcolm remains on the *Arizona*. Gordon was initially buried in Halawa Cemetery and then reinterred in the National Memorial Cemetery of the Pacific in the Punchbowl.

On February 22, 1942, the bells at the Community Presbyterian Church in Laguna Beach rang as Reverend Brahams presided over a memorial service for Gordon and Malcolm Shive. Even more than the hastily imposed coastal blackouts, their deaths brought the war home in sharp relief to Laguna Beach. Many remembered the barefoot lads who had roamed the beaches and hung out along the piers. Young Robert took it personally and tried to enlist. His mother didn't try to stop him, knowing that kind but firm recruiters would.

For her part, Lois never complained about her fate to Robert. She used part of the insurance money from her older sons' deaths to send Robert to military school and get him away from Frank Westgate, whose behavior had not moderated. The thing that Robert remembered most from that time was that his mother's brown hair turned gray almost overnight. She was forty-one and chose to mourn very personally. Robert did not recall his mother doing anything special in later years to commemorate Gordon and Malcolm's birthdays or that dreadful day of December 7. "Eventually," he said, "she just stopped talking about them."

In 1947, Robert Shive left the Southern California Military Academy during his junior year and fulfilled his mission to join the Navy. His permanent file contained the notation: "Last surviving son of a war-depleted family."

The Navy did not send him to a war zone during Korea because of it, but he later requested that the note be removed and he served three tours in Vietnam. From 1964 to 1967, he was stationed at Pearl Harbor in the shadow of his older brothers. Lois, who died in 1988, never visited him there.[14]

The fate of Gordon and Malcolm Shive's boyhood friend, Weston Balfour, was every bit as poignant. Having enlisted in the Army on Valentine's Day 1941, and passed through Hawaii for one last reunion with Gordon and Malcolm en route to the Southwest Pacific, Balfour wound up as an ordnance handler with the 24th Pursuit Group in the Philippines. Its squadrons of P-40 fighters were decimated by Japanese attacks on Philippine airfields on the same day as Pearl Harbor. Many of the group's survivors then fought as infantry on Bataan and came to endure the Bataan Death March. Wess was among them and survived a series of torturous POW camps before he ended up at Davao Penal Colony on Mindanao.

In September 1944, as General Douglas MacArthur advanced to retake the Philippines, the Japanese moved Balfour and 750 Allied prisoners from Mindanao to prevent them from being liberated and revealing the atrocities of their confinement. This contingent was put aboard the *Shinyō Maru,* a captured tramp steamer, and it sailed for Manila in a convoy of seven other ships.

Allied intelligence intercepted reports of 750 "soldiers" bound for Manila and assumed them to be Japanese. The American submarine *Paddle* (SS-263) intercepted the convoy and fired a spread of four torpedoes at the *Shinyō Maru* as it proceeded without Geneva Convention–mandated "prisoner of war" markings. Two torpedoes struck the ship, but the horror was only beginning. Guards machine-gunned the prisoners as they tried to abandon ship. Out of the total aboard, 668 were killed, including Wess Balfour. The care-free lads of Laguna Beach were short one more.[15]

As grim as the telegrams were that arrived, and the letters so lovingly written that were returned "unclaimed" or "undeliverable," the most heartbreaking deliveries were the packages that arrived in mailboxes or on doorsteps weeks and even months later. Some, like May Morse's early Christmas presents to her boys, were marked "return to sender." Others contained gifts intended for family members back home from sailors now dead.

Clyde Williams, a cornet player in the *Arizona*'s band, had bought his parents a set of drinking glasses adorned with hula dancers while shopping on liberty the afternoon of December 6. Clyde paid the store in Honolulu to wrap and mail them. When the package finally arrived in Okmulgee, Oklahoma, in February—long after the news of the fate of Clyde and his fellow musicians—the wrapping paper from the store was more than his parents could bear. The store was called the Japanese Bazaar.[16]

Sometimes, the reaction to a gift returned from Hawaii as unclaimed seemed unfathomable, but in the depths of enormous grief, it made perfect sense. Private, First Class, Russell Durio of Sunset, Louisiana, had been one of the Marines manning the secondary batteries along with Gordon Shive and Don Chandler. Russell definitely had a sweet tooth, and his family regularly sent him care packages from home. "Send all the cake and candy you all want," Russell encouraged them in one postscript.

On December 5, 1941, Russell's brother, A. D. Durio, mailed Russell a big box of Christmas cookies. According to family lore, their mother, Marie, and her two sisters-in-law had stayed up all night baking the cookies so Russell would have a big box to share with his buddies in the Marine Detachment. Years later, A. D. couldn't remember the exact kind, but he chuckled and noted that in that part of the South, they had to have had pecans and raisins in them.

After the initial news of the attack, the Durio family waited tensely like so many others. Because Russell's father was also the police chief of Sunset in addition to his garage business, the Durios had one of the few telephones in town. Late one night in January, the big brown box on the wall with an earpiece and hand crank rang. Simon Durio answered it, and after a moment, according to A. D., he "just slid down the wall" and collapsed on the floor, moaning, "I should have never signed those papers."

The official letter regretting to inform the family arrived on January 27, 1942. A few days later, the box of Christmas cookies was returned to Sunset stamped unclaimed. With A. D. helping him, Simon Durio took the unopened package into the backyard and buried it next to the foundation of an old chimney. Russell's body was never recovered.[17]

Neither were the bodies of Melvin and Luther Murdock. Just before the attack, twenty-three-year-old Melvin had sent his kid brother, Ken, the youngest of the five Murdock boys, twenty-five dollars to buy a new bicycle. Twenty-five-year-old Luther had been sending twenty-five dollars a month—about a quarter of his Watertender, First Class, salary after seven years in the Navy—home to his parents so they could purchase an electric refrigerator. C. W. and Sleatie were grateful, but all three Murdock boys had sent them gifts that they considered expensive. They would much rather have had all the boys home in Alabama. The last time the entire family had been together was a date etched on Sleatie's memory: November 10, 1939, in the wake of the boys' cross-country road trip and automobile accident. Now, the date of December 7, 1941, would also be indelible.

The hill country of northeastern Alabama rallied around the Murdock family, but as in so many homes across America, there was little one could say or do to assuage the grief. "This fine family is taking the tragedy most patriotically," the January 7, 1942, edition of the nearby *Fort Payne Journal* reported. "Mr. C. W. Murdock, Henagar, Route 3, the father, says now is the time for everyone to help the Red Cross all they can and to buy defense stamps and bonds." Sleatie put two Gold Stars in their window.[18]

Thomas Murdock did the best he could to find his brothers' bodies, at one point reportedly even donning a diving helmet himself and making an effort to locate their lockers amid the dark waters and mangled decks of the *Arizona*. It was a dangerous and futile task. So dangerous and futile, in fact, that further attempts to retrieve bodies from below decks were forbidden. Most of the bodies recovered in the harbor or found above decks by Ensign Joe Langdell's men and similar working parties were temporarily interred in Halawa Cemetery near Aiea Bay. After the war, they were reinterred in the National Memorial Cemetery of the Pacific.

Total casualties, including civilians, from the Japanese attack of December 7, 1941, were 2,403 killed and 1,178 wounded. Of the number of dead, almost one half—1,177 men—were on the *Arizona,* out of the complement of 1,514 assigned to the ship. The sinking of the *Arizona* remains the worst single military ship disaster in American history.

Of the 337 *Arizona* crew members who survived the attack, about two thirds were not aboard the *Arizona* that morning. They were ashore on liberty, staying in the Bachelor Officer Quarters on Ford Island, or temporarily assigned to other stations. Of the dead, more than nine hundred officers, sailors, and Marines—from Rear Admiral Isaac Kidd to just-reported-aboard Private Leo Amundson—remain entombed in the sunken hull of the *Arizona*.

CHAPTER 15

Those Left to Remember

AMONG THOSE WHO lived through December 7, 1941, when loved ones had not, there would always be a heavy dose of survivor's guilt. Why him, not me? It was particularly cruel to those brothers who lost their flesh and blood while serving aboard the same ship. Anthony "Tony" Czarnecki, the machinist's mate from Michigan, lost his younger brother Stanley, a fireman. Tony was ashore with his wife that weekend and never really got over it. "I think it bothered him his whole life," his son, David, recalled, "that his brother went down when he was on shore leave. I think he felt like he let his brother and his shipmates down."[1]

Tony Czarnecki's loss of his brother Stanley was compounded a few years later by the death of his brother Henry, who was one year Stanley's junior. Henry joined the Army and served as a Private, First Class, with the 85th Infantry Division in Europe. Henry was killed on April 22, 1945, as the division clawed its way into the Po Valley in northern Italy in the closing weeks of the war. He lies buried in the Florence American Cemetery in Italy along with forty-four hundred others. After Tony's death in 2004, his ashes were interred in the *Arizona*'s sunken hull to be near Stanley. "His last wish," said one of his sons, "was to be returned to USS *Arizona* to be with his brother and shipmates."

The legal status of brothers serving together aboard one ship during wartime is particularly perplexing. After the catastrophic losses on the *Arizona* and the *Juneau*, as well as the near misses of the six Patten brothers on the *Nevada* and their later service on the *Lexington* at Coral Sea, the Navy modified its long-standing policy of encouraging or at least acquiescing to brothers serving together, but it never absolutely prohibited the practice.

In the summer of 1942—after the *Arizona* losses, but before the Sullivans went down on the *Juneau*—the Bureau of Naval Personnel issued an informational bulletin forbidding commanding officers from forwarding requests from brothers to serve in the same ship or station. "The Bureau considers that it is to the individual family interest that brothers not be put on the same ship in war time," the instructions read, "as the loss of such a ship may result in the loss of two or more members of the family, which might be avoided if brothers are separated."

The bulletin went on to note "an instance of this was the loss of three brothers on the USS *Arizona* at Pearl Harbor, T. H. (Territory of Hawaii), on December 7, 1941." There had been many more brothers lost, of course, yet it does not seem that this prohibition against commanding officers forwarding such requests to serve with a brother was enforced in practice. Certainly, there was no effort made to separate brothers currently serving together.

After the five Sullivan brothers were lost in November 1942, a long-standing misconception developed among the general public that the Navy absolutely forbid brothers from serving together and went to lengths to reassign them to other ships. This was never the case. Rather, a Bureau of Naval Personnel circular two full years after the Sullivan tragedy addressed the "Return to the United States of Sons of War-Depleted Families," essentially a sole survivor policy.

This recognized "the sacrifice and contribution made by a family which has lost two or more sons who were members of the armed forces and has only one surviving, and he is serving in the Navy, Marine Corps, or Coast Guard." In that case, consideration would be given "to his return to, or retention in, the continental limits of the United States, except when he is engaged in nonhazardous duties overseas." None of this was automatic, however, and applications for such return or retention to duty within the United States had to be filed by the sailor himself or his immediate family. Out of a sense of service, many men never took advantage of these provisions in the final year of the war.

Indeed, within weeks of the Japanese surrender in September 1945, the Bureau of Naval Personnel issued another circular about "Members of Families Serving in the Same Ship or Other Activity." It noted: "With the end of the war with Japan, the Navy can now revert to its longtime policy of not prohibiting members of the same family from serving together aboard the same ship or at the same activity." Of course, it had never absolutely enforced that prohibition. "The Navy now has no objection to members of the same family serving in the same ship," the circular continued, "however, no assurance can be given that members of the same family can be kept together indefinitely."[2]

None of this offered any solace to those who had lost brothers while serving together on the same ship no matter how happy and fortunate that assignment had once appeared. James Lowell Flannery and Wendell Lee Flannery enlisted at Cincinnati within one month of each other in the fall of 1940, and after basic training each reported to the *Arizona*. James got his rating as a Storekeeper, Third Class, while Wendell earned his first stripe as a Coxswain. As their parents' hometown newspaper reported in summarizing their careers after the attack, "Through a stoke of good fortune both were assigned to the same ship and had the comfort of each other's company while off duty." Wendell survived; James did not.[3]

In Savonburg, Kansas, where the Becker family had moved from Nekoma, there was one more brother determined to serve. When Bob Becker finished his junior year at Savonburg High School, he dropped out and registered for enlistment in the Navy when he turned eighteen. Despite deferments as a farm laborer and because two of his brothers had been killed at Pearl Harbor, Bob insisted it was something he had to do. If his brothers had gone, he was going, too.

Bob's mother, Freda, was beside herself. "She was very upset," Bob recalled, but she also understood that her youngest son had to avenge the deaths of Marvin and Wesley. Freda added a Blue Star for Bob to her banner in the front window and prayed it would not turn to gold. "Losing a child," Freda confided to her daughter, Mary Ann, "is the worst kind of loss there is." Whatever his feelings, Bob's father, Bill, kept them to himself.[4]

On June 27, 1945, four days after his eighteenth birthday, Bob entered active duty and went through basic training at Great Lakes, just as his brothers had done. His class was told to learn as much about becoming landing craft operators as possible because before Christmas half of them would likely be killed in the planned invasion of Japan's home islands. The atomic bombs stopped that, and the farthest west Bob got was Guam. He mustered out the following summer, like his brother Wesley, a Seaman, First Class.

Upon his return home, Bob Becker served eight years in the Navy Reserve. He enrolled in nearby Humboldt High School for his senior year and graduated in 1947. At Humboldt High, he met Betty Mae Orcutt. They were married on Memorial Day, May 30, 1952, in New York City on the CBS-TV show *Bride and Groom*. The format included a pre-ceremony interview during which homage was paid to the Becker family's wartime service and particularly to Bob's two brothers Marvin and Wesley who had made the ultimate sacrifice.

Harvey Becker struggled with his brothers' sacrifice for the rest of his life. Harvey continued to serve in the Navy, initially on a minesweeper and then a destroyer, but the shock of Pearl Harbor and a measure of concomitant guilt plagued him. After his discharge, Harvey worked in California for Lockheed, building the air force's gigantic C-5 Galaxy transport. He and Marie eventually divorced. Harvey died in California in 1979 at the relatively young age of sixty-three.

Through the years, it was a tradition in Bob Becker's home that Christmas decorations were not set up until after Pearl Harbor Day. That day was to remain in solemn reflection, and the American flag always flew in front of his home in honored remembrance of his brothers. "The older I get," Bob remembered on the fiftieth anniversary of the attack, "the more I think about them. I think about when we were kids, especially Wesley. He was a good brother—and a good friend." They were indeed best "buds."[5]

Bob and Betty Becker lived and worked in the Kansas City area, spending sixty-four years together and raising a son and a daughter. Toward the end, their memories of the early years sharpened, but the present slowly ground away at their ties to the past. In the summer of 2012, a brush fire jumped the road at the southern edge of the Beckers' Savonburg farm and engulfed the buildings and many of the trees. Bill Becker's old tractors and truck were destroyed, and the same sheep shed that Bob and his father had been building on December 7, 1941, went up in flames.

Bob and Betty took it hard; it had been a tangible link to that dreadful day. And there was a cruel twist. Several decades before the fire, the county renamed its numbered grid of east-west roads after states. The fire that brought havoc to the Becker farm jumped Arizona Road.

It was long Bob Becker's request that when his time came, a graveside military service should be conducted not only for his sake, but also to honor Marvin and Wesley. Bob Becker, husband, father, and brother, died on November 29, 2016, at the age of eighty-nine. On December 3, four days prior to the seventy-fifth anniversary of Marvin and Wesley's deaths at Pearl Harbor, the surviving Becker family carried out Bob's wishes. The rifle volleys and notes of "Taps" that echoed across the cemetery near Savonburg were for all the Becker brothers.

When Russell Warriner awoke from the nightmare that was real of burning decks, about the only thing he had left was his Hamilton watch. Most of his clothing had been ripped and burned to tatters. The watch, minus all but a shred of its band, had been molded to his wrist by the heat. With his hands badly burned and burns over much of his body, Russ was transferred first to Naval Hospital Mare Island in California and then to Naval Hospital Great Lakes.

At Great Lakes, Navy doctors shook their heads and wanted to amputate. Warriner was adamantly opposed, and his brother Rudi arrived from Wisconsin to become his advocate, making certain that Russ not only got proper care but also kept his hands. Numerous operations to graft skin back onto his hands followed; movement in one would always be limited to a thumb.

Russ Warriner also found an advocate in his girlfriend, Elsa Schild. Two months after his medical discharge on July 7, 1942, Russ and Elsa married. They had a daughter and a son and spent fifty-six years together before Russ's death in 1998. But the toll of that December day remained with them always.

Before contemporary diagnoses of post-traumatic stress disorder, Russ suffered bouts of anxiety; at other times he would simply sit by himself and stare. A car backfiring was apt to send him jumping over the couch. Elsa was usually there to calm him; sometimes, she had to restrain him physically. Years later, their grandchildren would remember being told to play quietly "because of grandpa's nerves."

Russ tuned pianos for years, but Elsa was always the primary breadwinner and caregiver. She worked for the Beloit Corporation in human relations until her retirement at age sixty-five. Their son, Russell Walter, Jr., still has his dad's Hamilton watch.

The other Warriner brothers continued to serve. Ken, who had been on temporary duty at signal school in San Diego on December 7, remained in the Navy until 1946. Rudi entered the Army in 1943. Youngest brother Lyle joined up after the war, but was killed in an automobile accident while home on leave in 1947 at the age of nineteen.[6]

In Ostrander, Ohio, George and Mary Miller's subsequent wedding anniversaries would always be tinged with grief over the loss of "the boys," Jesse and Stanley. Like so many families, they had held out hope after hearing news of the attack that their sons were alive. Mary Vogt, who as a three-year-old had one fleeting memory of her uncle Jesse on his last visit home, recalled that her grandparents kept thinking that Jesse and Stanley "had been on shore leave or something. But that wasn't meant to be."

After their fate became certain, Mary Vogt didn't remember her grandparents speaking of her uncles very often. Theirs was a heavy and very personal grief. What Mary did recall very vividly was "the two gold stars that always hung on a faded banner in her grandparents' front window." But Mary Miller did something else, too.

Long after George and Mary Miller had passed on, a neighbor of theirs told their granddaughter this story. Every Memorial Day, she said, Mary Miller would leave her house carrying a bouquet of flowers and walk down a hill to the creek. Very gently, she would ease the flowers onto the flowing waters. Once, when the neighbor asked why she did so, Mary Miller told her: "Maybe they will float into a bigger creek, and maybe then to a river, and maybe into the ocean and finally float to the place where my two boys lay."

When Mary Vogt and her husband, Bob, visited Pearl Harbor on their own fortieth wedding anniversary, Mary dropped two flowers into the harbor. Remembering her grandmother as well as her lost uncles, she attached a simple, handwritten note: "These are from your mother."[7]

*   *   *

On February 10, 1942, in Grand Coteau, Louisiana, halfway between Sunset and Arnaudville, the friends and family of Russell Durio held a memorial service. The family of Russell's former basketball rival, Archie Arnaud, stoically did the same. A few months later, Russell Durio's younger brother, A. D., graduated from Sunset High School just like Russell had done. A. D. wanted to join the Marines, but he was still underage, and this time Simon Durio adamantly refused to be talked into signing for another son. Instead, A. D. soon got his draft notice from the Army. "I was so disappointed," A. D. recalled. He had wanted to be a Marine like his big brother.

A. D. Durio went off to basic training and became a medic with the First Cavalry Division. He sent his mother half of his pay to buy war bonds and shipped out to Ulithi and then to the Philippines, eventually preparing for an invasion of the Japanese mainland that never came. Instead, he spent fourteen months in Japan on occupation duty and then returned home to Sunset to work a plumbing and electrical business with his older brother, Howard. A. D. married Laurie LeGrange, and together they had three boys and a girl. As of 2018, he was hale and hearty at ninety-two.[8]

Some of those who survived the *Arizona* didn't survive the war. Seaman, First Class, Harry Frederick Bradshaw of Iowa and Watertender, Second Class, Dale Frederick Flory of Indiana were both killed when the oiler *Neosho* sank in May 1942 during the Battle of the Coral Sea. Flory had lost his brother, Max Edward Flory, on the *Arizona*.

The waters off Guadalcanal claimed more later that year: Gunner's Mate, Second Class, Roscoe Bryant Smith from

Texas went missing on August 9, when the destroyer *Jarvis* (DD-393) went down with all hands. Lieutenant, Junior Grade, Richard Clyde Glenn from Kansas perished along with the Sullivan brothers when the cruiser *Juneau* sank.

Two weeks later, Shipfitter, Second Class, Walter Franklin Bagby from Missouri was on the cruiser *New Orleans* (CA-32) when its bow was blown off by a Japanese torpedo in the Battle of Tassafaronga, and Seaman, First Class, William Robert Chappell from Ohio was among those killed when Japanese aircraft sank the destroyer *De Haven* (DD-469) on February 1, 1943, near Salvo Island.

The great typhoon off the Philippines in December 1944 claimed still others. Seaman, Second Class, Donald Arthur Culp from Washington State and Gunner's Mate, Second Class, Dayton Merrill Genest from California were both on the destroyer *Monaghan* (DD-354) when it capsized, with the loss of all but six of its crew.

Gunner's Mate, Third Class, Robert Kurtz Stanley of Oregon was killed when the destroyer *Maddox* (DD-622) sank within two minutes after a direct hit to its aft magazines by a German bomber during the invasion of Sicily in July 1943. Shipfitter, Second Class, Berwyn Robert Phipps of Illinois miraculously survived the sinking of both the *Neosho* and the *Maddox* and lived another fifty years.

A few of the survivors seemed to have led a charmed life. Machinist's Mate, First Class, Everett Reid, who had ridden in the captain's gig on his wedding day and been ashore with his wife celebrating his birthday on the night of December 6, transferred to the *Nevada*. After the ship was refloated and repaired, Reid saw service aboard it in the Aleutians, off Normandy, and at Okinawa. He retired from the Navy in 1957 as a twenty-year man and lived to be eighty-six.

Of all who had been at Pearl Harbor that dreadful day, twenty-three-year-old Frank Curre, the mess cook on the *Tennessee* from Waco, Texas, said what most of the survivors came to feel when he was well into his eighties. "There's a lot of stuff I don't remember much in my old age," Curre told the *Waco Tribune-Herald* in 2010, a month before making his last trip to Pearl Harbor. "But that day?" Curre said. "Everything that happened that day is tattooed on your soul. It never leaves you. You carry it with you the rest of your life."

Frank Curre died a year later at eighty-eight on the seventieth anniversary of the attack, December 7, 2011. "It's like he held on for today," his daughter said. It was "his special day."[9]

After his discharge in 1945, John "Andy" Anderson worked as a movie stuntman in Hollywood and rubbed shoulders with John Wayne while taking evening classes in meteorology. A friend convinced Anderson to join the Navy Reserve and he did so, serving for twenty-three years. After moving to Roswell, New Mexico, Anderson achieved local renown as "Cactus Jack," a likeable disc jockey playing country and western music. That job got him a handshake with a young Elvis Presley and Eddie Arnold. He went on to become a television meteorologist and a real estate agent. Anderson married Karolyn Barnett, whom he always considered "God's gift for him," and had four sons.

When John Anderson died on November 14, 2015, at the age of ninety-eight, he was the oldest survivor of the *Arizona*. He was also the last survivor of the seventy-eight brothers who had served together on the ship. A year later, on December 7, some of his ashes were interred in the well of Turret No. 4 near the remains of his twin brother, Jake.

"He was on top of everything until he passed away; he didn't miss a beat," his son, John Anderson, Jr., recalled. "He lived life to the fullest."[10]

In 2016, the five remaining survivors from the *Arizona* gathered at Pearl Harbor for the seventy-fifth anniversary of the attack and John Anderson's interment. Ken Potts, ninety-five, of Provo, Utah, had been a coxswain and was in Honolulu when the attack began. The other remaining survivors were all aboard the *Arizona* that morning.

Donald Stratton, ninety-four, of Colorado Springs, Colorado, and Lauren Fay Bruner, ninety-six, of La Mirada, California, were among the handful of survivors who went hand-over-hand along the line from the *Arizona*'s foremast to the *Vestal*. Louis Conter, ninety-five, of Grass Valley, California, had been a quartermaster standing watch on the quarterdeck. Conter retired from the Navy as a lieutenant commander after twenty-three years. Lonnie Cook, ninety-six, of Morris, Oklahoma, then a Seaman, First Class, was changing clothes in front of his locker in Turret No. 3. He followed the turret captain's orders to man his battle station and was among the few to escape.

As their numbers dwindled, the *Arizona* survivors were increasingly treated as heroes. Surely, they deserved it. But Lou Conter offered another view. "We're not the heroes," he told a reporter at the seventy-fifth anniversary. "The ones who are the heroes are the 1,177 who were killed that day."

"You've got to remember," Conter continued, "that we lived through it and came home and got married and had children and grandchildren and great-grandchildren, and lived a good life. They lost theirs immediately, and they're the ones who should be called the heroes."[11]

In addition to the ashes of John Anderson and Anthony

271

Czarnecki, forty other survivors have chosen to have their remains interred with more than nine hundred of their shipmates never recovered from the *Arizona*. While all Pearl Harbor survivors may have their ashes scattered over the harbor, only *Arizona* survivors may be interred on the ship. Urns are placed underwater in the well of the barbette for Turret No. 4.[12] By the seventy-seventh anniversary of the attack in 2018, only five crew members of the *Arizona* from that day were still alive.

Today, along what was once Battleship Row, white mooring quays still dot the waters off the eastern side of Ford Island. Near where the *West Virginia* and *Tennessee* lay on the morning of December 7, 1941, the battleship *Missouri*, some 250 feet longer than its older sisters, stands guard. Its bow points not toward the sea but to the gleaming white structure rising above the remains of the *Arizona*. Dedicated in 1962, the USS *Arizona* Memorial spans the sunken ship amidships like a covered bridge. The lone flagpole is attached to the superstructure of the *Arizona*.

The ship itself has long been designated a National Historic Landmark. Visitors arrive at the memorial via small boat from the mainland visitor center. Once assembled in hushed groups, they walk past seven large openings on either side of the span that look out across the harbor and down into the waters below. Etched on the walls of the Shrine Room at the far end of the memorial are the 1,177 names of the ship's company lost that day. It is a hallowed place that has seen poignant personal moments of remembrance and grief.

"There he is," one woman whispered softly to her daughter as they stood before the wall. "Who, Mom?" her daughter asked. "The first boy I ever kissed," came the reply. That boy was Galen Velia from Crawford County, Kansas. Galen had indeed given Ona Marie Wright, the girl who lived next door, a peck on her cheek as a birthday wish as he left home for the last time. Galen's older brother, Keith, was also assigned to the *Arizona*. Keith was in Honolulu that morning and survived. Galen's name ended up on the wall.[13]

Above Pearl Harbor at the National Memorial Cemetery of the Pacific in the Punchbowl, silence is usually the loudest sound. White granite markers float upon a sea of green grass below the grand staircase of the Court of Honor. Engraved into the stone at the base of the staircase are these words: "In these gardens are recorded the names of Americans who gave their lives in the service of their country and whose earthly resting place is known only to God."

The Courts of the Missing on either side of the staircase are arranged by conflict and service branch. Inscribed on the walls are the names of 18,095 Americans missing in action from World War II in the Central Pacific, including those from the *Arizona*. Other World War II missing from the Pacific, including Weston Balfour, are remembered in cemeteries in the Philippines and throughout the Southwest Pacific. On other walls in the Courts of the Missing, there are 8,210 names from the Korean War and 2,504 names from Vietnam. Fingers, some aging, others too young to have had a personal connection to those honored here, delicately trace the names carved into the marble slabs.

At the top of the wide staircase, a towering statue of Lady Columbia gazes out across the cemetery. She stands on the jutting bow of a ship and holds a laurel branch. The words at her feet are from a letter Abraham Lincoln wrote to a mother who had lost sons in battle: "The solemn pride that must be yours to have laid so costly a sacrifice upon the altar of Freedom."[14]

On March 4, 1942, while walking on the beach in Newport News and struggling with her great loss, Clara May Morse found a piece of paper with the typewritten lyrics to "The White Cliffs of Dover," a sentimental song of the early war years. "There'll be bluebirds over the white cliffs of Dover," it began, "tomorrow, just you wait and see." Far from cheering May, it stabbed her deeply and brought a flood of fresh grief. "I saw this lying on the walk," she scrawled on the bottom of the page, "but there never will be any bluebirds for me again."[15]

And there never were. May threw herself into the war effort. She visited wards at Naval Hospital Portsmouth multiple times and delivered magazines, candy, and cigarettes to the patients. Most were about the ages of her sons, Francis and Norman. One delivery May made was particularly soul wrenching. The boxes of candy and books she had mailed to Francis and Norman before Christmas—early, as instructed—had been returned to her unopened. Giving them again to others left her with a sense of mission but badly dazed nonetheless.

Returning to Denver, May entered the Red Cross Nurses' Aide Program and took her training at St. Anthony's Hospital. Like her boys, May worried about making the grade, in part because, as she wrote, "one derives a certain satisfaction from being able to do for others." She studied hard and graduated into the Nurse Corps on August 10, 1942.

Her boys' birthdays would always be difficult. "God how I feel I am so broken up, he never had a chance, he never had any life," May wrote in her diary on what would have been Norman's twenty-first birthday. Four months later, on November 22, what would have been Francis's twenty-third birthday, May worked five and a half hours at the hospital "in his memory," she said, but was "so miserable, nothing left for me now except hard work."[16]

Clara May Morse went on to work in a number of Denver hospitals and do extensive volunteer work. In the end, she was drawn back to the West Coast, where she had last seen Francis and Norman. She died in San Diego on November 6, 1981, a month shy of forty years after she had lost them. Her body was taken back to Lamar, Colorado, to lie beside her husband, Roy.

Between them, there is another marker over an empty plot. In an oval at its top, there is a raised silhouette of a ship and the words, "Battleship Arizona U.S.N. Pearl Harbor 1941." Beneath this oval are the names of Francis Jerome Morse and Norman Roi Morse, their birthdates, their final rates, and the date of their deaths, December 7, 1941.

"Thank God for the volunteer work and all work," May wrote on the thirteenth anniversary of Pearl Harbor. "It is a wonderful thing for me to be able to do Red Cross work after Pearl Harbor, my Pearl Harbor. Others will have their Pearl Harbors, I feel for them very much because I know. God how I do know."[17]

Brothers All

ADMIRAL CHESTER W. NIMITZ, who had once flown his flag from the *Arizona* as commander of Battleship Division One, flew into Pearl Harbor at 7:00 a.m. on Christmas Day, 1941. Three weeks removed from the attack, gunners throughout Oahu were still jumpy. A fighter escort met the admiral's big four-engine PB2Y Coronado over Molokai and shepherded it safely to a water landing just east of what remained of Battleship Row.

Climbing from the plane into a whaleboat for the short trip to the dock, Nimitz realized that he didn't dare sit down. The boat was fouled with debris and covered inside and out by a thick oily residue—a microcosm of what Nimitz saw as he looked out across the harbor.

There was the capsized hull of the *Oklahoma* looking like a beached whale, the sunken *West Virginia* squatting in the mud, and the tilted masts jutting above the wreckage that had once been the *Arizona*. The country would require a great deal of patience, Nimitz wrote his wife that evening, "because we are confronted with a most difficult period."[1]

At 10:00 a.m. on Wednesday, December 31, 1941, fifty-six-year-old Chester W. Nimitz stood on the deck of the submarine *Grayling* (SS-209) and read his orders assuming command of the Pacific Fleet. Amid the carnage of Pearl Harbor, the die had been cast. America was at war. Nimitz would lead the fleet, from battleship captains to the lowliest seaman, to victory and venerate those who remain entombed in the *Arizona*—brothers all.

Acknowledgments

My greatest debt in writing this book is to those who shared with me their family stories. I am most grateful to David Ishmael (Balfour Family); Dr. Robert S. Becker and Debbie Becker Hassed; Eddie Christiansen; A. D. Durio, Dan Durio, and Lorraine Justus; Karen Baker (Free Family); J. R. Givens, Barb Ickes, Bill Smith, and Jack Smith (Giovenazzo Family); Janice Brecht (Heidt/Streur Family); Camilla Meyer Saint; Sharon Duvick and Robert Vogt (Miller Family); Debra Murdock Rogers and Kenneth Dewayne Murdock, Jr.; Gary Shive and Catherine Shive Maynard; and Sara Miller, Russell W. Warriner, Jr., and Suzanne Warriner Cook.

My thanks as well to Admiral Harry B. Harris, Jr., commander, US Pacific Command, and his staff; Daniel Martinez, Scott Pawlowski, and the staff of the World War II Valor in the Pacific National Monument; Laura Orr and the Hampton Roads Naval Museum; Katie Young and the Special Collections of the University of Arizona Library; and the staffs of the Hoover Institution at Stanford University, the Library of Congress, the National Archives and Records Administration, the Naval History and Heritage Command, the Norlin Library at the University of Colorado, the Stephen H. Hart

Library at History Colorado, and the Denver Public Library. Thanks, as always, to the interlibrary loan services of my own Estes Valley Library, still the best small-town library in America.

Those deserving of special thanks for offering research leads or information include: Marcia Brauchler, Robert B. Brunson, Lonnie Cook, Olivia Cox, James Fleitas, Barbara Floyd, Dr. John Floyd, Janet Gehlhausen, Dean Harris, Tom Hone, Patricia Johnson, Meg Jones, Jerry Keenan, Joanne Larson, Richard Life (CAPT USN, Ret.), Amanda Minton, Strother Murdoch, Laura Orr, Ken Potts, Christy Pullara, Dr. Joseph Pullara, Pete Smith, Don and Randy Stratton, Dolph Swift, Tracy White, and Holly Zachariah. Once again, David Lambert provided his cartographic skills and enthusiasm, and I am in his debt for the maps.

I am particularly grateful to Dick Camp (LTC USMC, Ret.) for his insights and information on the Marine Detachment aboard the *Arizona,* and I am especially appreciative of Paul Stillwell (CDR USNR, Ret.), whose book *Battleship Arizona: An Illustrated History* and the oral history interviews he conducted in the 1980s were invaluable, as was his review of the manuscript.

I am also very grateful to John Parsley, my editor at Little, Brown for three prior books and under whose guidance and encouragement this project began. Thanks also to the Little, Brown team who worked directly on this book, publisher Reagan Arthur, editor Philip Marino, Gabriella Mongelli, Anna Goodlett, Mike Noon, Shannon Langone, Katharine Myers, and Jenny Shaffer.

First and foremost, my friend and mentor, Paul L. Miles, retired U.S. Army colonel and distinguished professor at both West Point and Princeton, provided his always insightful and informed advice. No less deserving for his constant encouragement and support is my longtime agent and friend, Alexander C. Hoyt. It doesn't seem possible that I could mean it more than I have already said, but thank you, Paul and Alex, so very much.

Appendices

A. BROTHERS SERVING ON USS *ARIZONA*, DECEMBER 7, 1941

(Based on National Park Service Information and independent research)

NAME (Survivors in Bold)	RATE	HOME STATE	DEATH BURIAL
ALLISON, Andrew K.	F1c	Tennessee	1941 USS *Arizona*
ALLISON, J. T.	F1c	Tennessee	1941 USS *Arizona*
ANDERSON, Delbert Jake	BM2c	Minnesota	1941 USS *Arizona*
ANDERSON, John Delmar	**BM2c**	**Minnesota**	**2015 USS *Arizona***
BALL, Masten A.	**F1c**	**Iowa**	**1985 Connecticut**
BALL, William V.	Sea1c	Iowa	1941 USS *Arizona*
BECKER, Harvey Herman	**GM2c**	**Kansas**	**1979 California**
BECKER, Marvin Otto	GM3c	Kansas	1941 USS *Arizona*
BECKER, Wesley Paulson	Sea1c	Kansas	1941 USS *Arizona*
BIRDSELL, Estelle	**MM1c**	**California**	**1989 Nevada**
BIRDSELL, Rayon Deloris	F2c	Missouri	1941 USS *Arizona*
BROMLEY, George Edward	SM3c	Washington	1941 NMCP
BROMLEY, Jimmie	Sea1c	Washington	1941 USS *Arizona*

NAME (Survivors in Bold)	RATE	HOME STATE	DEATH BURIAL
CHANDLER, Donald Ross	Pvt (USMC)	Alabama	1941 USS *Arizona*
CHANDLER, Edwin Ray	**Sea1c**	**Alabama**	**1982 California**
CHAPMAN, Naaman N.	Sea1c	Colorado	1941 USS *Arizona*
CHAPMAN, Noel B.	**Sea2c**	**Colorado**	**2004 Nebraska**
CHRISTIANSEN, Edward Lee	Bkr3c	Kansas	1941 USS *Arizona*
CHRISTIANSEN, Harlan Carl	**AS**	**Kansas**	**2002 Kansas**
CONLIN, Bernard Eugene	Sea2c	Illinois	1941 USS *Arizona*
CONLIN, James Leo	F2c	Illinois	1941 USS *Arizona*
CONRAD, Homer Milton, Jr.	Sea1c	Ohio	1941 USS *Arizona*
CONRAD, Walter Raleigh	QM2c	California	1941 USS *Arizona*
COOPER, Clarence Eugene	F2c	California	1941 USS *Arizona*
COOPER, Kenneth Erven	F2c	California	1941 USS *Arizona*
CZARNECKI, Anthony Francis	**MM1c**	**Michigan**	**2004 Michigan**
CZARNECKI, Stanley	F1c	Michigan	1941 USS *Arizona*
DOHERTY, George Walter	Sea2c	California	1941 USS *Arizona*
DOHERTY, John Albert*	MM2c	California	1941 USS *Arizona*
ELLIS, George William	**SC1c**	**Nebraska**	**2002 California**
ELLIS, Richard Everett	Sea1c	Nebraska	1941 USS *Arizona*
FLANNERY, James Lowell	SK3c	Ohio	1941 USS *Arizona*
FLANNERY, Wendell Lee	**Cox**	**Ohio**	**1999 Kentucky**
FLORY, Dale Frederick	**WT2c**	**Indiana**	**1942 Coral Sea**
FLORY, Max Edward	Sea2c	Indiana	1941 USS *Arizona*
HEIDT, Edward Joseph	F1c	California	1941 USS *Arizona*
HEIDT, Wesley John	MM2c	California	1941 USS *Arizona*
INGALLS, Richard Fitch	SC3c	New York	1941 USS *Arizona*

NAME (Survivors in Bold)	RATE	HOME STATE	DEATH BURIAL
INGALLS, Theodore A.	SC3c	New York	1941 USS *Arizona*
IVERSEN, Earl Henry	Sea2c	California	1941 USS *Arizona*
IVERSEN, Norman Kenneth	Sea2c	California	1941 USS *Arizona*
JONES, Daniel Pugh	Sea2c	Alabama	1941 USS *Arizona*
JONES, Woodrow Wilson	Sea2c	Alabama	1941 USS *Arizona*
JONES, Edmon Ethmer	Sea1c	Colorado	1941 USS *Arizona*
JONES, Homer Lloyd	SC3c	Colorado	1941 USS *Arizona*
KENISTON, Donald Lee	Sea2c	Ohio	1941 USS *Arizona*
KENISTON, Kenneth Howard	F3c	Ohio	1941 USS *Arizona*
KENNINGTON, Charles Cecil	Sea1c	Tennessee	1941 USS *Arizona*
KENNINGTON, Milton Homer	Sea1c	Tennessee	1941 USS *Arizona*
KRAMB, James Henry	Sea1c	New York	1941 USS *Arizona*
KRAMB, John David	Msmth1c	New York	1941 USS *Arizona*
LAKIN, Donald Lapier	Sea1c	Kansas	1941 NMCP
LAKIN, Joseph Jordan	Sea1c	Kansas	1941 NMCP
LIVERS, Raymond Edward	Sea1c	New Mexico	1941 USS *Arizona*
LIVERS, Wayne Nicholas	F1c	New Mexico	1941 USS *Arizona*
MILLER, George Stanley	Sea1c	Ohio	1941 USS *Arizona*
MILLER, Jessie Zimmer	Sea1c	Ohio	1941 USS *Arizona*
MORSE, Francis Jerome	BM1c	Colorado	1941 USS *Arizona*
MORSE, Norman Roi	WT2c	Colorado	1941 USS *Arizona*
MURDOCK, Charles Luther	WT1c	Alabama	1941 USS *Arizona*
MURDOCK, Melvin Elijah	WT2c	Alabama	1941 USS *Arizona*
MURDOCK, Thomas Daniel	**CY**	**Alabama**	**1979 California**
NICHOLS, Alfred Rose	Sea1c	Alabama	1941 USS *Arizona*
NICHOLS, Louis Duffie	Sea2c	Alabama	1941 USS *Arizona*

NAME (Survivors in Bold)	RATE	HOME STATE	DEATH BURIAL
O'BRYAN, George David	FC3c	Kentucky	1941 USS *Arizona*
O'BRYAN, Joseph Benjamin	FC3c	Kentucky	1941 USS *Arizona*
SHIVE, Gordon Eshom	PFC (USMC)	California	1941 NMCP
SHIVE, Malcolm Holman	RM3c	California	1941 USS *Arizona*
SKILES, Charley Jackson, Jr.	Sea2c	Missouri	1941 USS *Arizona*
SKILES, Eugene	Sea2c	Missouri	1941 USS *Arizona*
STARKOVICH, Charles	EM3c	Washington	1941 USS *Arizona*
STARKOVICH, Joseph, Jr.	F2c	Washington	1941 USS *Arizona*
VELIA, Galen Steve	SM3c	Kansas	1941 USS *Arizona*
VELIA, Keith Lloyd	**Sea2c**	**Kansas**	**1991 Kansas**
WARRINER, Kenneth T.	**Sea2c**	**Wisconsin**	**2001 California**
WARRINER, Russell Walter	**Sea1c**	**Wisconsin**	**1998 Wisconsin**
WELLS, Raymond Virgil, Jr.	Sea2c	Missouri	1941 USS *Arizona*
WELLS, William Bennett	Sea1c	Missouri	1941 USS *Arizona*

* Some lists of brothers identify John Andrew Doherty as the brother of George Walter Doherty and John Albert Doherty. This author could not confirm a relationship.

Abbreviations:

NMCP—National Memorial Cemetery of the Pacific

1c, 2c, 3c—First Class, Second Class, Third Class

AS—Apprentice Seaman

Bkr—Baker

BM —Boatswain's Mate

CGM—Chief Gunner's Mate

Cox—Coxswain

CY—Chief Yeoman

EM—Electrician's Mate

F—Fireman

FC—Fire Controlman
GM—Gunner's Mate
MM—Machinist's Mate
Msmth—Metalsmith
PFC—Private First Class (USMC)
Pvt—Private (USMC)
QM—Quartermaster
RM—Radioman
SC—Ship's Cook
Sea—Seaman
SK—Storekeeper
SM—Signalman
WT—Watertender

B. US BATTLESHIPS IN COMMISSION, 1941

Ship Name (No.)	Commissioned – De-commissioned	Disposition
Utah (BB-31)	August 31, 1911 – September 5, 1944	Sunk at Pearl Harbor
Wyoming (BB-32)	September 25, 1912 – August 1, 1947	Scrapped
Arkansas (BB-33)	September 17, 1912 – July 29, 1946	Sunk as post-war target
New York (BB-34)	April 15, 1914 – August 29, 1946	Sunk as post-war target
Texas (BB-35)	March 12, 1914 – April 21, 1948	Memorial, San Jacinto, TX
Nevada (BB-36)	March 11, 1916 – April 21, 1948	Sunk as post-war target
Oklahoma (BB-37)	May 2, 1916 – September 1, 1944	Sunk at Pearl Harbor*
Pennsylvania (BB-38)	June 12, 1916 – August 29, 1946	Sunk as post-war target
Arizona (BB-39)	October 17, 1916 –	Sunk at Pearl Harbor
New Mexico (BB-40)	May 20, 1918 – July 19, 1946	Scrapped
Mississippi (BB-41)	December 18, 1917 – December 17, 1956	Scrapped
Idaho (BB-42)	March 24, 1919 – July 3, 1946	Scrapped
Tennessee (BB-43)	June 3, 1920 – February 14, 1947	Scrapped

Ship Name (No.)	Commissioned – De-commissioned	Disposition
California (BB-44)	August 10, 1921 – February 14, 1947	Scrapped
Colorado (BB-45)	August 30, 1923 – January 7, 1947	Scrapped
Maryland (BB-46)	July 21, 1921 – April 3, 1947	Scrapped
Washington (BB-47)	Never commissioned	Sunk as target, 1924
West Virginia (BB-48)	December 1, 1923 – January 9, 1947	Scrapped
North Carolina (BB-55)	April 9, 1941 – June 27, 1947	Memorial, Wilmington, NC
Washington (BB-56)	May 15, 1941 – June 27, 1947	Scrapped

*Subsequently raised, stripped of guns and superstructure, and sold for scrap, but sank en route to San Francisco from Pearl Harbor, May 17, 1947.

Note: Hull numbers BB-49 through BB-54 were assigned and hulls laid down, but were scrapped in 1923 under the terms of the Washington Treaty.

Adapted from "The Battleships" at www.navy.mil/navydata/ships/battleships/bb-list.asp.

C. COMPARATIVE RANKS OF COMMISSIONED OFFICERS IN US MILITARY SERVICES

Pay Grade	Navy and Coast Guard	Army, Air Force, Marines
O-1	Ensign	Second Lieutenant
O-2	Lieutenant, Junior Grade	First Lieutenant
O-3	Lieutenant	Captain
O-4	Lieutenant Commander	Major
O-5	Commander	Lieutenant Colonel
O-6	Captain	Colonel
O-7	Rear Admiral (lower half)	Brigadier General
O-8	Rear Admiral (upper half)	Major General
O-9	Vice Admiral	Lieutenant General
O-10	Admiral	General

Note: The *rank* of commodore—one star and equivalent in grade to a brigadier general in the Army—was abolished by the US Navy in 1899, in part because it caused confusion with the *title* of commodore, the latter bestowed upon the commanding officer of a squadron of ships no matter what his rank. Consequently, during the pre–World War II period, naval officers jumped from captain to rear admiral (two stars). The rank of commodore was temporarily reestablished during World War II with similar confusion, especially as to convoy commodores. In 1981, the US Navy broke the rank of rear admiral into rear admiral lower half (one star) and rear admiral upper half (two stars).

D. WORLD WAR II–ERA GENERAL PROTOCOLS FOR NAMING US NAVY SHIPS

Battleships (BB)	States of the Union
Aircraft carriers (CV, CVL)	Famous battles; famous predecessor ships
Escort carriers (CVE)	Sounds and bays; battles of World War II
Heavy cruisers (CA)	Cities and towns
Light cruisers (CL)	Cities and towns
Destroyers (DD)	US Navy/Marine officers and enlisted men
Destroyer escorts (DE)	US Navy/Marine officers and enlisted men
Submarines (SS)	Fish and marine creatures
Minelayers (CM, DM)	Historic monitors of the US Navy
Minesweepers (AM)	Birds
Oilers (AO)	Rivers
Transports (AP)	Presidents; famous Americans; historic places
Hospital ships (AH)	Words of comfort
Ammunition ships (AE)	Volcanoes
Cargo ships (AK)	Stars; counties of the US
Repair ships (AR)	Mythological figures
Tugboats (ATA, ATF)	Indian tribes

E. COMMAND ORGANIZATION, US PACIFIC FLEET, BATTLE FORCE, CIRCA DECEMBER 7, 1941

US PACIFIC FLEET
Admiral Husband E. Kimmel
Pennsylvania (BB-38) — Fleet Flagship

Battle Force, Pacific Fleet — Vice Admiral William S. Pye
California (BB-44) — Battle Force Flagship

Battleships, Battle Force — Rear Admiral Walter S. Anderson
West Virginia (BB-48) — Flagship

Battleship Division One — Rear Admiral Isaac C. Kidd
Arizona (BB-39) — Flagship
Nevada (BB-36)
Oklahoma (BB-37

Battleship Division Two — Rear Admiral David W. Bagley
Tennessee (BB-43) — Flagship
Pennsylvania (BB-38)
California (BB-44)

Battleship Division Four — Rear Admiral Walter S. Anderson
West Virginia (BB-48) — Flagship
Colorado (BB-45)
Maryland (BB-46)

Cruisers, Battle Force — Rear Admiral H. Fairfax Leary
Honolulu (CL-48) — Flagship

Destroyers, Battle Force — Rear Admiral Milo F. Draemel
Detroit (CL-8) — Flagship

Aircraft, Battle Force — Vice Admiral William F. Halsey
Enterprise (CV-6) — Flagship

Carrier Division One — Rear Admiral Aubrey W. Fitch
Saratoga (CV-3) — Flagship
Lexington (CV-2)

Carrier Division Two — Vice Admiral William F. Halsey
Enterprise (CV-6) — Flagship

Notes

A NOTE ABOUT SOURCES AND ABBREVIATIONS

Action Reports of Ships at Pearl Harbor are compiled on the Naval History and Heritage Command website under Archives, Digitized Collection, Action Reports, WWII Pearl Harbor Attack, and listed by individual ship; these are noted herein as "USS *Ship Name* Action Report."

Pearl Harbor Attack Hearings Before Congress are compiled at http://www.ibiblio.org/pha/congress/ and noted herein as "PHA, Part, Page."

Specific family documents from private sources are identified with names and dates of the correspondence and material and noted as being from "*Name* Family Papers." General information gathered from multiple family sources and interviews is noted as being from "*Name* Family Papers."

CHAPTER 1 – "AT 'EM *ARIZONA*"

1 John Willard Evans Oral History, December 5, 1996, box 54, folder 3, no. 247, USS *Arizona* Collection (AZ517), Special Collections, University of Arizona Libraries; Donald Stratton, with Ken Gire, *All the Gallant Men: The First Memoir by a USS Arizona Survivor* (New York: William Morrow, 2016), 36.

2   "Arizona Afloat as 75,000 Cheer," *New York Times*, June 20, 1915; Esther Ross Hoggan obituary, *Los Angeles Times*, August 27, 1979.

3   Paul Stillwell, *Battleship Arizona: An Illustrated History* (Annapolis: Naval Institute Press, 1991), 10.

4   Michael Howard, *War in European History* (Oxford: Oxford University Press, 1976), 124.

5   "The Mighty Arizona Now a Part of Navy," *New York Times*, October 18, 1916.

6   "At 'em *Arizona*" newsletters, box 37, folder 9, USS *Arizona* Collection (AZ517), Special Collections, University of Arizona Libraries.

7   Franklin D. Roosevelt, "Shall We Trust Japan?" *Asia: The American Magazine on the Orient* 23, no. 7 (July 1923): 475.

8   Arthur W. Radford, "Aircraft Battle Force," in Paul Stillwell, ed., *Air Raid: Pearl Harbor! Recollections of a Day of Infamy* (Annapolis: Naval Institute Press, 1981): 19; Albert A. Nofi, *To Train the Fleet for War: The U.S. Navy Fleet Problems, 1923–1940* (Newport, Rhode Island: Naval War College Press, 2010), 151–54. Rear Admiral Ernest J. King led a similar attack against Pearl Harbor during Fleet Problem XIX in 1938 with similar results.

9   Walter R. Borneman, *The Admirals: Nimitz, Halsey, Leahy, and King—The Five-Star Admirals Who Won the War at Sea* (New York: Little, Brown, 2012), 114–15.

10   Stillwell, *Battleship Arizona*, 124, 127; Nofi, *To Train the Fleet for War,* 155–60.

11   Grace Person Hayes, *The History of the Joint Chiefs of Staff in World War II: The War Against Japan* (Annapolis: Naval Institute Press, 1982), 4–8.

12   Stillwell, *Battleship Arizona*, 144.

13   Morris J. MacGregor, Jr., *Integration of the Armed Forces, 1940–1965* (Washington: Center of Military History, United States Army, 1981), 4–6, 11–12, 58–61. See also Richard E. Miller, *The Messman Chronicles: African Americans in the U.S. Navy, 1932–1943* (Annapolis, Naval Institute Press, 2004).

14   Stillwell, *Battleship Arizona*, 143.

15   Stillwell, *Battleship Arizona*, 155–58.

16   "At 'em *Arizona*" newsletter, April 17, 1937, box 37, folder 11, USS *Arizona* Collection.

17   Stillwell, *Battleship Arizona*, 197–98.

18   http://www.public.navy.mil/surfor/ddg100/Pages/name-sake.aspx#.WDztmneZORs

19   Everett Owen Reid Oral History, December 5, 2001, box 54, folder 4, no. 397, USS *Arizona* Collection.

20   *Arizona* Log in Stillwell, *Battleship Arizona*, 327–31.

21   George C. Dyer, *On the Treadmill to Pearl Harbor: The Memoirs of Admiral James O. Richardson* (Washington, DC: Naval History Division, 1973), 425, 435; William D. Leahy Diary, William D. Leahy Papers, Manuscript Division, Library of Congress, Washington, DC, October 8, 1940.

22   *Arizona* Log in Stillwell, *Battleship Arizona,* 217, 330–31. Kidd reported on January 23, 1941, at San Pedro.

23   "Tucson High Boy Died with Admiral," *Tucson Daily Citizen*, November 27, 1958, 4. Van Horn reported aboard the *Arizona* on August 13, 1941.

24   Stillwell, *Battleship Arizona*, 216, 331.

CHAPTER 2 – "MY BROTHER JOINED UP..."

1   Naval Station Great Lakes History, Naval Installations Command.

2   *The Bluejackets' Manual, United States Navy*, 10th ed., 1940 (Annapolis: United States Naval Institute, 1940), 3.

3   Marvin Becker to Willard Hansen, November 14, 1940, Becker Family Papers.

4   Wesley Becker to Bob Becker and Freda Becker, October 13, 1941, Becker Family Papers.

5   Herbert V. Buehl, "Tour of Duty Remembrances, December 7, 1940–December 7, 1941," unpublished manuscript (#SC1449), Wisconsin Historical Society, 10–11, accessed at http://content.wisconsinhistory.org/cdm/ref/collection/tp/id/75126.

6   Wesley Becker to Bob Becker and Freda Becker, October 13, 1941, Becker Family Papers.

CHAPTER 3 – UNSETTLED SEAS

1   Joe Klein, *Woody Guthrie: A Life* (New York: Knopf, 1980), 217–18.

2   Molly Kent, *USS* Arizona'*s Last Band: The History of U.S. Navy Band Number 22* (Kansas City, MO: Silent Song, 1996), 133–34.

3   Kent, *USS Arizona's Last Band*, 140, 145, 221.

4   Kent, *USS Arizona's Last Band*, 156.

5   Log in Stillwell, *Battleship Arizona*, 332.

6   Kent, *USS Arizona's Last Band*, 174–76, 186.

7   Kent, *USS Arizona's Last Band*, 174–76.

8   *Arizona* Log in Stillwell, *Battleship Arizona*, 332.

9   Postcard Book, Free Family Papers.

10 Stillwell, *Battleship Arizona*, 226.

11 Nikki Patrick, "Keeping the Memory of Pearl Harbor Alive," *Morning Sun* (Pittsburg, Kansas), December 7, 2001, Pearl Harbor's 60th Anniversary supplement.

12 Van Valkenburgh to Faith Van Valkenburgh Vilas, November 4, 1941, quoted in Meg Jones, *World War II Milwaukee* (Charleston, South Carolina: History Press, 2015), 19.

13 Stillwell, *Battleship Arizona*, 227.

14 Kent, *USS Arizona's Last Band*, p. 191.

15 William F. Halsey and J. Bryan III, *Admiral Halsey's Story* (New York: McGraw-Hill, 1947), 73–74; Borneman, *The Admirals*, 202–05.

16 *Press Conferences of President Franklin D. Roosevelt, 1933–1945*, Franklin D. Roosevelt Presidential Library & Museum, online edition at http://www.fdrlibrary.marist.edu/archives/collections/franklin/?p=collections/findingaid&id=508, no. 787, November 28, 1941.

17 United States Department of State, *Papers Relating to the Foreign Relations of the United States, Japan: 1931–1941*, vol. 2 (Washington, DC: Government Printing Office, 1931–1941), 768–70.

18 *New York Times*, December 2, 1941.

19 Edwin T. Layton, *"And I Was There": Pearl Harbor and Midway—Breaking the Secrets* (New York: William Morrow, 1985), 237–40.

20   *Press Conferences*, no. 788, December 2, 1941.

21   May Morse to Francis Morse, December 2, 1941, Morse Collection, box 1, folder 3.

22   May Morse to Norman Morse, December 2, 1941, Morse Collection, box 1, folder 3.

23   Kimmel to Stark, December 2, 1941, PHA, part 16, 2253–56; for Japanese submarines see http://www.ww2pacific.com/japsubs.html.

24   Layton, *"And I Was There,"* 249–52, but see Beardall's testimony about this conversation at PHA, part 11, 5284, which Layton reverses and attributes the question "When?" to Beardall.

CHAPTER 4 – CHASING GHOSTS

1   Dick Camp, *Battleship Arizona's Marines at War: Making the Ultimate Sacrifice, December 7, 1941* (St. Paul, Minnesota: Zenith Press, 2006), 13.

2   Michael T. Snyder, "Pearl Harbor: Marines Officer Was Lone Casualty from Pottstown," *Pottstown Mercury* (Pennsylvania), December 4, 2011, posted at http://www.pottsmerc.com/article/MP/20111204/TMP08/312049977.

3   California marriage records show an October 31, 1949, date of marriage between Lois Shive and Frank Westgate, although Lois used "Westgate" as her name in the 1940 census. http://search.ancestry.com/cgi-bin/sse.dll?indiv=1&db=CAMarriageRecs&h=21262856&tid=&pid=&usePUB=true&_phsrc=QGb10&_phstart=successSource&usePUBJs=true&rhSource=2469.

4   Telegram, Shive to Westgate, May 1940, Shive Family Papers.

5   Shive Family Papers.

6   Gordon Shive to Malcolm Shive, April 30, 1941, Shive Family Papers.

7   Chandler Family Papers.

8   Stratton, *All the Gallant Men*, 63; Jasper, *USS Arizona*, 82–83.

9   Jasper, Joy Waldron, James P. Delgado, and Jim Adams. *The USS Arizona: The Ship, the Men, the Pearl Harbor Attack, and the Symbol that Aroused America* (New York: St. Martin's Press, 2001),

10   Buehl, "Tour of Duty Remembrances," 5 –6.

11   Stillwell, *Battleship Arizona*, 228; Kleber S. Masterson, *"Arizona* Survivor," in *Air Raid: Pearl Harbor!*, 171.

12   Stratton, *All the Gallant Men*, 64; Jasper, *USS Arizona,* 83–84.

13   *Chicago Daily Tribune*, December 4, 1941, 1, 10, 11. For one account of the disclosure of FDR's plan see Thomas Fleming, "The Big Leak," *American Heritage*, December 1987, vol. 38, no. 8. http://ariwatch.com/Links/RainbowFive.htm.

14   *New York Times*, December 4, 1941, 12.

15   *New York Times*, December 4, 1941, 16.

16   *New York Times*, December 4, 1941, 24.

17   Layton, *"And I Was There,"* 255.

CHAPTER 5 – WEEKEND DREAMING

1   *The Bluejackets' Manual, United States Navy*, 10th ed., 1940 (Annapolis, Maryland: United States Naval Institute, 1940), 135–36.

2   Layton, *"And I Was There,"* 263.

3   PHA, part 26, 343–46. Task Force 12 ships escorting *Lexington* were the heavy cruisers *Chicago*, *Portland*, and *Astoria* and the destroyers *Porter*, *Drayton*, *Flusser*, *Lamson*, and *Mahan*.

4   Bill Dye, author's interview, Estes Park, Colorado, January 26, 2012.

5   PHA, part 26, 148.

6   PHA, part 12 (Joint Committee Exhibits 1 through 6), 345–46.

7   *Press Conferences*, no. 789, December 5, 1941; *New York Times*, December 5, 1941, 4.

8   Frances Perkins, "The President Faces War," in *Air Raid: Pearl Harbor!,* 113–15.

9   Walter R. Borneman, *MacArthur at War: World War II in the Pacific* (New York: Little, Brown, 2016), 71–72.

10   USS *Pennsylvania* Action Report.

11   The Patten story is told in Clarence Floyd Patten III and Dale E. Sporleder, *124 Years Before the Navy Mast: The Patten Family* (Carmel, Indiana: Huntington, 2006).

12   Stratton, *All the Gallant Men*, 68; Stillwell, *Battleship Arizona*, 228.

13   Stillwell, *Battleship Arizona*, 158.

14   Stillwell, *Battleship Arizona*, 228.

15   A. D. Durio, author's interview, Arnaudville, Louisiana, November 16, 2017, and Durio Family Papers.

CHAPTER 6 – "BY THIS TIME NEXT WEEK..."

1   *New York Times*, December 6, 1941, 1–2.

2   Gallup Poll Survey, no. 254-K, question no. 4, interview date 11/27–12/1/41, at http://ibiblio.org/pha/Gallup/Gallup%201941.htm. The poll broke down yes, 52 percent; no, 27 percent; no opinion, 21 percent.

3   Gordon W. Prange, *At Dawn We Slept: The Untold Story of Pearl Harbor* (New York: Penguin, 1991), 464–67; see also PHA, part 14, 1414–15.

4   United States Department of State, *Foreign Relations of the United States Diplomatic Papers, 1941. The Far East*, vol. 4 (Washington, DC: US Government Printing Office, 1941), 723–25.

5   Joseph C. Harsch, *At the Hinge of History: A Reporter's Story* (Athens: University of Georgia Press, 1993), 72–73; William Waldo Drake, "I Don't Think They'd Be Such Damned Fools," in *Air Raid: Pearl Harbor!*, 269.

6   Stillwell, *Battleship Arizona*, 228.

7   Stillwell, *Battleship Arizona*, 228.

8   Stratton, *All the Gallant Men*, 67.

9   *Honolulu Advertiser*, December 6, 1941, 1.

10 *Honolulu Advertiser*, December 6, 1941, 6.

11 *Honolulu Advertiser*, December 6, 1941, 16.

12 Football schedules, scores, and standings compiled from various sources.

13 *New York Times*, December 3, 1941, 34. The St. Louis Cardinals did indeed win the World Series in 1942.

14 Stillwell, *Battleship Arizona*, 229–30; Barb Ickes, "2 Silvis Brothers—1 dies, 1 survives attack on Pearl Harbor," *Quad-City Times* (Davenport, Iowa), December 7, 2016. Ickes is the great-granddaughter of George and Concetta Giovenazzo and daughter of Teresa Faye Giovenazzo Ickes.

15 Marvin Becker to Willard Hansen, November 25, 1941, Becker Family Collection.

16 Frances Pullara, "Remembering Pearl Harbor," Redondowriter Blog, December 7, 2004. http://redondowriter.typepad.com/sacredordinary/2004/12/remembering_pea.html

17 Edward "Bud" Heidt to Donna Streur, November 29, 1941, Streur Family Papers.

18 Wesley Heidt to Genevieve Dunlap, November 22, 1941, quoted in Laura Orr, "Pearl Harbor Experiences," unpublished manuscript, Hampton Roads Naval Museum, 8.

19 Edward "Bud" Heidt to Julia Heidt Duncan, November 24, 1941, Program Subject Files within record group 64, records of the National Archives and Records Administration.

20 *Tucson Daily Citizen*, November 27, 1958, 4.

CHAPTER 7 – LUCK OF THE DRAW

1 *Fort Payne Journal* (Alabama), November 15, 1939.

2 Kent, *USS Arizona's Last Band*, 201–03.

3 *New York Times Book Review*, December 7, 1941, 37.

4 *Honolulu Advertiser*, December 6, 1941, 9.

5 *Honolulu Advertiser*, December 7, 1941, 13.

6 Kent, *USS Arizona's Last Band*, 202–06; http://archive.mcclendon-winters.com/Obits/streight,asa.htm.

7 Prange, *At Dawn We Slept*, 474–76; Layton, *"And I Was There,"* 290; see PHA, part 10, 4662 for "This means war" quote.

8 Kleber S. Masterson, "Arizona Survivor," in *Air Raid: Pearl Harbor!*, 172.

9 Everett Owen Reid Oral History, December 5, 2001, box 54, folder 4, no. 397, USS *Arizona* Collection; Stillwell, *Battleship Arizona*, 231.

10 http://tree.wellswooster.com/getperson.php?personID=I40767&tree=Earle; December 7, 1941, Experience of John H. Earle (Col., USMC Ret.); Camp, *Battleship Arizona's Marines at War*, 69–74.

11 Shive to Westgate, March 31, 1941, Shive Family Papers.

12 Shive to Balfour, April 18, 1941, Shive Family Papers.

13   Shive to Balfour, November 2, 1941, Shive Family Papers.

14   Shive to Balfour, November 26, 1941, Shive Family Papers.

CHAPTER 8 – DAWN

1   Prange, *At Dawn We Slept*, 485–87, but see PHA, part 12, 245 for text and part 12, 248 for execute wording.

2   PHA, part 14, 1334.

3   Holly Zachariah, "Recalling the Miller Boys," *Columbus Dispatch*, November 12, 2011, http://www.dispatch.com/content/stories/local/2011/11/12/recalling-the-miller-boys.html.

4   USS *Ward* Action Report; PHA, part 37, 704 for radio log; and part 22, 319 for Kimmel's Roberts Commission testimony.

5   *New York Times*, December 7, 1941, 1.

6   *New York Times*, December 7, 1941, 4E.

7   *New York Times*, December 7, 1941, 61.

8   *New York Times*, December 7, 1941, section 5 (Sports), 1.

9   Camp, *Battleship Arizona's Marines at War*, 73–74.

10   Undated family memoir, Clara May Dyer Morse Collection (manuscript no. 453), History Colorado, Denver, Colorado, box 1, folder 4.

11   Note dated December 16, 1936, Morse Collection, box 1, folder 1.

12   Francis Morse to May Morse, August 29, 1938, Morse Collection, box 1, folder 4.

13   Note dated April 24, 1939, Morse Collection, box 1, folder 3.

14   Prange, *At Dawn We Slept*, 499–501. One of the twelve aircraft turned back to California during the night with engine trouble.

15   Larry Kimmett and Margaret Regis, *The Attack on Pearl Harbor: An Illustrated History* (Seattle: Navigator Publishing, 1991), 30.

16   Stillwell, *Battleship Arizona*, 231.

17   Kent, *USS Arizona's Last Band*, 213–15.

18   Stillwell, *Battleship Arizona*, 233; Dick Camp, "And the Band Played On: The Marine Detachment, USS *Arizona*," *Leatherneck*, vol. 89, no. 12 (December 2006).

19   Prange, *At Dawn We Slept*, 481, 508–09.

20   Kent, *USS Arizona's Last Band*, 219–22.

21   Prange, *At Dawn We Slept*, 510.

CHAPTER 9 – "ANDY, WHO ARE THOSE GUYS?"

1   Shaun McKinnon, "John Anderson, one of the last USS *Arizona* survivors, dies at 98," *Arizona Republic* (Phoenix), November 15, 2015, https://www.azcentral.com/story/news/local/best-reads/2015/11/16/pearl-harbor-uss-arizona-survivor-john-anderson-dies/75878586/.

2   Stillwell, *Battleship Arizona*, 244–45.

3   Kimmett and Regis, *The Attack on Pearl Harbor*, 36–41; USS *Oklahoma*, *West Virginia*, *California*, *Nevada*, *Oglala*, and *Helena* Action Reports; Russell McCurdy Oral History, December 4, 1996, box 54, folder 3, no. 241, USS *Arizona* Collection.

4   John Anderson Oral History, December 9, 1981, box 54, folder 1, no. 43, USS *Arizona* Collection; Stillwell, *Battleship Arizona*, 264–65.

5   Stillwell, *Battleship Arizona*, 264–65; USS *Vestal* Action Report; Kimmett and Regis, *Attack on Pearl Harbor*, 46–50; USS *Arizona* Action Report, statement of Douglas Hein.

6   Stillwell, *Battleship Arizona*, 246.

7   "Attack at Pearl Harbor, 1941," EyeWitness to History, http://www.eyewitnesstohistory.com/pearl.htm.

8   Henry Donald Davison Oral History, December 4, 1986, box 54, folder 1, no. 176, USS *Arizona* Collection.

9   George Phraner, "George Phraner's Brush with Death Aboard the USS *Arizona*—Pearl Harbor, HI," http://iloveww2warbirds.com/pearl-harbor-survivor-story/.

10 Orr, "Pearl Harbor Experiences," 6.

11 Kimmett and Regis, *Attack on Pearl Harbor*, 107.

12 Frank Curre, "Living to Tell the Horrible Tale of Pearl Harbor," from StoryCorps, NPR Morning Edition, November 11, 2011 https://www.npr.org/programs/morning-edition/2011/11/11/142216387/ .

13 Mark Carlson, "Eyewitnesses on Battleship Row," *World War II History*, December 2016, http://warfarehistorynetwork.com/daily/wwii/eye-witnesses-on-battleship-row/.

14 Howard French Interview in Gordon W. Prange with Donald M. Goldstein and Katherine V. Dillon, *Dec. 7, 1941: The Day the Japanese Attacked Pearl Harbor* (New York: McGraw-Hill, 1988), 134, 140–41.

15 Robert H. Meyer, unpublished manuscript, May 15, 2001, Meyer Family Papers.

16 Warriner Family Papers.

17 Buehl, "Tour of Duty Remembrances," 3–4, 14–15.

18 Prange, *At Dawn We Slept*, 505, 507.

19 Halsey, *Admiral Halsey's Story*, 76–77.

20 PHA, part 8, 3819, 3835–38.

21 Stanley Weintraub, *Long Day's Journey into War, December 7, 1941* (New York: Dutton, 1991), 238–39; Prange, *At Dawn We Slept*, 555; PHA, part 14, 1411.

22 Harsch, *At the Hinge of History*, 73–75.

23 Stillwell, *Battleship* Arizona, 244–45.

CHAPTER 10 – "MY BROTHER'S UP THERE!"

1   Becker Family Papers.

2   *Honolulu Star-Advertiser*, December 8, 1979, 19.

3   Camp, *Battleship Arizona's Marines at War*, 80, 82, 84, 96; USS *Tennessee* Action Report.

4   Shive to Balfour, November 26, 1941, Shive Family Papers.

5   Camp, *Battleship Arizona's Marines at War*, 87, 89.

6   Stillwell, *Battleship Arizona*, p. 233.

7   John Anderson interview, Don Smith NewsVideo; Michael E. Ruane, "One died at Pearl Harbor, the other lived. Seventy-five years later, they'll be reunited," *Washington Post*, December 6, 2016 at https://www.washingtonpost.com/local/one-died-at-pearl-harbor-the-other-lived-seventy-five-years-later-theyll-be-reunited/2016/12/05/79fdeee8-aaa0-11e6-977a-1030f822fc35_story.html?utm_term=.0563f6ee69b7.

8   Weintraub, *Long Day's Journey*, 549.

9   John Crawford interview in Prange, *Dec. 7, 1941*, 145.

10 Prange, *At Dawn We Slept*, 514.

11 USS *Vestal* Action Report; Stratton, *All the Gallant Men*, 87, 96, 98–105; Russell Lott Oral History, December 4, 1996, box 54, folder 2, no. 240, USS *Arizona* Collection. Alvin Dvorak died of his wounds weeks later while en route to treatment in California. The other five survived, and after recovering, all returned to service, four on destroyers and one, Earl Riner, on the aircraft carrier *Lake Champlain* (CV-39).

12   Patten and Sporleder, *124 Years Before the Navy Mast*, 170–72.

13   Anderson Oral History, December 9, 1981, USS *Arizona* Collection; USS *Arizona* Action Report, statement of J. A. Doherty.

14   Leland Howard Burk reminiscences at http://www.ussarizona.org/index.php/features/arizona-survivor-stories/1556-burk-leland-howard-story.

CHAPTER 11 – "ABANDON SHIP!"

1   Kimmett and Regis, *The Attack on Pearl Harbor*, 68–73; Meyer Family Papers; USS *Nevada* Torpedo and Bomb Damage Report at http://www.researcheratlarge.com/Ships/BB36/PearlHarborDamageReport/#SectionII.

2   https://www.otrcat.com/air-raid-pearl-habor.

3   Jan Landon, "A Brother Lost," *Topeka Capital Journal*, December 2, 2001, at http://cjonline.com/stories/120201/mid_christiansen.shtml#1.

4   Clyde Jefferson Combs Oral History, December 5, 1996, box 54, folder 3, no. 246, USS *Arizona* Collection.

5   Clinton Howard Westbrook Oral History, December 4, 1996, box 54, folder 3, no. 245, USS *Arizona* Collection.

6   Andy Lindstrom, "Day of Infamy," *Tallahassee Democrat*, December 7, 1991, 1, 4A.

7   USS *Arizona* Action Report, Statement of J. A. Doherty.

8   Samuel Glenn Fuqua, Medal of Honor citation at https://history.army.mil/html/moh/wwII-a-f.html#FUQUA.

9   Hazel Ashcraft, "Arizona survivor Earl Pecotte remembers fateful day of sinking," *Jonesboro Sun* (Arkansas), December 1, 1991; Stillwell, *Battleship Arizona*, 234.

10   Stillwell, *Battleship Arizona*, 235, 238; Russell McCurdy Oral History, December 4, 1996, box 54, folder 3, no. 241, USS *Arizona* Collection.

11   Glenn Lane Oral History, December 6, 1996, box 54, folder 2, no. 239, USS *Arizona* Collection.

12   Miller, *The Messman Chronicles*, 181; *Congressional Record*, Extension of Remarks, E1186 (June 16, 2006) at https://www.congress.gov/crec/2006/06/16/CREC-2006-06-16-pt1-PgE1186.pdf.

13   Orr, "Pearl Harbor Experiences," 8.

14   Ashcraft, "Arizona survivor Earl Pecotte;" Stillwell, *Battleship Arizona*, 234.

15   Larry "Silas" Elliott Oral History, December 8, 1991, box 54, folder 2, no. 223, USS *Arizona* Collection.

CHAPTER 12 – THE WAITING

1   Jack Rogo Letter in Prange, *Dec. 7, 1941*, 331.

2   See Prange, *At Dawn We Slept*, 541–50, for analysis of the failure of the Japanese to launch a third strike. See also, Samuel Eliot Morison, *Strategy and Compromise* (Boston: Little, Brown, 1958), 67, for Morison's appraisal that the Japanese attack was "only a qualified tactical success because no aircraft carrier was sunk, and the installations and fuel tanks at Pearl Harbor were hardly touched."

3   Weintraub, *Long Day's Journey*, 245–47.

4   Diary, December 7, 1941, *The Diaries of Henry Lewis Stimson in the Yale University Library* (New Haven: Yale University Library, 1973).

5   Cordell Hull, *The Memoirs of Cordell Hull* (New York: MacMillan, 1948), 1096–97; Dean Acheson, *Present at the Creation: My Years in the State Department* (New York: Norton, 1969), 35. Hull himself took exception to reports of his language and wrote in his memoirs that no "cussing out" could have made his feelings any stronger to the Japanese.

6   Camp, *Battleship Arizona's Marines at War*, 103–04.

7   Weintraub, *Long Day's Journey*, 277, 308; "Rubinstein Soloist in Brahms Concerto," *New York Times*, December 8, 1941, 30; concert program at: http://archives.nyphil.org/index.php/artifact/b753cbcd 7915-44359a0c-fa13fe7b5309-0.1/fullview#page/1/mode/2up.

8   Weintraub, *Long Day's Journey*, 305–06; "55,051 See Dodgers Beat Giants," *New York Times*, December 8, 1941, 32.

9   "Nye Slow Giving News to Firsters," *Pittsburgh Post-Gazette*, December 8, 1941, 13; "America Firsters Jeer President as Nye and Others Conceal Awful Truth," *Pittsburgh Press*, December 8, 1941, 2, 18; James A. Kehl, "The Next Page: With the attack on Pearl Har-

bor, a collapse of 'isms,'" *Pittsburgh Post-Gazette*, November 30, 2014, at http://www.post-gazette.com/opinion/Op-Ed/2014/11/30/The-Next-Page-With-the-attack-on-Pearl-Harbor-a-collapse-of-isms/stories/201411300177.

10 Klein, *Woody Guthrie*, 214, 225–26.

11 Shive Family Papers.

12 May Morse to Norman Morse, December 7–8, 1941, Morse Collection, box 1, folder 3.

13 May Morse to Francis Morse, December 7–8, 1941, Morse Collection, box 1, folder 3.

14 Giovenazzo Family Papers.

15 Pullara, "Remembering Pearl Harbor," Redondowriter Blog, December 7, 2004.

16 "Japs Open War on U.S. with Bombing of Hawaii," *Los Angeles Times*, December 8, 1941, 1.

17 Becker Family Papers.

18 Durio Family Papers.

19 Winston S. Churchill, *The Second World War*, vol. 3, *The Grand Alliance* (Boston: Houghton Mifflin, 1950), 604–05.

20 Stimson Diaries, December 7, 1941; Prange, *At Dawn We Slept*, 557–59; *Washington Post*, December 8, 1941.

21 Prange, *At Dawn We Slept*, 568.

22 Meyer Family Papers; Andre B. Sobocinski, "Navy Medicine at Pearl Harbor (Dec. 7, 1941)," Navy Medicine Live blog http://navymedicine.navylive.dodlive.mil/archives/3809.

23 Ruth Erickson interview in Prange, *Dec. 7, 1941*, 231.

24 Camp, *Battleship Arizona's Marines at War*, 105–06.

25 Stillwell, *Battleship Arizona*, 253; Leon Grabowsky Oral History interview (#OH0131), East Carolina Manuscript Collection, J. Y. Joyner Library, East Carolina University, Greenville, North Carolina. Masterson identified Ensign James Ashton Dare as being with him instead of Grabowsky in his account in "*Arizona* Survivor," *Air Raid: Pearl Harbor!*, 172–74.

CHAPTER 13 – "YESTERDAY, DECEMBER 7 . . ."

1   *Honolulu Advertiser*, December 8, 1941, 1, 8.

2   "Day of Infamy" speech at http://docs.fdrlibrary.marist.edu/tmirhdee.html.

3   "The Only U.S. Politician to Vote Against War With Japan 75 Years Ago Was This Remarkable Woman," *Washington Post*, December 8, 2016; *Emporia Gazette* (Kansas), December 10, 1941, 4.

4   Patten and Sporleder, *124 Years Before the Navy Mast*, 177, 179. With the *Nevada* going nowhere any time soon, Ted's six brothers aboard the battleship were temporarily assigned to the carrier *Lexington*. Five months later, it sank at the Battle of the Coral Sea, and the Patten family endured another tense time before learning that once again all six brothers were safe.

5   Mary Buckhelt, "For Feller, Navy Decision Was Easy," at http://www.espn.com/espn/page2/story?page=buckheit/091112&sportCat=mlb; *New York Times*, December 15, 2010; *Life*, May 12, 1941, 51.

6   Joseph Kopcho Langdell Oral History, December 5, 1996, box 54, folder 4, no. 251, USS *Arizona* Collection; Elahe Izadi, "The USS *Arizona*'s last surviving officer has died. How the Pearl Harbor hero recalled the day of infamy," *Washington Post*, February 10, 2015, at https://www.washingtonpost.com/news/morning-mix/wp/2015/02/10/the-uss-arizonas-last-surviving-officer-has-died-howthe-pearl harbor-hero-recalled-the-day-of-infamy/?utm_term=.3aa31fbdc71f; Stillwell, *Battleship Arizona*, 255–56.

7   Example of postcard at: http://www.navyhistory.org/2013/12/i-am well-letter-follows-at-first-opportunity-pearl-harbor-survivor postcard/.

8   Stillwell, *Battleship Arizona*, 267–68.

9   Landon, "A Brother Lost," *Topeka Capital Journal*, December 2, 2001; Patrick, "Keeping the memory of Pearl Harbor alive," *Morning Sun* (Pittsburg, Kansas), December 7, 2001.

10 *Press Conferences*, no. 790, December 9, 1941; Fireside Chat no. 19, December 9, 1941, http://docs.fdrlibrary.marist.edu/120941.html.

11 Prange, *Dec. 7, 1941*, 337.

CHAPTER 14 – "THE SECRETARY OF THE NAVY REGRETS . . . "

1   Borneman, *The Admirals*, 212–13.

2   *Kansas City Star* (Missouri), December 4, 1991.

3   *Shawnee Mission Post* (Kansas), December 6, 2013.

4   Barb Ickes, "2 Silvis Brothers" "Silvis Sailor Listed as Missing, Safe, Reported a Casualty," *Daily Dispatch* (Moline, Illinois), February 16, 1942.

5   *Daily Dispatch* (Moline, Illinois), January 21, 1944; Ickes, "2 Silvis Brothers."

6   Diary, December 25, 1941, Morse Collection, box 2.

7   Fuqua to Morse, December 28, 1941, Morse Collection, box 1, folder 3.

8   Jacobs to Morse, January 30, 1942, Morse Collection, box 1, folder 4.

9   Knox to Morse, February 2, 1942, Morse Collection, box 1, folder 4.

10 Pat Kinney, "Albert Sullivan's widow looks back," *Waterloo-Cedar Falls Courier* (Iowa), November 11, 2012 at http://wcfcourier.com/news/local/albert-sullivan-s-widow-looks-back/article_e0e04cf3-954d51d8-817d-3d8fda4d67f8.html.

11 Unknown clipping, Free Family Papers.

12 Westgate to Shive, January 10, 1942, Shive Family Papers.

13 Homann to Westgate, January 27, 1942, Shive Family Papers.

14 Amy Wilson and Andy Alison, "The Brothers," *Orange County Register* (Anaheim), May 20, 2001; since 1983, it has been the Laguna Presbyterian Church.

15 Shive Family Papers; Balfour Family Papers.

16 Kent, *USS Arizona's Last Band*, 203.

17 Durio Family Papers.

18 Julia D. Brown, ed., *A History of World War II Veterans from DeKalb County, Alabama* (Fort Payne, Alabama: Landmarks of DeKalb County, 2008) at http://www.landmarksdekalbal.org/publications-landmarks-dekalb-county-alabama/world-war two-veteransbook/murdock-brothers/. The fourth Murdock brother, Verlon Aaron, followed his brothers into the Navy and was stationed in Los Angeles at the time of the attack. The youngest brother, Kenneth Dewayne, although only fourteen, dropped out of school, lied about his age, and enlisted just prior to December 7, 1941. While in

basic training, his true age was discovered; he was promptly discharged and never served. Thomas Murdock retired from the Navy years later as a lieutenant commander.

CHAPTER 15 – THOSE LEFT TO REMEMBER

1 https:www.nps.gov/valr/learn/historyculture/names-of-uss-arizona-brothers.htm.

2 Bureau of Naval Personnel (BuPers) Information Bulletin no. 304, July 1942; BuPers Circular Letter, no. 345–44, 15 November 1944; and BuPers Circular Letter no. 281–45, 28 September 1945 at "The Sullivan Brothers: U.S. Navy Policy Regarding Family Members Serving Together at Sea," Naval History and Heritage Command, www.history.navy.mil/browse-by-topic/disasters-and-phenomena/the-sullivan-brothers-and-the-assignment-of-family-members/sullivan-brothers-policy-family-members.

3 *Press-Gazette* (Hillsboro, Ohio), December 23, 1941, 1; *Portsmouth Times* (Ohio), December 7, 1942.

4 *Shawnee Mission Post* (Kansas), December 6, 2013; Becker Family Papers.

5 *Kansas City Star* (Missouri), December 4, 1991; Becker Family Papers.

6 Warriner Family Papers.

7 Zachariah, "Recalling the Miller Boys," *The Columbus Dispatch*, November 12, 2011.

8 Author's interview with A. D. Durio, Arnaudville, Louisiana, November 16, 2017.

9 Regina Dennis, "Waco Native Frank Curre, a Pearl Harbor Survivor, Dies on 70th Anniversary of Attack," *Waco Tribune-Herald*, December 8, 2011, at http://www.wacotrib.com/news/waco-native-frank curre-apearl-harbor-survivor-dies-on/article_993c338e-2adf 59d3-9bcd7737d072a4b9.html.

10 *Pioneer Press* (St. Paul, Minnesota), November 17, 2015, http://www.twincities.com/2015/11/17/for-mer-minnesotan-oldest-survivor-of-uss-arizona-attack-dies-at-98/.

11 Keith Rogers, "On Pearl Harbor anniversary, 2 who lived join fallen

USS *Arizona* comrades beneath the waves," *Las Vegas Review-Journal*, December 7, 2016 at https://www.reviewjournal.com/news/military/on-pearl-harbor-anniversary-2-who-lived-join-fallen uss-arizonacomrades-beneath-the-waves/.

12 USS *Arizona* Interments, World War II Valor in the Pacific National Monument, at https://www.nps.gov/valr/learn/historyculture/ussarizonainterments.htm.

13 Amanda Minton, "Our History: Galen Steve Velia and the USS *Arizona*," *Morning Sun* (Pittsburg, Kansas), December 4, 2017, http://www.morningsun.net/news/20171204/our-history-galensteve-velia-and-uss-arizona.

14 American Battle Monuments Commission, at http://www.abmc.gov/cemeteries-memorials/americas/honolulu-memorial#.WgM2q7aZORs.

15 Lyrics, Morse Collection, box 1, folder 1.

16 Diary, July 12, July 19, November 22, 1942, Morse Collection, box 2.

17 Diary, December 7, 1954, Morse Collection, box 2.

EPILOGUE: BROTHERS ALL

1 Borneman, *The Admirals*, 220–21.

Bibliography

I. OFFICIAL HISTORIES, PUBLICATIONS, AND REPORTS

Action Reports of Ships at Pearl Harbor, Naval History & Heritage Command.

Congressional Record

Hayes, Grace Person. *The History of the Joint Chiefs of Staff in World War II: The War Against Japan*. Annapolis: Naval Institute Press, 1982.

MacGregor, Morris J., Jr. *Integration of the Armed Forces, 1940–1965*. Washington: Center of Military History, United States Army, 1981.

Morton, Louis. *Strategy and Command: The First Two Years*. Vol. 1 of *The United States Army in World War II: The War in the Pacific*. Washington: Center of Military History, United States Army, 1962.

Pearl Harbor Attack Hearings Before Congress at http://www.ibiblio.org/pha/congress/.

United States Department of State. *Foreign Relations of the United States Diplomatic Papers, 1941. The Far East*, vol. 4. Washington, DC: US Government Printing Office, 1941.

United States Department of State. *Papers Relating to the Foreign Relations of the United States, Japan: 1931–1941*, vol. 2. Washington, DC: Government Printing Office, 1931–1941.

United States Navy. *The Bluejackets' Manual*, 1940 Tenth Edition. Annapolis: United States Naval Institute, 1940.

II. PERSONAL MEMOIRS AND DIARIES

Acheson, Dean. *Present at the Creation: My Years in the State Department*. New York: Norton, 1969.

Churchill, Winston S. *The Second World War,* vol. 3, *The Grand Alliance*. Boston: Houghton Mifflin, 1950. (Chartwell Edition)

Grew, Joseph C. *Ten Years in Japan*. New York: Simon and Schuster, 1944.

Halsey, William F. and J. Bryan III. *Admiral Halsey's Story*. New York: McGraw-Hill, 1947.

Harsch, Joseph C. *At the Hinge of History: A Reporter's Story*. Athens: University of Georgia Press, 1993.

Hull, Cordell. *The Memoirs of Cordell Hull*. New York: MacMillan, 1948.

Kimmel, Husband E. *Admiral Kimmel's Story*. Chicago: Henry Regnery, 1955.

Layton, Edwin T. *"And I Was There": Pearl Harbor and Midway—Breaking the Secrets*. New York: William Morrow, 1985.

Stimson, Henry Lewis. *The Diaries of Henry Lewis Stimson in the Yale University Library*. New Haven: Yale University Library, 1973. Microfilm.

Stimson, Henry L. and McGeorge Bundy. *On Active Service in Peace and War*. New York: Harper & Brothers, 1948.

Stratton, Donald, with Ken Gire. *All the Gallant Men: The First Memoir by a USS* Arizona *Survivor*. New York: William Morrow, 2016.

III. SECONDARY SOURCES

Borneman, Walter R. *The Admirals: Nimitz, Halsey, Leahy, and King—The Five-Star Admirals Who Won the War at Sea*. New York: Little, Brown, 2012.

Borneman, Walter R. *MacArthur at War: World War II in the Pacific*. New York: Little, Brown, 2016.

Brown, Julia D., ed., *A History of World War II Veterans from DeKalb County, Alabama.* Fort Payne, Alabama: Landmarks of DeKalb County, 2008.

Camp, Dick. *Battleship Arizona's Marines at War: Making the Ultimate Sacrifice, December 7, 1941.* St. Paul, Minnesota: Zenith Press, 2006.

Dyer, George C. *On the Treadmill to Pearl Harbor: The Memoirs of Admiral James O. Richardson.* Washington, DC: Naval History Division, 1973.

Howard, Michael. *War in European History.* Oxford: Oxford University Press, 1976.

Jasper, Joy Waldron, James P. Delgado, and Jim Adams. *The USS Arizona: The Ship, the Men, the Pearl Harbor Attack, and the Symbol That Aroused America.* New York: St. Martin's Press, 2001.

Jones, Meg. *World War II Milwaukee.* Charleston, South Carolina: History Press, 2015.

Kent, Molly. *USS Arizona's Last Band: The History of US Navy Band Number 22.* Kansas City, Missouri: Silent Song, 1996.

Kimmett, Larry and Margaret Regis. *The Attack on Pearl Harbor: An Illustrated History.* Seattle: Navigator Publishing, 1991.

Klein, Joe. *Woody Guthrie: A Life.* New York: Knopf, 1980.

Miller, Richard E. *The Messman Chronicles: African Americans in the US Navy, 1932–1943.* Annapolis: Naval Institute Press, 2004.

Morison, Samuel Eliot. *Strategy and Compromise.* Boston: Little, Brown, 1958.

Nofi, Albert A. *To Train the Fleet for War: The US Navy Fleet Problems, 1923–1940.* Newport, Rhode Island: Naval War College Press, 2010.

Patten, Clarence Floyd, III and Dale E. Sporleder. *124 Years Before the Navy Mast: The Patten Family.* Carmel, Indiana: Huntington, 2006.

Pogue, Forrest C. *George C. Marshall: Ordeal and Hope, 1939–1942.* New York: Viking, 1966.

Prange, Gordon W. *At Dawn We Slept: The Untold Story of Pearl Harbor.* New York: Penguin, 1991.

Prange, Gordon W. with Donald M. Goldstein and Katherine V. Dillon. *Dec. 7, 1941: The Day the Japanese Attacked Pearl Harbor.* New York: McGraw-Hill, 1988.

Slackman, Michael. *Remembering Pearl Harbor: The Story of the USS Arizona Memorial.* Honolulu: USS *Arizona* Memorial Museum Association, 1998.

Stillwell, Paul, ed. *Air Raid: Pearl Harbor! Recollections of a Day of Infamy.* Annapolis: Naval Institute Press, 1981.

Stillwell, Paul. *Battleship Arizona: An Illustrated History.* Annapolis: Naval Institute Press, 1991.

Weintraub, Stanley. *Long Day's Journey into War, December 7, 1941.* New York: Dutton, 1991.

IV. ARTICLES

Ashcraft, Hazel. "Arizona survivor Earl Pecotte remembers fateful day of sinking," *Jonesboro Sun* (Arkansas), December 1, 1991.

Benson, Lee. "Provo resident returns to Pearl Harbor 75 years later," *Deseret News* (Salt Lake City), December 6, 2016.

Camp, Dick. "And the Band Played On: The Marine Detachment, USS *Arizona*," *Leatherneck*, vol. 89, no. 12 (December 2006).

Carlson, Mark. "Eyewitnesses on Battleship Row," *World War II History*, December 2016.

Curre, Frank, "Living to Tell the Horrible Tale of Pearl Harbor," from StoryCorps, NPR Morning Edition, November 11, 2011.

Dennis, Regina. "Waco Native Frank Curre, a Pearl Harbor Survivor, Dies on 70th Anniversary of Attack," *Waco Tribune-Herald*, December 8, 2011.

Izadi, Elahe. "The USS *Arizona*'s last surviving officer has died. How the Pearl Harbor hero recalled the day of infamy," *Washington Post*, February 10, 2015.

Ickes, Barb. "2 Silvis Brothers—1 dies, 1 survives attack on Pearl Harbor, *Quad-City Times* (Davenport, Iowa), December 7, 2016.

Kehl, James A. "The Next Page: With the attack on Pearl Harbor, a collapse of 'isms,'" *Pittsburgh Post-Gazette*, November 30, 2014.

Kinney, Pat. "Albert Sullivan's Widow Looks Back," *Waterloo-Cedar Falls Courier* (Iowa), November 11, 2012.

Landon, Jan. "A Brother Lost," *Topeka Capital Journal*, December 2, 2001.

McKinnon, Shaun. "John Anderson, One of the Last USS *Arizona* Survivors, Dies at 98, *Arizona Republic* (Phoenix), November 15, 2015.

Minton, Amanda. "Our History: Galen Steve Velia and the USS *Arizona*," *Morning Sun* (Pittsburg, Kansas), December 4, 2017.

Motsinger, Carol. "The Miller Boys, Brothers in Life, in Arms, in Death," *Cincinnati Enquirer*, December 3, 2016.

Patrick, Nikki. "Keeping the Memory of Pearl Harbor Alive," *Morning Sun* (Pittsburg, Kansas), December 7, 2001, Pearl Harbor's 60th Anniversary supplement.

Phraner, George. "George Phraner's Brush with Death Aboard the USS *Arizona* – Pearl Harbor, HI." http://iloveww2warbirds.com/pearl-harbor-survivor-story/.

Pullara, Frances. "Remembering Pearl Harbor," Redondowriter Blog, December 7, 2004. http://redondowriter.typepad.com/sacredordinary/2004/12/remembering_pea.html

Rogers, Keith. "On Pearl Harbor anniversary, 2 who lived join fallen USS *Arizona* comrades beneath the waves," *Las Vegas Review-Journal*, December 7, 2016.

Roosevelt, Franklin D. "Shall We Trust Japan?" *Asia: The American Magazine on the Orient* 23, no. 7 (July 1923), 475–78.

Ruane, Michael E., "One died at Pearl Harbor, the other lived. They'll be reunited 75 years later," *Washington Post*, December 6, 2016.

Snyder, Michael T. "Pearl Harbor: Marines Officer Was Lone Casualty from Pottstown," *Pottstown Mercury* (Pennsylvania), December 4, 2011.

Wilson, Amy and Andy Alison, "The Brothers," *Orange County Register* (Anaheim), May 20, 2001.

Zachariah, Holly. "Recalling the Miller Boys," *Columbus Dispatch*, November 12, 2011.

V. PERSONAL PAPERS AND MANUSCRIPT
COLLECTIONS

USS *Arizona* Collection (AZ 517). Special Collections, University of Arizona Libraries, Tucson, Arizona.

Charles Claude Bloch Papers, Naval Historical Foundation Collection, Manuscript Division, Library of Congress, Washington, DC.

Leon Grabowsky Oral History Interview (#OH0131), East Carolina Manuscript Collection, J. Y. Joyner Library, East Carolina University, Greenville, North Carolina.

William Frederick Halsey Papers, Manuscript Division, Library of Congress, Washington, DC.

Husband Edward Kimmel Papers, 1907–1999, American Heritage Center, University of Wyoming, Laramie, Wyoming.

William D. Leahy Diary, William D. Leahy Papers, Manuscript Division, Library of Congress, Washington, DC.

Clara May Dyer Morse Collection (#453), History Colorado, Denver, Colorado.

Press Conferences of President Franklin D. Roosevelt, 1933–1945, Franklin D. Roosevelt Presidential Library & Museum, on-line edition at http://www.fdrlibrary.marist.edu/archives/collections/franklin/?p=collections/findingaid&id=508.

Walter Campbell Short Papers, Hoover Institution Archives, Stanford University, Palo Alto, California.

VI. FAMILY PAPERS, INTERVIEWS, AND UNPUBLISHED
MANUSCRIPTS

Specific family documents from private sources are identified in the notes with names and dates of the correspondence and material, and noted as being from "*Name* Family Papers." General information gathered from multiple family sources, emails, and interviews is noted as being from *"Name* Family Papers."

Family Papers

Becker Family Papers
Chandler Family Papers
Christiansen Family Papers
Durio Family Papers
Free Family Papers
Giovenazzo Family Papers
Hansen Family Papers
Meyer Family Papers
Miller Family Papers
Murdock Family Papers
Shive Family Papers
Streur Family Papers
Warriner Family Papers

Interviews by the Author

(Does not include family telephone and email exchanges)
Becker Family Teleconference, May 9, 2017
Lonnie Cook, by telephone, September 26, 2017
A. D. Durio, Arnaudville, Louisiana, November 16, 2017
Bill Dye, Estes Park, Colorado, January 26, 2012
J. R. Givens, San Diego, California, September 8, 2017
Ken Potts, by telephone, March 13, 2018
Don and Randy Stratton, Colorado Springs, Colorado, October 26, 2017
Warriner Family Teleconference, August 7, 2017

Unpublished Manuscripts

Buehl, Herbert V. "Tour of Duty Remembrances, December 7, 1940 – December 7, 1941," unpublished manuscript

(#SC1449), Wisconsin Historical Society, Madison, Wisconsin. http://content.wisconsinhistory.org/cdm/ref/collection/tp/id/75126.

Orr, Laura "Pearl Harbor Experiences," unpublished manuscript, Hampton Roads Naval Museum, Norfold, Virginia.

VII. ONLINE RESOURCES

"American Battle Monuments Commission," http://www.abmc.gov/cemeteries-memorials/americas/honolulu-memorial#.WgM2q7aZORs.

"Day of Infamy Speech," http://docs.fdrlibrary.marist.edu/tmirhdee.html.

"John H. Earle Experience," http://archive.mcclendon-winters.com/Obits/streight,asa.htm.

"Fireside Chat #19, December 9, 1941," http://docs.fdrlibrary.marist.edu/120941.html.

"For Feller, Navy Decision Was Easy," http://www.espn.com/espn/page2/story?page=buckheit/091112&sportCat=mlb.

"Fuqua Medal of Honor Citation," https://history.army.mil/html/moh/wwII-a-f.html#FUQUA.

"Gallup Poll," http://ibiblio.org/pha/Gallup/Gallup%201941.htm.

"Japanese Submarines at Pearl Harbor," http://www.ww2pacific.com/japsubs.html.

Leland Howard Burk reminiscences, http://www.ussarizona.org/index.php/features/arizona-survivor-stories/1556-burk-leland-howard-story.

"Names of USS *Arizona* Brothers," https://www.nps.gov/valr/learn/historyculture/names-of-uss-arizona-brothers.htm.

"Naming Ships," http://www.fas.org/man/dod-101/sys/ship/names.htm.

"Navy Medicine at Pearl Harbor (Dec. 7, 1941)," http://navymedicine.navylive.dodlive.mil/archives/3809.

"New York Philharmonic Program," http://archives.nyphil.org/index.php/artifact/b753cbcd-7915-4435-9a0c-fa13fe7b5309-0.1/fullview#page/1/mode/2up.

"Asa Everett Streight Obituary," http://archive.mcclendon-winters.com/Obits/streight,asa.htm.

"The Sullivan Brothers: US Navy Policy Regarding Family Members Serving Together at Sea," Naval History & Heritage Command, www.history.navy.mil/browse-by-topic/disasters-and-phenomena/the-sullivan-brothers-and-the-assignment-of-family-members/sullivan-brothers-policy-family-members.

"Survivors Postcard," http://www.navyhistory.org/2013/12/i-am-well-letter-follows-at-first-opportunity-pearl-harbor-survivor-postcard/.

"USS *Arizona* Interments, World War II Valor in the Pacific National Monument," https://www.nps.gov/valr/learn/historyculture/ussarizonainterments.htm.

VIII. NEWSPAPERS AND MAGAZINES

Chicago Daily Tribune

Cincinnati Enquirer

Columbus Dispatch (Ohio)

Daily Dispatch (Moline, Illinois)

Deseret News (Salt Lake City)

Emporia Gazette (Kansas)

Honolulu Advertiser

Jonesboro Sun (Arkansas)

Kansas City Star (Missouri)

Las Vegas Review-Journal

Life

Los Angeles Times

Morning Sun (Pittsburg, Kansas)

Newsweek

New York Times

Orange County Register (Anaheim)

Pioneer Press (St. Paul, Minnesota)

Pittsburgh Post-Gazette

Pittsburgh Press

Press-Gazette (Hillsboro, Ohio)
Pottstown Mercury (Pennsylvania)
Quad-City Times (Davenport, Iowa)
Shawnee Mission Post (Kansas)
Tallahassee Democrat
Time
Topeka Capital Journal
Tucson Daily Citizen
Wall Street Journal
Washington Post
Waterloo-Cedar Falls Courier (Iowa)

Index

(Page references in *italics* refer to illustrations.)

About the Author

Walter R. Borneman is the author of nine works of nonfiction, including *MacArthur at War, The Admirals, Polk,* and *The French and Indian War.* He holds both a master's degree in history and a law degree. He lives in Colorado.